THE ITINERARY OF
LUDOVICO DI VARTHEMA
OF BOLOGNA

THE ITINERARY OF
LUDOVICO DI VARTHEMA
OF BOLOGNA

FROM 1502 TO 1508

AS
TRANSLATED FROM THE ORIGINAL ITALIAN EDITION OF 1510, BY

JOHN WINTER JONES
IN 1863

WITH
A DISCOURSE ON VARTHEMA
AND HIS TRAVELS IN SOUTHERN ASIA BY
SIR RICHARD CARNAC TEMPLE

ISBN : 978-93-5324-579-5 (HB)

First Published, London, 1863

Published, 2020

Published by

Facsimile Publisher
12 Pragati Market
Ashok Vihar, Ph-2
Delhi-110052
E-mail: books@facsimilepublisher.com

Printed at: G. Print Process, Delhi.

The Itinerary of Ludovico Di Varthema of Bologna

Sir Richard Carnac Temple

THE ITINERARY
OF
Ludovico di Varthema of Bologna
from 1502 to 1508

AS

Translated from the Original Italian Edition of 1510, by *John Winter Jones, F.S.A.* in 1863 for the Hakluyt Society

WITH

A Discourse on Varthema and his Travels in Southern Asia

by

SIR RICHARD CARNAC TEMPLE, BT.
C.B., C.I.E., F.B.A., F.S.A., F.A.S.B.

1928

THE ARGONAUT PRESS
11 & 13 SOUTHAMPTON ROW
LONDON

PREFACE

THERE are three points in the Eastern travels of the great Italian wanderer, Ludovico di Varthema, that give them an unusual interest. The first is their date between 1502 and 1508: that is to say, he was on his way over the East within four years of the opening of the sea-route to India by Vasco da Gama. Secondly, he travelled through the Arabian desert to Mecca and thence all over Yemen and Hadramaut, passing on to Hormûz and Persia as far as Shîrâz, and afterwards all round the Indian coasts as far as Pulicat near Madras on the eastern part of it, including Ceylon in his journeys. From Pulicat he went across the Bay of Bengal to Bengal itself and Pegu, along the western coast of the Malay Peninsula to Mergui and Malacca and the Malay Archipelago, visiting Sumâtra, Java, Banda, the Moluccas and "Borneï." Considering his period, it was an exceptionally hazardous and wonderful achievement. Thirdly, within fifty years of its accomplishment strong doubts were cast over the credibility of Varthema's accounts of it by another traveller of note, Garcia da Orta, a Spaniard in Portuguese employ. These doubts have ever since been expressed by scholar after scholar. For these reasons, Sir Richard Temple, who has had a long personal knowledge of much of the area traversed by Varthema, has examined his statements in detail, and has come to the conclusion that he has been maligned.

Another matter that has affected the value of Varthema's book on his travels is that it achieved a great success at once, passing from edition to edition in various languages. It had also a wide influence, as it preceded the accounts of Barbosa and other Portuguese travellers on their proceedings in India and the East. It was first published in Italian at Rome in 1510, and then in Latin in 1511, and from the Latin it was translated into delightful Elizabethan English by Richard Eden in 1577. But unfortunately it has not been possible to use Eden's book for the present edition, as the Latin rendering, and therefore his, varies greatly from the original Italian, and contains mistakes not to be found in Varthema's own work. Sir Richard Temple was therefore obliged to set Eden's translation aside and adopt that of John Winter Jones made in 1863 from the original Italian edition of 1510.

This last translation was in the same year admirably edited for the Hakluyt Society by the great Arabic scholar, G. P. Badger, long resident at Aden, and the thanks of the present editor and publishers are due to that Society for the interest taken in their labours. But Badger's remarks are necessarily often out of date, and were made on much less information than is now available. So Sir Richard Temple, while using Badger's valuable notes as far as possible, has consequently gone his own way in remarking on Varthema's story.

Like many travellers of his date, he acquired a working knowledge of colloquial Arabic, deliberately setting himself to learn it, and he spent a year and a half on the West Coast of India in the neighbourhood of Calicut and Cochin as a factor of the Portuguese Viceroy, thus acquiring some acquaintance with Malayalam, the language of that region. He is fond of showing off his knowledge by giving numerous sentences in both Arabic and Malayalam, of course incorrectly in a haphazard Italian transliteration. As he has translated these sentences after a free fashion in every case, scholars in the above languages can make out the originals for themselves—Badger has given in correct form those that are quoted in Arabic—and so no attempt has been made in this edition to give the originals correctly in footnotes or otherwise. But the correct form of place and personal names and of individual words—and occasionally very brief explanations—have been added to the text in square brackets. No footnotes have been used, as it is hoped that the long "Discourse" at the commencement of the book will explain to the reader all the many difficulties in the text.

Certain geographical puzzles arise in perusing Varthema's pages. Among these is the term "the city of Banghella," representing some town in Bengal. This has been used by other early writers, and has long been a source of scholarly dispute. However, as Varthema has in several other instances used the name of a country for a town in it which he visited—*e.g.* Cioromandel (Coromandel) for Negapatam, and Tarnassari (Tenasserim) for Mergui, and so on—and as it is not of much consequence to decide in this volume which town it was in Bengal that he stayed at, the question of its identity has been left vague. But it has greatly exercised Badger, as it did Dames later on when editing Barbosa's *Book*. They both left long notes on it, and other scholars, European and Indian alike, have examined it at length without much practical result. Varthema also refers to "Capellan," another name that has roused controversy, but as without doubt it means the Ruby Mines District of Upper Burma, it has been left unsolved as a name. On the other hand, attempts have been made in the "Discourse" to settle such puzzles as the situation of Sarnau, Bornei, and "Eri." Other difficulties of a minor nature are numerous, but they have all been dealt with as they occur in the text.

Varthema's travels have naturally been discussed by many scholars, and their results have been considered in this edition of his book, but the works that have been principally used are, besides John Winter Jones's translation, the Aungervyle Society's reprint (1884) of Richard Eden's *Navigations and Voyages of Lewis Wertomannus In the Yeare of our Lorde* 1503, G. P. Badger's edition for the Hakluyt Society of *The Travels of Ludovico di Varthema*, and Ch. Schefer's edition (1888) of J. Balarin de Raconis' French translation "sous le roi François Ier" of *Les Voyages de Ludovico di Varthema* (Vol. ix of the *Recueil de Voyages*). Alberto Bacchi della Lega's edition, published at Bologna (1885), of *Itinerario de Ludovico Varthema, nuovamente posa in luce* is a reprint without notes, published in *Scelta di Curiosità letterarie inedite o rare dal secolo XIII. al XVII.*

Varthema's own division of his work into "books" and "chapters" is somewhat haphazard and confusing, so it has been ignored, and a straightforward arrangement with chapters has been substituted for the better convenience of the reader. But a list of his chapters has nevertheless been added for general information.

The Argonaut Press has been especially fortunate in again securing the valuable services of Sir Richard Temple, whose wide experience and personal knowledge of so much of the countries visited by Varthema greatly enhance the value of the present edition.

N. M. PENZER

VARTHEMA'S DIVISION OF HIS WORK INTO BOOKS AND CHAPTERS

THE BOOK CONCERNING ARABIA DESERTA

THE SECOND BOOK OF ARABIA FELIX

The Chapter concerning the Sultan of all the above-mentioned cities, and wherefore he is called by the name Sechamir.

The Chapter concerning apes and some animals like lions, very hostile to man.

Discourse touching some places in Ethiopia.

The Chapter concerning Zeila, a city of Ethiopia, and of the abundance of it, and concerning some animals of the said city, such as sheep and cows.

The Chapter concerning Barbara, an island of Ethiopia, and of its people.

THE BOOK CONCERNING PERSIA

The Chapter concerning Diuobandierrumi, and Goa, and Giulfar, Lands of Meschet, a port of Persia.

The Chapter concerning Ormus, a city and island of Persia, and how they get very large pearls at it by fishing.

The Chapter concerning Eri in Corazani of Persia, and of its riches, and of the abundance of many things and especially of rhubarb.

The Chapter concerning the river Eufra, which I believe to be the Euphrates.

The Chapter concerning Sambragante (as it is called), a very large city, like Cairo, and of the persecution by the Soffi.

THE FIRST BOOK CONCERNING INDIA

The Chapter concerning Combeia, a city of India, abounding in all things.

The Chapter concerning the estate of the Sultan of the very noble city of Combeia.

The Chapter concerning the manner of living and customs of the King of the Joghe.

The Chapter concerning the city of Cevul, and its customs, and the bravery of its people.

The Chapter concerning Dabuli, a city of India.

The Chapter concerning Goga, an island of India, and the King of the same.

The Chapter concerning Decan, a very beautiful city of India, and of its many and various riches and jewels.

The Chapter concerning the activity of the King in military affairs.

The Chapter concerning Bathacala, a city of India, and of its fertility in many things, and especially in rice and sugar.

The Chapter concerning Centacola, Onor and Mangolor, excellent districts of India.

The Chapter concerning Canonor, a very great city in India.

The Chapter concerning Bisinegar, a very fertile city of Narsinga in India.

The Chapter showing how elephants generate.

The Chapter concerning Tormapatani, a city of India; and concerning Pandarani, a place one day distant; and concerning Capogatto, a similar district.

THE SECOND BOOK CONCERNING INDIA

The Chapter concerning Calicut, a very large city of India.

The Chapter concerning the King of Calicut and the religion of the people.

The Chapter concerning the manner of eating of the King of Calicut.

The Chapter concerning the Brahmins, that is, the priests of Calicut.

THE THIRD BOOK CONCERNING INDIA

THE CHAPTERS CONCERNING OUR RETURN

THE BOOK CONCERNING ETHIOPIA

CONTENTS

MAPS AND ILLUSTRATIONS

MAPS

ILLUSTRATIONS

THE ITINERARY OF LUDOVICO DI VARTHEMA IN SOUTHERN ASIA

DISCOURSE ON VARTHEMA AND HIS TRAVELS

BY

SIR RICHARD CARNAC TEMPLE, B^t

As in the case of his contemporary the Portuguese Magellan, and as in that of the Englishman Drake, both of a later generation, the birthplace of Varthema is not exactly known. Indeed, as regards Varthema, it is not known at all, nor are any of the other facts about his personality so far discovered of any historical value. His name is variously spelt as Varthema and Barthema, both with and without the *h*, and all that can be said definitely about him is that he was an Italian gentleman and was eventually knighted by the Portuguese. Not even from his book can any clear information be gathered about his life before he started on his travels. He writes in one place, when he was in Calicut on the west coast of India, that "my father was a physician in my country," but this was said in the course of conversation with a "Moorish" merchant, who had asked to see him when he was ill. Varthema proceeded to treat this unlucky man, as "that which I knew, I knew by the practice which he [my father] had taught me," and in all truth his practice, as described by himself, was ignorant enough, but fortunately for him the patient recovered. It is therefore quite possible that the statement as to his father being a physician was untrue.

¶ On another occasion, when in a very dangerous position, trying to escape from a caravan near Mecca, Varthema says to a "Moor," or Muhammadan friend, "I am a Roman," and when he added, "I was the most skilful maker of large mortars in the world" he was assisted to escape. Obviously, even less reliance can be placed on this statement, as the term Rūmī (Roman) would mean to a "Moor" any kind of European, most likely one from Asia Minor or Constantinople. On yet another occasion, however, when describing a sea-fight between Muhammadans and Portuguese off Cannanore, he incidentally remarks: "Truly I have found myself in some battles in my time, but I never saw any men more brave than the Portuguese." Here he seems to be relating a fact, and it may be assumed that before he had started on his travels he had been a soldier by profession. Such an assumption is supported by the interest he displays in his book in military weapons and organization, and by the part he took during the Portuguese fights which occurred just before his return homewards from the west coast of India, as on that account the Viceroy, Dom Francisco d'Almeida, knighted him—an honour subsequently confirmed by Manoel of Portugal.

¶ Lastly he remarks at Malacca: "If I had not had a wife and children I would have gone with them," *i.e.* further east with some Oriental friends he had picked up in Bengal. This statement completes the facts that have been ascertained about Varthema. It is not known where or when he died. He is usually described as "of Bologna," because that is his own description of himself in the dedication of his book. But he has also been said to have been "of Rome," because of the statement above quoted, or perhaps because the first edition of his book was printed in Rome.

THE BOOK

¶ Varthema's book was a great success. The copyright was secured to him for ten years by the Cardinal Chamberlain at the Court of Rome at the special mandate of Pope Julius II, and it soon began to run through various editions in several languages. The first was in Italian at Rome in 1510 and the second in 1517 also at Rome. The third was published in Venice in 1518 and the fourth in Milan in 1519. The fifth was also published in Milan in 1523 and the sixth and seventh in Venice in 1535, the latter being a close reprint of the sixth. It was produced in Latin in 1511 and other Latin editions followed in 1610 and 1611. A German edition appeared in 1515, followed by others in German in 1516, 1518, 1548, 1610 and 1615. In Spanish the book was printed in 1520, 1523, 1570 and 1576: in French in 1556: in Dutch in 1563, 1615 and 1655; and lastly in English there was a translation by Richard Eden in 1577, and it was noticed in *Purchas his Pilgrimage* in 1625. So Varthema reaped the reward which he hints that he hoped for—his name, though not his personal life, became widely known in Europe.

¶ In 1863 John Winter Jones, Librarian of the British Museum, translated the original Italian edition of 1510 into English, and George Percy Badger, the well-known Orientalist and Arabic scholar, annotated the translation for the Hakluyt Society. This is the edition used for the text of the present volume. Since Badger's edition, the great French scholar, Ch. Schefer, produced a valuable edition in French with many annotations in 1882. A translation into English was brought out in 1884, and another Italian edition was printed in 1885.

¶ As early as 1550 Garcia da Orta, a Spanish physician in Portuguese employment and writer on Indian drugs, threw doubts on the reliability of Varthema's statements, which will be dealt with presently, and as these doubts have continued ever since on the faith of Garcia's statements, it is as well to say here something of him and his work. He was born about 1490 (or a few years later) at Elvas, near the Spanish frontier on the way to Badajos. He was patronized by the de Sousa family and studied at Salamanca and Alcala de Henares in 1515–1525. From 1526 he was for some years a village doctor at Castello de Vide, near Elvas. In 1532 he was appointed lecturer in the Lisbon University. In 1534 he went out to India as physician with Martin Affonso de Sousa, leaving the Tagus on 12 March, 1534, and reaching Goa in September. In India he became personally well acquainted with the countries bordering on the west coast. He was at Diu when it was ceded to the Portuguese and accompanied de Sousa from Kâthiâwâr nearly to Ahmadâbâd. He acted as physician to Bahrâm Nizâm Shâh at Ahmadnagar. He accompanied de Sousa in a campaign from Cochin against the Zamorin, and in Ceylon. This seems to be the extent of his personal knowledge of India and the East. He is believed to have died at Goa about 1570.

¶ Garcia had a house and a garden of many medicinal herbs at Goa and about 1554 he was granted a long lease of the Island of Bomba, which he sublet. After de Sousa left India, Garcia was physician to the Viceroy Pedro Mascarenhas in 1554–1555. In 1558 he formed a friendship with the licentiate Dimas Bosque, who came to India with the Viceroy Constantino de Braganza, and it was probably owing to Bosque's influence that his great work on the drugs and simples of India was undertaken. It was finished in the time of Francisco Coutinho (1561–1564), to whom it was dedicated, and was published at Goa on 10 April, 1563. The first edition, full of typographical errors, is very rare. A second was published at Goa. The title of the book was *Colloquios dos simples e drogas de cousas medecinais da India, compostos pello Doutor Garcia da Orta.* There was an epitome in Latin, in 1567, an Italian translation in 1582 and a French translation in 1619. An imperfect edition was printed by F. A. de Varnahagen at Lisbon in 1872. In 1891 and again in 1895 the Conde de Ficalho published what is now the standard edition of Garcia da Orta at Lisbon, and this was translated by Sir Clements Markham in 1913 and issued as *Colloquies on the Simples and Drugs of India.* This is the edition which has been used in this volume when discussing Garcia's animadversions on Varthema's work.

ITS CREDIBILITY

¶ It is right to commence the examination of Varthema's travels with a note on the credibility of his statements, owing to the doubts just mentioned, which have been felt ever since the days of Garcia da Orta, who wrote between 1558 and 1561, *i.e.* about 50 years after the date of Varthema's book of travels. The importance of settling this doubt may be gauged from the following facts. If Varthema is entirely to be believed, he was the first European to go to Mecca with a *hajj* (pilgrim) caravan through the Arabian desert and to write an account of the pilgrimage, Schiltberger's travels there, *c.* 1425, being doubtful. He was also the first European to give an account of a journey to the Spice Islands beyond Java in the Malay Archipelago, and the first man to refer to the conditions of a voyage south of Java, and even south of Australia and Tasmania, long before those lands were discovered. The travels, which he describes as having been undertaken between 1502 and 1508—Vasco da Gama sighted Mount Deli on the south-west coast of India as late as 1498—may be divided into four parts: those in Arabia, those in Persia, those along the coasts of India and the Malay Peninsula, and those in the Malay Archipelago. No doubt has been cast on his accounts of Arabia and the west coast of India, but disbelief has been strongly expressed as to his having actually travelled, as he describes, in Persia, the east coast of India, and the Malay Peninsula and Archipelago. Two out of the three points in his travels of importance historically have, therefore, been held to be apocryphal—to the mind of the present writer wrongly.

The whole travel is clearly not only remarkable for the date—beginning of the sixteenth century—but also important, and Varthema's accounts are straightforward. Further, despite obvious mistakes, they are wonderfully accurate. Yet he has been always set down as untrustworthy and a liar, because his *bona fides* is doubted by the Spanish doctor of medicine, Garcia da Orta, who was himself another remarkable traveller not long after Varthema. As already explained, Garcia went to India direct from Portugal to Goa in 1534 and is believed to have died at Goa about 1570. Between 1558 and 1561 he wrote a famous book on drugs, which was edited by the Conde de Ficalho in 1895 and translated by Sir Clements Markham in 1913. As above said, it is entitled *Colloquios dos simples e drogas de cousas medecinais da India, compostos pello Doutor Garcia da Orta.*

¶ This book contains *inter alia* a colloquy (the ninth) between Garcia and one Ruano on *Benjuy* (*Styrax Benzoin*). In the course of the discussion Ruano says: "I answer what a Milanese [Varthema: 'Milanese' then meant any northern Italian] states. . . . This author is Ludovico Vartomano, and he says that the best [*benjuy*] of all comes from Malacca. Tell me whether this is true." To this Garcia replies: "You believe this Milanese, to whom I do not give credence. . . . As for Ludovico Vartomano, I have spoken here and in Portugal with men who knew him in India, and said that he went about in the dress of a Moor, and that he returned to us and did penance for his sins. They told me that he never went beyond Calicut and Cochin, nor did we then frequent the seas which we now navigate. As for what he says about Sumatra, he never was there. It is true that the good kind [of *benjuy*] is worth much in its own land. That which now comes is that which we call *Benjuy de boninas*. I did take this Ludovico, whom you quote, for a truthful man. But afterwards I looked into his book and found that he wrote in it what was false. For speaking of Ormuz, he said that it was an island and one of the richest cities there could be, and that it had the softest water in the world. Yet in Ormuz there is no water but what is brackish, and all the provisions come from beyond the island, nor is it very good water that does come from outside. Also when this Ludovico speaks of Malacca he says that there is neither wood nor water. This is all false, for there is plenty of good water and abundance of wood. From this you will see how little he is to be trusted as regards anything in India. Then turning to what this Milanese says about the *Benjuy* of Macedonia, I may say to you that it is possibly *storax*. May God grant you salvation; for I have laboured to obtain knowledge, yet I have never heard of *storax* coming from anywhere but Ethiopia, whence the myrrh also comes." It is on the faith of these statements that Varthema has been put down as a liar and not worthy of credence. It will be seen from what follows that Garcia has made a mistake.

¶ Varthema returned to Italy in 1508, and at once published a quarto book, *Itinerario de Ludovico di Varthema Bolognese...nel anno MDX a di* vi *de Decembrie*. This work had a great success and was repeatedly re-issued and translated into many languages, amongst others at once into Latin by Madrignanus: *Ludovici Patritii Romani novum Itinerarium...Mediolani octavo calen. Junias MDXI* [25 May, 1511]. In 1577 Richard Eden produced in the most delightful English *The Navigation and Voyages of Lewis Wertomannus, translated out of Latine into Englysshe*. Both the Latin and the English editions differ from the Italian, and contain mistakes which are not in Varthema's own book. The most amusing error is perhaps the following. "The Thyrde Booke, Cap. 5" of Eden is entitled: "Of Sainct Bragant, a citie bygger than Babylon, and the kyng of Persia, named the Sophie." But Varthema's own book has "the chapter concerning Sambragante (as it is called) a very large city like Cairo, and of the persecution by the Soffi." The Soffi was Shâh Isma'îl as-Safavî, the founder of the Safavî (Sophie, Soffi) dynasty of Persia, but the amusing mistake is in "Sainct Bragant." Varthema's Sambragante is a natural error for Samarkand, through Sambrakand. This the Latin translator "improved" by printing it "Sam Bragant," a term which Eden translated as "Sainct Bragant," thus introducing a new Saint to the Calendar.

¶ Now the Spanish edition of Varthema was translated from the Latin translation of 1511 and published in 1520 by Christoval de Arcos, who says that he could not procure the Italian edition and that it was full of errors. It was this incorrect Spanish edition that Garcia da Orta used. As to that part of it which immediately concerns us, it will be perceived, firstly, that Garcia notes that Varthema said that the best *benzoin* comes from Malacca. But what Varthema actually said was: "A great quantity of *benzoin* is also produced here [Pedîr in Sumâtra, not Malacca], which is the gum of a tree. Some say, for I have not seen it myself, that it grows at a considerable distance from the sea, on the mainland" (Hakluyt Society's edition, p. 234). Eden's translation from the Latin edition runs as follows: "Here also groweth the Laser tree, whiche bryngeth forth the precious gumme named *Laserpitium* or *Belzoe*, as the inhabitauntes and merchauntes tolde vs: but because I haue not seene it, I wyll speake no more of it." The place under consideration is "Sumatra or Taprobana." It must be seen therefore that Varthema is quite straightforward in his statement and does not say what Garcia attributes to him.

¶ Again Garcia writes of Varthema that, in speaking of Hormûz, he said that it had "the softest water in the world." But what Varthema says (*op. cit.* p. 95) is: "In this island there is not sufficient water or food, but all comes from the mainland." He says in fact what Garcia asserts to be the truth in almost the same words. Eden (*op. cit.* p. 98) has of "Ormus or Armusium," that "it hath a great scarcenesse of freshe water."

¶ Lastly Garcia remarks that "this Ludovico" said that in Malacca "there is neither wood nor water. This is all false." But what Varthema said (*op. cit.* p. 225) was that "this country [Melacha] is not very fertile," an opinion in which he is backed by de Barros. He then goes on to talk of many animal and vegetable products. Eden's translation (p. 24) says: "This region is not euery where fruitefull." Here again is Garcia clearly wrong and not in the least justified in his strong animadversion on the veracity of Varthema. It is possible that he was misled by the Spanish translation of the Latin translation of Varthema's original Italian account of his travels.

¶ If the matter rested there it would hardly be worth so careful an examination as the above, but owing to Garcia da Orta's fame poor Varthema has apparently ever since been held to be untrustworthy. In that famous work, *Hobson-Jobson*, by himself and A. C. Burnell, Sir Henry Yule (a really great authority) remarks, in the "Fuller Titles of books quoted," under "Varthema, Ludovico di": "Neither Mr Winter Jones nor my friend Dr Badger, in editing Varthema, seem to have been aware of the disparagement cast on his veracity in the famous *Colloquios* of Garcia da Orta (f. 29 v. and f. 30). These affect his statements as to his voyages in the further East; and deny his ever having gone beyond Calicut and Cochin; a thesis which it would not be difficult to demonstrate out of his own narrative." This observation shows how easy it is to decry a writer on the faith of statements made by former critics, and because so great a scholar as Sir Henry Yule has suggested the inaccuracy of Varthema without, it is now clear, enquiring into the accusing text, he has influenced later scholars.

¶ But the matter does not rest even here, for other English scholars have been misled. W. T. Sinclair and Donald Ferguson, in translating and annotating the travels of Pedro Teixeira, 1586–1605, for the Hakluyt Society in 1912, give in Appendix A a translation of "*A Short Narrative of the Origin of the Kingdom of Hormuz*, extracted from the History written by Torunxa [Turun Shâh] King of the same." In the *Addenda* and *Corrigenda* attached to the volume (p. 269) there is an addition to the notes on Ra'îs Saifu'ddîn, the boy "king" of Hormûz at the time of its capture by d'Albuquerque in 1507. Here Teixeira's editors write (p. 269): "Varthema, who professes to have visited Hormûz *circa* 1504, relates circumstantially, as having occurred while he was on the island, the murder of the Sultan by his eldest son, the latter, in his turn, being slain by an Abyssinian slave, who, after occupying the throne for twenty days, resigned it in favour of a younger brother of the parricide (Hakluyt Society's edition of Varthema, pp. 96–99). The whole story looks like an invention of this hare-brained traveller." In the passage quoted above from the Hakluyt Society's edition, Varthema indulges in a wild and lurid tale, which he relates as having happened in his own day, at Hormûz, *i.e.* at the time when Saifu'ddîn was *ra'îs* or chief. But in telling it he was not so hare-brained as it would appear at first sight, for certainly worse things of the same sort are said to have occurred when Shâh 'Abbâs, the Great, of Persia lay dying about a century later, and there are signs of the tale being a memory of something of the same kind at the death of the Caliph Kaim of Baghdâd in the eleventh century. It is likely that the tale was told to Varthema by his Persian friend, one Khwâja Junair (Caziazenor) of Herât-i-Khâra, whom he had met as a Hâjî at Mecca and afterwards again at Shîrâz.

¶ So far the authorities dealt with are English, but in the introduction to Schefer's edition of Varthema (1882), we find a great French scholar doubting the truth of parts of his accounts as to Persia, and as to Malacca, Pedîr (Sumâtra) and the Moluccas. The Persian part of his remarks need not be dealt with here, as a solution of the questions raised by Varthema's statements is offered later on in the text of this *Discourse.* Also the question of Varthema's credibility is not so important here as in the matter of the visit which he states he made to Banda and the Moluccas. On this point Schefer writes: "As to the travels of Varthema to Malacca, Pedîr and the Molucca Islands I must express the same doubts as I have for his stay at Ormuz and his excursion into the interior of Persia." And then he adds: "M. Tiele, *De Europeërs in den maleischen Archipel*, expresses the same doubts as those above stated." Here then we have a well-known Dutch writer casting doubts on Varthema's journey to the Spice Islands. But next Schefer goes on to state in his support the remarks above quoted from Garcia da Orta. It will be perceived that the evil of Garcia's animadversions is still poisoning the minds of his successors.

¶ There are various ways of testing Varthema's statements. One of the best is a careful survey of those as to the time spent at various points of the journey, because in his day the monsoons governed the voyages of the native craft in which he travelled. A series of dates (as the outcome of such a survey) at which he arrived at various places mentioned on his journeys is attached. From a perusal thereof it will be seen that it is possible for Varthema to have made the journeys that he says he made. It should be borne in mind in perusing the accompanying table that the fair weather for sailing in the Indian Ocean and the Bay of Bengal is during the North-east Monsoon, October to middle June. In the South-west Monsoon from middle June to October *nâkhudâs* or native skippers will not sail if they can help it. There is, however, no monsoon near the Equator, *e.g.* at Malacca or in Sumâtra, though strong seasonal winds blow at the Moluccas and in the Banda Sea. From Calicut to Quilon there are inland passages for small vessels through the backwaters along the west coast, practically all the way. Cape Comorin can be doubled by small vessels in the South-west Monsoon by watching the weather and at any rate after the middle of August.

APPROXIMATE DATES

AT WHICH VARTHEMA ARRIVED AT CERTAIN PLACES DURING HIS JOURNEYS

Italy to Egypt and Syria, 1502–1503			
		Beyrout	25 Jan.
Venice	(left) 1 Dec.	Tripoli	1 Feb.
Alexandria	(arrived) Dec.	Aleppo	13 Feb.
Cairo	Jan.	Damascus	25 Feb.

Arabia Deserta, 1503

Damascus (left) 8 Apr.
Al-Mazarîb (arrived) 11 Apr.
'Akabat ash-Shâmî 16 Apr.
Khaibar 7 May
Medîna 11 May
Mecca 22 May
Hudda 12 June
Jedda 14 June

Arabia Felix, 1503–1504

Jîzân 1 July
Kamarân 16 July
Aden 21 July
Radâ'a al-'Arab 3 Oct.
Aden 3 Feb.
Lâhaj 10 Feb.
'Az'az and Damt 13 Feb.
Al-Makrâna 15 Feb.
Sanâ'a 19 Feb.
Ta'iz 21 Feb.
Zabîd 25 Feb.
Dhamâr 26 Feb.
Aden 3 Mar.

"Ethiopia," 1504

Zaila 17 Mar.
Berbera 22 Mar.

Gujarat (*India*), 1504

Diû 13 Apr.
Gogo (Gôghâ) 18 Apr.

Persia, 1504

Dhofâr and Muscat 24 Apr.
Hormûz 1 May
Herât-i-Khâra and Shîrâz, and back to Herât-i-Khâra and Hormûz (till) Oct.

India (*Cambay to Calicut*), 1504–1505

Jûâ and Cambay 10 Oct.
Châul 25 Oct.
Dabul and Goa 1 Nov.
Bîjâpur 10 Nov.
Sadâsivagarh and Anjediva 16 Nov.
"Centacola" and Onore 18 Nov.
Mangalore and Cannanore 21 Nov.
Vijayanagar 6 Dec.
Cannanore, Dharmapatan, Pantalâyinî and Kapata 21 Dec.
Calicut 1 Jan.

India (*East Coast*) *and Ceylon*, 1505

Kâyankullam and Quilon 15 Jan.
Kâyal and Negapatam 20 Jan.
Jaffna (Ceylon) 25 Jan.
Pulicat 3 Feb.

Tenasserim, 1505

Mergui 1 Mar.

Bengal, 1505

Satgâon 15 Mar.

Pegu, 1505

Pegu 1 Apr.

Malacca and Sumâtra, 1505

Malacca 21 Apr.
Pedîr (Sumâtra) 28 Apr.

Spice Islands, 1505

Banda 13 May
Moluccas 21 May
Buru and Java 1 June

Return to India, 1505–1506

Malacca 21 June
Negapatam 18 July
Quilon 10 Aug.
Calicut 27 Aug.
Cannanore 5 Sept.
Cochin 9 Sept.
Fight off Cannanore 16 Mar.

In Calicut and Cochin, 1506–1507

Factor in Calicut and Cochin (till) Nov. 1507
Fight off Cannanore Aug. 1507
Attack on Ponâni 24 Nov. 1507
Leaves Cochin 6 Dec.

Homeward Journey, 1507–1508

Mozambique 18 Dec. 1507
Lisbon Oct. 1508
Rome Dec. 1508

¶ Another good test of such journeys as Varthema made is finance, as in his time voyages required money as much as they do nowadays. He started from Italy evidently with money enough to take him from Venice to Damascus. There he joined a *hajj* caravan for Mecca as one of the *mamlûk* guard, and he must have received pay. At Mecca he escaped from the caravan in a natural manner, and proceeded to Jedda and on to Aden on his earnings as a *mamlûk*. At Aden he was imprisoned for a long while as a Christian masquerading as a Muslim *hâjî*, and lost everything. But a wife of his captor eventually befriended him at Radâ'a al-'Arab, and gave him funds, with which he wandered about Yemen, and finally he escaped quite naturally at Aden. He had still money enough to take him to Hormûz and Shîrâz in Persia. There he met a rich merchant, a fellow *hâjî*, whom he had known at Mecca. This man not only befriended him, but financed the rest of his journeys in India and further east, and brought him back to Calicut. At Calicut Varthema deserted his friend, again with loss of any funds he had. But he joined the Portuguese and his information was most useful to Dom Lourenço, the son of the Viceroy, Francisco d'Almeida, which last appointed him a factor at Calicut. In this office he amassed sufficient funds to take him home. Varthema's financial position throughout is thus quite naturally explained.
¶ A third point in favour of Varthema's veracity is his description of the nutmeg tree at Banda and of the clove tree at the Moluccas. It seems impossible to believe that such descriptions are from hearsay conversations with Muhammadan merchants or skippers, especially as in describing *benzoin* and camphor Varthema frankly states that his information is what he only heard, as he had not seen the trees. For the above reasons it has been assumed in this volume that he spoke the truth, which is not to say that he made no mistakes. How could they be avoided in the case of a European travelling to the East at his date?

VARTHEMA'S CHARACTER AS REVEALED IN HIS BOOK

¶ Apart from its general credibility Varthema's book reveals some aspects of his character. There is no other evidence for gauging it. He had undoubtedly a craving for travel, leaving wife and children at home for an indefinite period without apparent compunction to satisfy it. So great was his love of wandering that it never occurs to him to grumble at difficulty or discomfort, though indeed the many hardships he had to endure were by no means light. He did not attempt to make money out of his wanderings—differing here from the majority of the old travellers—

and in their pursuit he had courage to face any hazard, infinite determination, unremitting persistence, and extraordinary resource when in dangerous positions, allowing no scruples and no feeling for others to stand in his way. He threw over friends and even benefactors without hesitation if they interfered, however unwittingly, with his object for the time being, sometimes with a callous disregard as to what might happen to them in consequence. Callousness, in fact, seems to have been a part of his character, and he even chuckles over the cruel deception of a kindly friend, whom he deserted in order to forward his own ends, yet he showed unselfish kindness to the child of a fellow-countryman in distress. Like most other men, he must have possessed a complex character.

¶ His book is seldom verbose. On the contrary, his accounts of what he saw are often too brief, as he seems to have had the fear of being a bore always in his mind. He also evidently wrote with the fear of the Pope's chamberlain before him, and worded some parts of his story so as to make sure of their passing unchallenged. Especially is this the case when he is speaking of Muslims and Hindus. Then he evidently thought it wise to use terms of disparagement to prove that he was a good Christian, though beyond question he had played at being a Muhammadan throughout a great part of his eastern travels. Self-centred as no doubt he shows himself to have been, he is not boastful of his achievements, though he describes the fights and battles he saw or was concerned with somewhat in the vainglorious style usual in his day. Occasionally he muddles a tale—especially while in Persia, as to his sojourn in which he had some reason for saying as little as possible; and at times—as in the case of his description of "Eri" in Persia and perhaps of "Bornei" in the Malay Archipelago—one suspects that his general reading has been brought into play to supplement his experiences, to the confusion of those who came long afterwards to study his writings. And all the while he tells us so little about himself—and that little has to be carefully searched out—that he hardly appears before us at all in human form. Clearly he was a man obsessed by one great idea—his travels—and anxious to tell the world what he had seen, with a natural sneaking desire running all through his story to make for himself a lasting name.

THE ITINERARY

¶ Varthema, in the dedication of his book to "the most illustrious and most excellent Lady, the Countess of Albi and Duchess of Tagliacozzo, Madame Agnesina Feltria Colonna," tells us frankly that he travelled to places "least frequented by the Venetians," simply because of his ardent longing to do so, and that he desired "to give a very faithful description of his voyage." At the back of this last desire there seems to have been the very human hope that he would thus preserve for himself a high name in the future, as the "privilege" granted him by "Raphael, by Divine grace, Bishop of Portueri, Cardinal of St George, Chamberlain of our Most Holy Lord the Pope, and of the Holy Roman Church," puts it: "Those who have devoted themselves to such studies have always been held in the highest honour, and have been abundantly rewarded."

IN EGYPT AND SYRIA

¶ In this frame of mind, Varthema sails, he does not tell us from what port in Italy, to Alexandria, and thence, partly by way of the Nile, he proceeds to Cairo, which disappoints him as to size. He finds the city under the Burjî Mamlûk dynasty, the monarch of the day being the celebrated al-Ashraf Saifu'ddîn, usually known as Kânsûh al-Ghôrî, whom he calls the "Grand Sultan," and who is served by "the Mamelukes, and the Mamelukes are lords over the Moors," a common medieval and even modern European name for all Muhammadans. The *mamlûks* were foreign slaves of any country, race or religion, forcibly converted to Islâm and often of high rank in the land of their birth. As a body they were used as soldiers by their captors, and some of them constantly rose to high position in many Muhammadan countries, not infrequently, as in Egypt, to the throne itself. The Burjî Mamlûks were so called because they were quartered in the towers of the citadel (*burj*) of Cairo, and they provided Sultâns of Egypt from 1309 to 1517. Kânsûh al-Ghôrî, *i.e.* Kânsûh of Ghôr in Afghânistân, was the great opponent of the Portuguese when they first appeared in India and the East, and there is mention of some of his proceedings in the pages of Varthema.

¶ Beyond his remarks as to the "Grand Sultan" and the "Mamelukes" there is nothing in Varthema's book about Cairo, and he goes thence, chiefly by sea, to Syria. Kânsûh al-Ghôrî had some claim to be entitled "Grand Sultan," as his territories comprised Syria as far as Taurus in Cilicia on the north and the Euphrates on the east, besides Egypt and Arabia.

¶ The first place Varthema touches at in Syria is Beyrout, which he calls by its proper name Barûtî, and there he finds one of the many buildings in Syria and Palestine connected with the story of St George and the Dragon. He passes on thence, presumably by sea to Tripoli, which

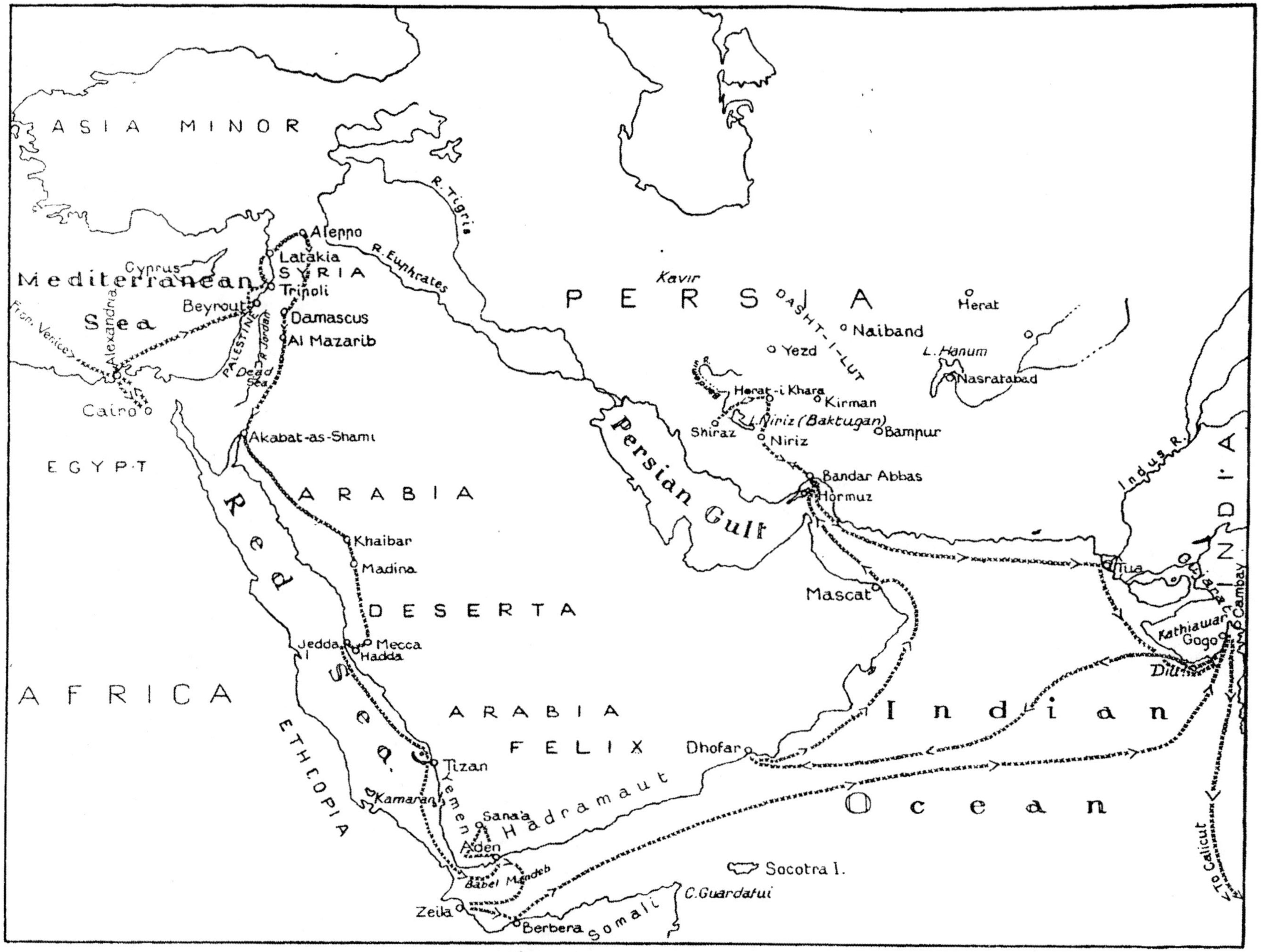

VARTHEMA'S ITINERARY IN SYRIA AND ARABIA

he notices is "subject to the Grand Sultan" of Egypt. From Tripoli he goes, probably again by sea to Latakîa, and thence over the hills to Aleppo (Halab), where he remarks on the great trade carried on thence with Persia, which he calls Azemia ('Ajam), by the Azamini ('Ajamî, Persian subjects). He next makes his way southwards by the east of the mountains to Damascus, but he goes partly over the hills by Hamâ, which he calls Aman, and Menîn, passing Homs unnoticed. He remarks, however, on the fruit and grapes for which these places have been famous from the earliest times. Oddly enough, he does not mention the Orontes (Nahr al-'Asî), which runs through Hamâ, the Hamath of Scripture and the Epiphania of Greek and Roman writers. But he notices with some acumen that Greek Christians were numerous in Menîn.

¶ Varthema gives a long account of Damascus, "in which I resided some months in order to learn the Moorish [*i.e.* the Arabic] language." He did not leave it till April, 1503. He finds "this city entirely inhabited by Moors and Mamelukes and many Greek Christians," and the *mamlûks* he describes as "renegade Christians who have been purchased by the said lord," *i.e.* by the Mamlûk Governor of Damascus. This is an interesting aspect of the *mamlûk* question, and on it Badger has a quotation from *Travels in Africa, Egypt, Syria, etc.* (pp. 53–56, 76) by an old traveller, Browne, in 1722, which is worth quoting here: "These military slaves are imported from Georgia, Circassia and Mingrelia. A few have been prisoners, taken from the Austrians and Russians, who have exchanged their religion for an establishment....Particular attention is paid to the education of these slaves. They are instructed in every exercise of agility or strength, and are in general distinguished by the grace and beauty of their persons....They have no pay [but this was by no means always the case], as they eat at the table of their master.... Any military officer may purchase a slave, who becomes *ipso facto* a *mamlûk*. After a proper education, the candidate thus constituted a *mamlûk*, receives a present of a horse and arms from his master, together with a suit of clothes, which is renewed every year in the month of Ramadhân [the Muslim Lent]."

¶ The Mamlûk Governor of Damascus Varthema describes as a Florentine, whose name is still unknown; but such men rose and fell so quickly in the days of Mamlûk rule in Egypt, that it is quite possible for many of them, even the most powerful temporarily, to have become completely forgotten. In this case, however, research into local history, such as may now be possible since Damascus is included in French mandated territory, may unearth this particular individual, if what Varthema writes is correct: "Afterwards he died in Damascus, and the people held him in great veneration as a holy man, possessing great knowledge, and from that time forward the castle has always been in the possession of the Sultan."

¶ After telling us a naïve story of the Oriental process of bribery, by which an *amirra*, *i.e.* an *amîr* or nobleman, obtained the governorship of Damascus, Varthema gives an interesting account of the city itself and of such sights as resident Christian monks would show to travellers. He has also a long account of the *mamlûks* and their overbearing ways towards the populace and an incorrect—perhaps naturally so—view of the Muhammadan law of divorce.

IN ARABIA DESERTA

¶ Leaving Damascus on 8 April, 1503, Varthema starts on a truly astonishing journey to Mecca by the Transjordanian and Arabian route, being the only European to traverse the intervening country until many years later. We learn incidentally also that he must have become one of the *mamlûks* in Damascus for the purposes of the journey, a fact which accounts for his interest in that body. He was, of course, obliged to clothe the story in Christian raiment for such an audience as his book must necessarily have. That he really became a Muslim for his travels in the East at any rate, there can be no doubt, for towards the end of his journeys in 1507 he remarks to a Persian merchant in Calicut in western India: "I should like to see them all [the Portuguese] of our Mahommedan faith." He also shows a considerable knowledge of Muhammadan ceremonies and doctrines, and could lead the prayers, as it was the custom to make *mamlûks* and strangers do. The actual circumstances leading to his becoming a *mamlûk* he describes as follows: "I being desirous of beholding various scenes and not knowing how to set about it, formed a great friendship with the captain of the said Mamelukes of the caravan, who was a Christian renegade, so that he clothed me like a Mameluke and gave me a good horse, and placed me in company with the other Mamelukes; and this was accomplished by means of the money and other things which I gave him, and in this manner we set ourselves on the way."

¶ As one of sixty *mamlûks*, who were guards of a very large caravan of 40,000 persons, as he conjectures, Varthema was given the Islamic name of Yûnus (Iunus) or Jonah, and by this name he was known to all Orientals throughout his many journeys. The great caravan which he thus joined consisted clearly of pilgrims to Medina and Mecca, performing the *hajj* or pilgrimage incumbent on all Muslims capable of going through it, and it followed the regular route of such pilgrimages from Syria. Varthema thus became not only a Muslim, but one of the most honoured and respected among them—a *hâjî* or pilgrim who had been to Mecca. Disguised then as a *mamlûk* he starts from Damascus with the caravan, and in three days he reaches al-Mazarîb, the *rendezvous* of all caravans going southwards to Arabia, and there he stays three days more—the usual stop is ten days. This enabled him to observe the az-Za'abî Arabs, or Zambei as he calls them, of that place. Of this tribe, which consisted of desert raiders, he gives a remarkably graphic and correct description, obviously from direct observation.

¶ Twelve days' march from Damascus, but apparently fifteen *en route* including the stop at al-Mazarîb, the caravan reached a valley, probably the pass known as 'Akabat ash-Shâmî on the Hajj route. This name differentiates the Syrian (Shâmî) pass from 'Akabat Aila, the Egyptian pass, a little to the west of it and between it and the Dead Sea. It is in appearance "a region of dead cities," such as are still known as the Cities of Lût or Lot in the great Persian desert. Varthema naturally mistook it for the land of Sodom and Gomorrah. Here Arabs, whom he estimated at 24,000, demanded payment for water, just as their ancient forefathers had demanded it in the days of Moses from the Israelites in the neighbouring 'Akabat Aila. This brought about a fight, lasting two days, in which the caravan was victorious, though in the end the water had to be paid for. April 29 had, it may be conjectured, now been reached.

¶ The caravan wandered on for another eight days and by 7 May, it may be presumed, it "found a mountain, which appeared to be ten or twelve miles in circumference, in which mountain there dwell four or five thousand Jews," who were clad and coloured like Bedouin Arabs (Badawî) and are described as being possessed of a fanatical hatred of all Arabs, and they had reason. Their habitation was the Khaibar Oasis, to the north of Medîna, and its name is said to be taken from a Hebrew word, *khabar*, a castle. The Jewish inhabitants noted by Varthema were probably originally refugees from the north in consequence of the many persecutions they met with at the hands of enemies of all kinds. They are first heard of in A.D. 568 and are mentioned by Abu'l-Faraj 'Ali in his *Aghânî* or *Songs* in the tenth century. They were reduced to great poverty by Muhammad in 628 and driven out by the Caliph 'Umar *ibn* al-Khattâb, but they were back again by 1173, when Benjamin of Tudela found a colony of them. But Burckhardt in the early nineteenth century, and afterwards Burton, reported them as having entirely disappeared. Varthema's statement about them as numbering

4000 or 5000 in 1503, even if exaggerated, is therefore of some historical importance.

¶ Leaving Khaibar, the caravan reached Medîna in three days more, halting for a day outside to clean itself up before entering the holy city. So it may be assumed that Medîna was entered on 11 May. Varthema calls it by its full name, Medinathalnabi, *i.e.* Medînatu'n-Nabî, the City of the Prophet, which is a specially interesting form of the name, as it gave rise to a natural but puzzling mistake in a popular geography of the seventeenth century, Nansen's (Danish) *Compendium Geographiæ*, ed. 1646, wherein it appeared as Medîna Talnaby, and was therefore thought to be two separate cities of Arabia. Later on in his travels Varthema is examined by the Sultan of Aden, and then makes use of an expression, which seems to show the origin of the mistake of taking Medînatu'n-Nabî as two places. He is asked a question as to whence he came and gives his answer in Arabic with a very free translation into Italian which has been Englished by Winter Jones as follows: "*Ana aji Medînatu'n-Nabî wa Mecca, wa ba'ad ana aji balûdak*, I had been to Medina, to Naby, where Mahomet is buried, and then I had to come to see His Highness." The translation should have been: "I came to the City [*Medîna*] of the Prophet and to Mecca, and then I came to your country." But it will be seen that Varthema's rendering makes Medîna and Naby two separate cities.

¶ Varthema's description of Medîna is accurate, so far as it goes, and he describes the earthen fortifications built by Kâsim ad-Daula al-Ghôrî of Cairo, the gardens of Kûba and the underground water-supply. The caravan remained three days, and at this point he interpolates a short passage to observe with some acumen: "Now, some who say that the body of Mahomet is suspended in the air at Mecca must be reproved. I say that it is not true. I have seen his sepulchre in this city, Medinathalnabi." Then, after telling us that they wished to see everything, he describes at length the place "where Mahomet and his companions were buried," remarking that it was obligatory to employ a guide (*dalâl* or *muzawwir*).

¶ The description of the Hujra or Tomb of Muhammad, but said to have been the chamber of 'Aisha, his favourite wife, is remarkably accurate, if compared with the later accounts of Burckhardt and Burton. Here Varthema makes, however, a mistake in saying that it also contains the tombs of 'Alî, Abû-bakr, 'Othmân ('Usmân), 'Omar ('Umr) and Fâtima. Of these, Fâtima was Muhammad's daughter, 'Alî his son-in-law, and the others his companions. However, 'Alî and 'Usmân were buried elsewhere and Fâtima outside the enclosure. Also it is a libel on Abû-bakr to say, as Varthema does, that he was "cardinal and wanted to be pope."

Varthema further mentions that Muhammad's library was kept in the Hujra, but apparently it is not there now, but in the Bâbu's-Salâm. He says, too, that these books caused "this *canaille* to cut each other to pieces," *i.e.* they caused violent differences of opinion, the term *canaille* applied to them being used perhaps as much with an eye on his audience as from personal feelings, as Varthema more than once speaks of Muslims in terms of abuse. He then tells us a story to "explain the sect of Mahomet," mentioning the dome over the Hujra and referring roughly to the Muslim belief in the "pillar of heavenly light" over it. In the course of the tale he gives a conversation in execrable Arabic between the *mamlûk* captain of the caravan and the "superior of the mosque."

¶ "We being tired of these things and vanities of Mahomet," the caravan next went on to Mecca, reaching it in ten days and arriving there on 22 May. Varthema here notes casually that "twice we fought with 50,000 Arabs," and gives a remarkable reference to then current politics in Arabia: "We arrived at Mecca, and there was a very great war, one brother with another, for there are four brothers, and they fought to be Lords of Mecca." This is a neat reference, showing accurate knowledge of the conditions met with. The chiefship of Mecca—the title of the chief being first Amîr and then Sultân and lastly Sherîf—was held by election from among descendants of 'Alî, through his eldest son Hasan, and then in two lines through the latter's two sons, Zaid and Hasan al-Musanna, a condition of affairs which led to frequent fights for supremacy. The Chief of Mecca was first under the nominal suzerainty of the Caliphs (Khalîfa) of the 'Umayyî and 'Abbâsî dynasties, and then in Varthema's time under that of the Mamlûks of Egypt, as he says. According to the *Kurratu'l-Ayûn*, an Arabic Chronicle of Yemen (Southern Arabia), supported by the *Rûa ar-Rûa*, another Chronicle (quoted by Badger), there had been one of the frequent great fights among the followers of the two factions between March and May, 1503. This makes it likely that the "50,000 Arabs" Varthema's caravan fought with between Medîna and Mecca were adherents of one or both sides.

¶ His account of the journey between Medîna and Mecca is somewhat confused and not easy to follow. He begins by talking of "a very fine well in which there was a great quantity of water, which well, the Moors say, was made by St Mark the Evangelist, by a miracle of God, on account of the want of water which prevails in that country." St Mark, however, is not now known to the Muslims of Southern Arabia, but it is possible that Varthema is referring to some current local Christian legend he heard. Then he interpolates with "I must not forget to mention," an interesting account of the flat desert between al-Akhdar on the Hajj route and "the Mountain of the Jews" at Khaibar, and gives a folktale about the carvings on Mt Athâlith, which he calls "a spur of Mount Sinai," *en route* to the west of al-Hijr, which is connected with the life of Muhammad and is mentioned in the *Korân*. It is an accursed spot to devout Muslims and a source to them of great fear, as Varthema points out. He also mentions "our pilots, great observers of their compasses and charts," probably meaning thereby the *ḳibla-nâma*, small portable compasses used by desert guides in Arabia to find the direction of Mecca.

¶ Varthema next enters into a long and extraordinarily accurate account of Mecca, considering that he had no predecessors and no special knowledge of Arabia or Oriental literature. His mistakes are not many and they are unimportant, and as to some details, he is more than usually interesting and closely observant; *e.g.*, he remarks on the Saniya Kuda, the pass into the Mecca Plain: "We found a mountain, where there was a road cut by human labour, and then we descended into the plain." This pass has a hard causeway leading to an opening in the hills, which has an artificial appearance; and Burckhardt writes of it that "on the other side the opening, the road descends into the plain of Sheikh Mahmoud, so named from the tomb of a saint, round which the Syrians generally camp," and no doubt Varthema's caravan did so encamp.

¶ He begins his account of the town by a description of Mount Arafât, on which, according to Muslim tradition, Abraham (Ibrâhîm) proposed to sacrifice Ishmael (Isma'îl), not Isaac (Isḥâk) as Varthema says. He then remarks: "You must know that, in my opinion, the curse of God has been laid upon the said city, for the country produces neither grass nor trees, nor any one thing," an observation occasionally indulged in by jocular Muhammadans in milder form to the present day. Then, after briefly describing the pilgrims and merchandise of the place, Varthema passes on to a more congenial theme, "the Pardoning in Mecca." This causes him to explain the Ka'ba or Holy House and to describe the *tawaf* or circumambulation thereof and also the well of Zemzem, of world-wide renown. He then refers to the "first tower" they walked round as "the first house that Abraham built," according to Muslim tradition. In his description, Burton, however, thinks that Varthema has fallen into some confusion by giving the ceremonies in the wrong order, but this after all is a minor fault.

¶ After this he descants on the sacrifices at Mecca and tells us of the Khutbatu'l-wakfa, the great Sermon on Mount Arafât, and the subsequent rush homewards, he says to protect the caravans, but the usual reason given is to say the evening prayer at the Mosque of Musdalîfa, three hours distant, in imitation of Muhammad. Half-way on the road he mentions the wall at al-Mûna, known as the Shaitân al-Kabîr, the Great Devil, and built up with the stones cast by pilgrims at the devil (Shaitân) in remembrance of a legend; but Badger, in a valuable footnote, shows that "maledictory lapidation" of this kind is a very old and common custom in the East. Lastly, as regards the city generally, he notices the great number of doves that are never disturbed because of "that dove which spoke to Mahomet in the form of the Holy Spirit."

¶ Lastly, Varthema makes a remarkable observation "concerning the unicorns in the temple of Mecca, not very common in other places." He describes the unicorns as if he had seen them: resembling a dark bay horse with a stag's head, slender legs like a goat's and cloven hoofs. "These two animals were presented to the Sultan of Mecca as the finest things that could be found in the world at the present day, and as the richest treasures ever sent by a king of Ethiopia, that is, by a Moorish king." Ethiopia is generally used to designate Abyssinia, but that has always been a Christian and not a Muhammadan country, and Varthema probably means Berbera, which he afterwards visits as an "island of Ethiopia." This story of the unicorns has always been a puzzle, and it will be observed that the description of them is the old established one in folklore. Badger gives many quotations from every part of the world in favour of the following judgment by him on the whole story: "I am still disposed to rely on the credibility of Varthema and to believe that he saw at Mecca two ordinary specimens of the famous unicorn." It may be as well to leave the matter there.

¶ Varthema tells us that he was in Mecca twenty days, *i.e.* till, say, 12 June, and shows his anxiety to leave the Syrian Hajj caravan in order to continue his journey to the East with the return caravan for India via Jedda. Fortunately, he comes across "a Moor," who knew him for a foreigner, as he had been in Genoa and Venice, no doubt as a merchant. To him Varthema describes himself as a Roman, *i.e.* a European, and as "the most skilful maker of mortars in the world," and, therefore, most useful to the Muhammadans against the Europeans, then newly arrived in the East as a powerful people. Next follows a conversation in which he shows his knowledge of the early Portuguese movements in the Red Sea in 1502, the year before his journey. He then deserts the Hajj caravan and lives in concealment with the family of his new friend—a very dangerous proceeding. The "Moor" adds to his services by directing him to "the King, who is in the parts of India Major, and who is called the

King of Deccan," *i.e.*, to the *mamlûk*, Yûsuf 'Adilshâh, the founder of the 'Adilshâhî kingdom of Bîjâpûr, who ruled between 1489 and 1510. His friend apparently took his place in the returning Syrian Hajj caravan, which he thus joined free of duty on his goods, owing to the influence of Varthema with the "Captain" thereof. Varthema himself then on a Friday starts with the Indian caravan, reaches "a certain city in Arabia (Hudda)" where it remains all night, and next day, Saturday, about midnight it arrives in Jedda on the Red Sea, about 40 miles from Mecca, *i.e.* say, on 14 June, 1503.

¶ Jedda is found to be very like an Italian city, so "we will therefore not dwell long on a description of it," and indeed it is still superior to any city in Southern Arabia. Varthema also notes correctly that, in his time, neither Christians nor Jews were admitted into it, a rule that remained in force till the nineteenth century. For this reason he hid himself all day in the Mosque, covered up and groaning as if in pain. He was thus left alone as "a dying Moor," and a bad time he must have had in such a place at such a season. He here gives proof once more of his general accuracy, for he tells us correctly that the city was under the rule of "a lord of Cairo," who is "a brother of Barachet, that is of the Sultan of Mecca. They are subject to the Grand Sultan of Cairo." The actual ruler of Egypt at that time was the *mamlûk*, al-Ashraf Kânsûh al-Ghôrî, and the Barakât family ruled in Mecca under his suzerainty.

¶ After fourteen days at Jedda, Varthema makes arrangements with "the master of a vessel which was going towards Persia" and "three days afterwards [say, on 1 July] we set sail." Then with acute observation he tells us "that the Red Sea is not red," and gives a correct account of the navigation at the southern end of it, which is difficult owing to the many islands that obstruct the way.

IN ARABIA FELIX

¶ Varthema had now done with Arabia Deserta and had fairly started on his further journey. After six days the ship arrived, about 6 July, at Jîzân or Gîzân on the Arabian coast of the Red Sea, which he remarks, in his assumed bigoted manner, is "subject to a Moorish lord and is a district very fruitful and good, like Christian countries." He gives a long list of semi-Oriental fruits found there, "so that it is a paradise." He also accurately notes that the grain used in the place, a millet, was called *dora* (*ḍhura*), though elsewhere in Southern Arabia it is known as *ta'âm*.

¶ Leaving Jîzân on 11 July, the ship sails down the coast to a place he calls al-Baidâwî, the inhabitants of which he says are Baduin, apparently in mistake for the desert Arabs known as al-Badawî (Bedouin). They proved to him, as they have to others, a wild, predatory tribe, and with them Varthema describes a fight in his somewhat vainglorious manner. About 16 July the ship reaches Kamarân, an islet now used as a quarantine station for pilgrims to Mecca, and long frequented by native craft trading between India, Persia and the Red Sea. This island he remarks "is subject to the Sultan of the Ammani," by which name he may mean here the Imâm of Sanâ'a, the ruler of the chief town of Southern Arabia and its dependencies, rather than Yemenî, the people of Yemen. As far as this point from Jedda he rightly remarks that navigation must be by day for sailing vessels, owing to the number of islands, but onwards to the mouth of the Red Sea the passage is open.

¶ Going southwards through the Little Strait, just as native craft still do, Varthema gives a remarkably accurate account of the appearance of the land on both sides as far as Cape Babel Mandeb (Bâbu'l-Mandab). The mouth of the Red Sea is here divided into the Great and Little Straits by the island of Perim, but Varthema gives its name as Bebmendo, *i.e.* Bâbu'l-Mandab, the Gate of Lamentation. It took his ship two days to get through the Little Strait and three days more to reach Aden, at which ancient port he did not arrive till, say, 21 July. He seems to have had an inkling of the danger he now ran from the South-west Monsoon, which rages in the Indian Ocean at that season.

¶ The ship anchored off the little island of Sîra, which legend says is the spot whither, according to Muhammadan tradition, Cain (Kâbîl) fled after the murder of Abel (Hâbîl), and was there presented by Satan (Shaitân) with the lute and other musical instruments for his amusement. The traveller is much taken with the appearance of Aden from that anchorage and calls it "the strongest city that was ever seen on level ground," and again he says: "This city is extremely beautiful." The fortifications he describes were those of 'Othmân az-Zanjîlî, a rapacious governor, who was appointed by Turân Shâh *ibn* Aiyûb, brother of the famous Saladin (Salâhu'ddîn), Sultân of Egypt, in A.D. 1175. It was mid hot-season when Varthema was at Aden, and he remarks that the market was held "at two o'clock midnight," *i.e.* at the second watch, say from nine to twelve.

¶ Varthema's description of Aden is kindly, as he had no reason to love the place, because here it was that he came to great trouble. This is his story of it: "The second day after my arrival in the said city I was taken and put in irons, and this occurred through one of my companions, who said to me: 'Christian dog, son of a dog.' Some Moors heard this speech, and through this I was taken with great violence to the palace of the Vice-Sultan, and they immediately consulted whether they should at once put me to death, because the Sultan was not in the city. They said that I was a spy of the Christians. But as the Sultan of the country (Aden, Yemen) never puts anyone to death, these people respected my life, and kept me sixty-five days with eighteen pounds' weight of iron on my feet." Both Varthema and his companion, and also a "Moor," were thus imprisoned, and he uses "we" thereafter in describing events.

¶ On the third day after their captivity had commenced, say 6 July, some sailors who had escaped from an attack by the Portuguese on their ship, a fact corroborated by the *Kurratu'l-Ayûn* as having occurred in A.H. 908, *i.e.* A.D. 1502, said that "we had come there as spies" and demanded blood. Badger, quoting Greene, *Collection of Voyages*, i, 51 f. and Ramusio, i, 136 ff., has tried to fix this attack down to the results of one made by Estevão da Gama off Mount Deli on the west coast of India, on a ship belonging to Kânsûh al-Ghôrî on 29 September, 1502, in which 300 "Moors," including 30 women, were destroyed by the Portuguese. This resulted in six more "Moorish" ships being chased and captured by 22 and 26 October, 1502, and Badger conjectures that it must have been some refugees from these ships that had reached Aden before July 1503 and raised a disturbance against Varthema.

¶ After being kept in prison at Aden, the two companions were sent to the Sultân who was at Radâ'a al-'Arab, which they reached about 3 October, 1503. This place is sixty miles east of Aden and some eighty miles south-east of Sanâ'a. At Radâ'a they find the Sultân al-Malik adh-Dhâfîr of Aden, whose full name was 'Amir *ibn* 'Abdu'l-Wahhâb, known also as Shêkh 'Amir, or Sechamir as Varthema calls him. He was preparing an attack on the Imâm (ruler) of Sanâ'a. Taken before the Sultân, Varthema is unable to repeat the Muslim Creed through fear and is consequently thrust back into prison closely guarded. Two days later, say 5 October, the Sultân takes the field with "3000 horsemen, sons of Christians as black as Moors." These were clearly *mamlûks* "of Prester John's country," *i.e.* Abyssinians or perhaps Somâlîs. They are accurately described even to the minute points of using the *mesuech* (*miswâk*), or twig tooth-brush to clean their teeth, Oriental fashion, and the head-dress of horns made of their own hair. Varthema also shows his accuracy of report by never mentioning the use of fire-arms by the Arab troops he met with. They were not introduced into Southern Arabia till just after his visit, *i.e.* in 1515, by Egyptian troops.

¶ Prester John, the Preste João of Duarte Barbosa, or High Priest John, was a universal name in medieval Europe for a mysterious Christian potentate somewhere in the Asiatic wilds, including Ethiopia or Christian Abyssinia. In reality, he and his Christian people were the Tartar, properly Tâtâr, tribe of the Onguts of Kânsû in China. The first Christian chief of this tribe was a Nestorian Sergîs or Sergius, *i.e.* George, who was believed to have helped the Crusaders against the Muhammadans in the eleventh century. He had a son Johanan or John, whence "Prester John," which became eventually a general term designating any far distant Oriental Christian potentate.

¶ Varthema next gives a long account of what happened, while in custody at Radâ'a, between him and the "queen," *i.e.* one of the wives of 'Amir *ibn* 'Abdu'l-Wahhâb. There is a suspicion of rhodomontade here, as there is in all such stories of this period. He makes himself out a greater hero than he was in all probability, but at any rate his tale accounts for his escape. He and his companions in prison arrange by casting lots that one of them should pretend madness, and the lot falls on Varthema. He then tells a rather interesting story of the consequent events, which end in the "queen" falling in love with him. She seems to have been a simple sort of woman and persuades her husband to let him go free. He then induces the "queen" to let him visit a "holy man" in Aden to be cured of his madness. This seems a reasonable request to her, as "holy men" teemed in Arabia at that time and were held in the highest esteem. So she gives him "a camel and twenty-five seraphim" or *ashrafî* (gold coins, ducats). He sees the holy man, and as he finds he must wait for a month for a ship to "India," to gain time and also to escape the attentions of the people of Aden, he writes to the "queen" and tells her that he is cured and wishes to visit the whole of her husband's kingdom. This he proceeds to do and thus escapes, it may be assumed, about the beginning of February, 1504. The tale sounds improbable, but on the whole there must be truth in it, as it accounts for the money Varthema obviously had for his further travels. As long as he was a *mamlūk* he must always have had pay besides what money he had in hand when he became one, but when he was made a prisoner he must have lost it all, and plenty of it was necessary to him after he escaped.

¶ He kept his eyes open as usual while in captivity, for he notices correctly fat-tailed sheep at Radâ'a and indeed at several places in Arabia and Ethiopia, *i.e.* the opposite African coast. He notices also the grapes for which Radâ'a is famous, and after the Mediterranean fashion he translates *jûz hindî*, *i.e.* coconuts, which he does not describe, as nutmegs.

¶ To kill time for a month and to keep wandering so as to avoid detection, Varthema takes a zigzag path about Yemen and the Aden country, journeying at random. Thus he makes journeys aggregating 600 miles, going first north-west from Aden to Lâhaj, 'Az'az and Damt about 130 miles, thence east to al-Makrâna and Yarîm 40 miles, thence north to Sanâ'a 40 miles and then south 110 miles more to Ta'iz, thence north-west 70 miles to Zabîd and east-north-east another 70 miles to Dhamâr, and finally south 120 miles back to Aden. It was obviously haphazard travelling merely for the sake of safety in movement.

¶ Journeying then to the north-west, about 10 February, 1504, he reaches Lâhaj, and correctly notes that it did not produce grapes. He then passes on to 'Az'az and gives a confused account of the blood-stained feuds between the orthodox Sunnîs and the heretical sect of the Zaidîs in those parts, and about 13 February he reaches Damt. Then turning sharp to the east he reaches on the 15th a fortress, al-Makrâna, where he says Sultân 'Amir kept his treasure and a wife, a statement supported by the native Chronicle *Rûa ar-Rûa*. Travelling still to the east, he reaches Yarîm next day and describes the seedless *sultâna* grapes of that place. He then turns northwards and goes to Sanâ'a, the capital of Yemen, at which he arrived on 19 February. Here he describes the unsuccessful assault on the fortress by Sultân 'Amir in 1502, and correctly asserts that the walls are extraordinarily thick. He has also a folktale about the madness of one of the sons of the ruler, Imâm Ahmad *ibn* al-Imâm an-Nasîr.

¶ Leaving Sanâ'a he goes a long way to Ta'iz, reaching it on 21 February, where he describes with accuracy the roses and the rose-water (*'atar*) trade, and remarks on "a temple there, built like Santa Maria Rotonda at Rome, and many other very ancient palaces." The rose-water trade still flourishes, there are many mosques and public buildings, and Niebuhr, travelling in 1760, describes Varthema's "temple," the Mosque of Isma'îlu'l-Mulk, as "the Cathedral of Ta'iz." Turning again north-west, he goes to Zabîd, arriving on 25 February, and correctly tells us that he found it a flourishing place. It was taken from Sultân 'Amir by Egyptian and Turkish troops soon after Varthema's visit, in 1516, in circumstances of peculiar atrocity, but it was soon recovered by the Imâm of Sanâ'a. He then went a hard day's journey to the north-east to Dhamâr. Thence in five days, *i.e.* on 3 March, he reaches Aden once more through the Yemen woods, the numerous apes of which made a great impression on him, and so did the hyaenas, which he calls "certain animals like lions." The Lord of the whole country is described as the Sultân of the Ammânî, *i.e.* Yemenî, the inhabitants of Yemen.

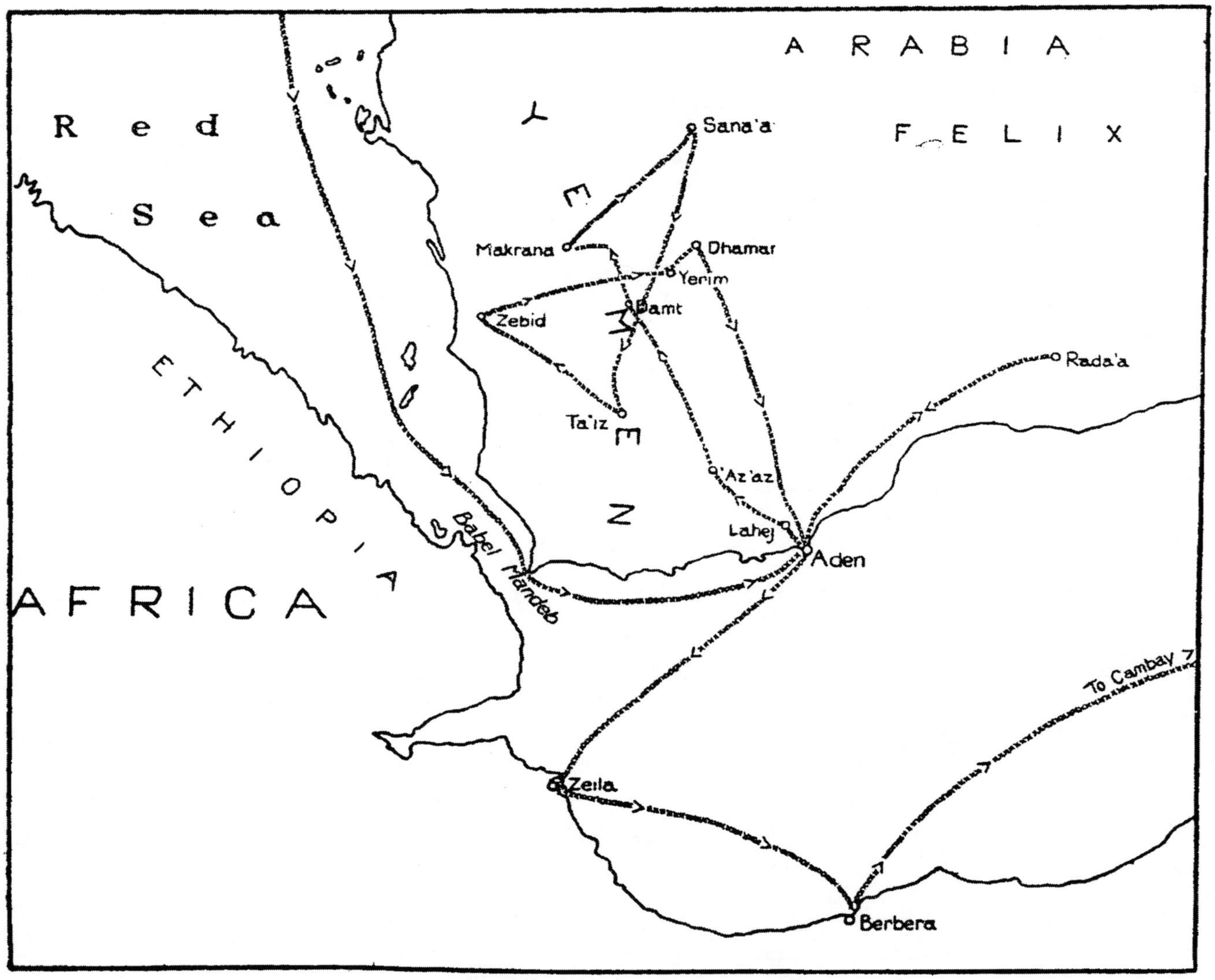

VARTHEMA'S ITINERARY IN YEMEN

¶ It is hardly surprising that Varthema is somewhat confused as to time after he was taken prisoner at Aden, but a careful reading of his account shows that the dates given above must be approximately accurate. He thus continued his voyage for "India" about 3 March, 1504, when the North-east Monsoon was in full force, and fine weather was to be expected. The Arab commander knew what he was doing when he fixed the date for departure from Aden. It is important to preserve as accurate a time table as possible in such travels as these, since the weather at various seasons in Eastern seas and countries greatly governs the movements of wayfarers, and so is a test of the accuracy of old travellers' tales.

¶ By "India" Varthema meant the only part of India then known to Europeans in general, *i.e.* the south-west coast about Calicut, and this accounts for his statement: "I spoke secretly with the captain of a ship, and told him that I wished to go to India, and if he would take me I would give him a handsome present. He replied that, before he went to India, he wished to touch at Persia. With that I was satisfied and so we agreed." In the sequel he did actually go to India before he reached Persia, *i.e.* he touched first at Cambay in Gujarât *en route*: but Cambay is nowhere near the "India" that he had read about.

IN "ETHIOPIA"

¶ Deserting his cavalcade, Varthema leaves Aden in a hurry and in secret: "As soon as I had arrived in Aden, I placed myself in the mosque pretending to be ill, and remained there all day. In the evening I went to find the captain of the ship, so that he put me on board secretly." Thus on 4 March, 1504, he starts for his goal—India—in a convoy of twenty-five vessels laden with madder, the trade in which from Aden is still carried on. The weather, however, proves to be against them—they probably met with a *balât* or north-westerly gale, such as occasionally occurs in the fine weather—and so they have to put into Zeila about 17 March. Varthema says it is "in Ethiopia," *i.e.* on the African coast across the water not far from Aden. He describes the place as a slave-dealing port for "those people of Prester John (Africans), whom the Moors take in battle." He also descants on the oil made there from *zerzalino*, *i.e. juljulân* or sesamum, known in India as gingelly oil. He also remarks two sorts of sheep—fat-tailed and twisted-tailed; the latter with heavy dewlaps is the *oryx*, which he calls "a certain kind of cows, which had horns like a stag and were wild." The rhinoceros he further describes as "cows, which had a single horn in the forehead, which horn is a *palmo* and a half in length, and turns more towards the back of the cow than forwards." Lastly, he gives a fairly accurate description of the town and of the Somâlîs that inhabit it.

¶ On the weather becoming again possible, the ships set sail about 22 March and reached "an island which is called Barbara." Berbera, however, is not an island, though the anchorage might have made it appear to be one, or Varthema may have mistranslated *jazîra*, used usually for an island, but also on occasion for a peninsula or a harbour. He found the place "small but good and very well peopled." In this he was more fortunate than he knew, as from April to October Berbera is deserted, though it is filled by a large crowd of African traders from October to April, and it was very near the end of the busy season that Varthema's convoy was in the place. The ship remains only one day at Berbera and sails for India and Persia presumably about 1 April.

IN GUJARAT (INDIA)

¶ Varthema now crosses the northern part of the Indian Ocean without touching at any point on the Arabian or Persian coasts, and about 13 April reaches the island of Diu, off the coast of Gujarât in India, though to him it is not "India," as explained above. Diu, he tells us, "is called Diuobandierrumi, that is, Diu, the port of the Turks," meaning thereby Diu Bandar ar-Rûmî, Diu the Port of the Rûmîs, *i.e.* of foreigners from Rûm or Turkey, or perhaps better the Nearer East, or foreigners in general. He says that it was "subject to the Sultan of Combeia," *i.e.* Kambâya or Kambâyat (Cambay), and that "the captain of this Diu is one named Menacheaz," thus giving a neat reference to the notorious foreign *mamlûk* of uncertain origin, Malik 'Aiyâz, an important personage then on the west coast of India, who greatly impressed the Portuguese, and of whom there are long accounts by both Barbosa and de Barros. He also notices that the small sailing vessels in use thereabouts were called *thalae*, *i.e.* *at-talâyî* or *atalâya*, coast-guard boats.

¶ The ship stays only two days at Diu and goes on to Gogo or Gôghâ, which Varthema calls Goa, in Kâthiâwâr, then included in the Kingdom of Gujarât. He arrives at Gogo in three days, say by 18 April, and notes that the Gogo district, *i.e.* Kâthiâwâr, is "fat and wealthy," and says incorrectly that the inhabitants are "all Mahommedans," but he could not have remained there long; and again he puts to sea, crossing the Indian Ocean westwards beyond the entrance to the Persian Gulf.

IN PERSIA

¶ The ship in fact proceeds to Giulfar, *i.e.* Julfâr, which it reaches about 24 April. The reading Giulfar is variously written in MSS. as Diulfar and Diufar and represents Zuffâr or Dhofâr, the Arab port for horses and frankincense on the 'Omân coast. It is briefly described as "most excellent and abounding." Hence the ship goes eastward again to Muscat, which is merely called "another port." Departing thence, say about 1 May and so still in fine weather, Varthema at last reaches "the noble city of Ormus [Hormûz]," in Persia proper.

¶ The island of Hormûz (Perûn) he finds "extremely beautiful," a remark which is true of the evening light at the southern end of the Persian Gulf, as says the proverb: "If the world were a ring, Hormûz would be the jewel of that ring"; or he may have had in mind the extraordinary ruggedness of the coast behind the island. However, what most attracted his attention is the pearl fishery "at a distance of three days' journey," and he gives an accurate account of the method used by the fishermen to bring up the pearl oystershells from the sea. His description of the place generally also shows that he writes from personal knowledge. He then indulges in a long story about the "Sultan of Ormus," then apparently a boy, named Saifu'ddîn, with an adroit *mamlûk* as governor. It is a wild tale, but not so unlikely as it would at first appear, since it might well be the popular form of the horrible domestic occurrences, a century later on, at the end of the reign of the famous Shâh 'Abbâs, the Great, of Persia. It may even be a memory of the tales of the Caliph Kaim of Baghdâd and the rise of the Seljûk Dynasty in Persia in the eleventh century. One cannot help suspecting that Varthema heard it in Arabic from his friend "Cazazionor [also Cogiazenor], a Persian merchant," whom he met "in this city of Schirazo" [Shîrâz] and of whom more presently.

¶ So far Varthema can be followed safely as a traveller relating what he saw. His story is detailed and gives the impression of having been written from notes made soon after the events occurred, and it is possible to follow his dates. This cannot, however, be said of what he now tells us of his further journeys in Persia. He informs us that "departing thence [Ormus] I passed into Persia [*i.e.* the mainland], and travelling for twelve days I found a city called Eri, and the country is called Corazani, which would be the same as to say 'The Romagna.' The King of Corazani dwells in this city." There can be no doubt that by this description Varthema means Herât in Khurâsân, but he says nothing of the route, which is roughly 300 miles to Kirmân through the mountains, then onwards 200 miles more to Naiband still in the mountains, then across the terrible Persian desert, the Dasht-i-Lût, then some 300 miles through sand and mountains to Herât. Yet he has nothing to say of the hill country or the desert or even of Kirmân, a truly remarkable place. Had his route avoided the Dasht-i-Lût, it would have taken him through mountains past Bâmpur and Nasratâbâd and that wonderful sheet of water and marsh, the Hâmun-i-Helmand, which he would hardly have failed to remark, and it would have been much longer than any route via Kirmân. Yet he says he was only twelve days on it.

¶ He next tells us "I quitted this place [Eri] and travelled twenty days on the mainland, finding cities and castles very well peopled. I arrived at a large and fine river, which is called by the people there Eufra, but, so far as I can judge, I believe that it is the Euphrates [Ufrât, Furât], on account of its great size. Travelling onwards for three days to the left hand, but following the river, I found a city which is named Schirazo [Shîrâz]." That is to say, he means that he arrived in Shîrâz via a river on which it is situated in twenty-three days from Eri. The only remarkable river, however, hereabouts is the Bendemîr, which Varthema might have thought was the Euphrates, but Shîrâz is not situated on it. He says, moreover, nothing of his journey, and there is no direct route from Herât to Shîrâz unless a cross-country journey is taken via Naiband and Yezd, but that would cross the Dasht-i-Lût and also a *kavir* or desert marsh, and would moreover lead the traveller over great mountains. It would be over 600 miles in length and would provide a mighty experience, and yet Varthema says nothing of it except that he did it in twenty days. There is no doubt, then, that if his statements are to be accepted in any form, some other site than Herât must be found for his "Eri," despite his account of it fitting that place.

¶ Assuming that Varthema really did visit Shîrâz, the following statements afford a clue as to what happened. He met there a man whom he had known at Mecca as a *hâjî* or pilgrim. With this man he planned a wild journey across Persia to Samarkand, which was abandoned as the country was too disturbed: "And with this we set ourselves on our way, and returned towards Eri. . . . . We returned [thence] to the city of Ormus at the end of eight days." This settles the doubt as to "Eri" being Herât. It was clearly on a route between Hormûz and Shîrâz. With the help of Sir Percy Sykes, who has an intimate knowledge of this part of Persia, the following solution of the problem of Varthema's proceedings has been arrived at. He seems to have gone from Hormûz Island to a spot near what has since become well-known as Bandar 'Abbâs, and travelled thence to Tarûn, thence to Nîrîz, and thence via Tashk to Herât-i-Khâra, a fertile district not far to the east of Lake Nîrîz or Baktegân. This is the place he calls "Eri" or Heri, the old name for the great Herât, now in Afghânistân. From Herât-i-Khâra he goes, again past Tashk, to the Bendemîr River and thence to Shîrâz. Then after staying at Shîrâz for fifteen days he returns to "Eri," *i.e.* Herât-i-Khâra, where his Persian friend has a house, and from this place he eventually returns with the Persian to Hormûz. Such a series of journeys would be quite within possibilities, and would not occupy an unreasonable amount of time.

¶ In the light of these reflections it may be remarked that Varthema's very brief account of "Eri in Corazani" is fairly correct, though Herât-i-Khâra, of course, is nowhere near Khurâsân. His description of Shîrâz, so far as it goes, is also accurate, especially as the mart for turquoises and balas rubies from Badakhshân, and it was also a mart, as he says correctly, for *lapis lazuli*, antimony and musk. As to this last he has an exaggerated account, no doubt by report, of the evil effect the smell of it has on some constitutions. He describes the Persians as "the most cunning men in intellect and at falsifying things of any nation in the world," but at the same time as "the best companions and the most liberal of any men who inhabit the earth." This character may be due to his good fortune in coming across the Persian merchant, who was obviously a man of wealth and glad of his company, for Varthema's funds must have been much exhausted by the time he reached Shîrâz, and no doubt his further journeys, even in India, were financed through his friendship with that trader. After meeting his Persian friend, he plans to go with him to Samarkand and gives an acceptable reason for desisting, viz. because the country was in an uproar over the recent foundation of the Safavî rule by Shâh Isma'îl and his determination to establish the Shî'a faith throughout his dominions.

¶ This friend's name is given as Cazazionor or Cogiazenor, *i.e.* Khwâja Junair or Junaid—Varthema frequently writes *z* for *j* (Italian *gi*). Schefer guesses another possible Persian name, Khoja (= Khwâja) Jauhar, as the equivalent of "*le mot defiguré de Cozazionor*." He is described as a Persian merchant of "Eri," *i.e.* Herât-i-Khâra: "When we had arrived at his house [at Eri]," writes Varthema. From this friend he would hear much about the great Herât and Samarkand, which he calls Sambragante by an almost natural corruption. The Khwâja (a common title for merchants) would also be able to tell him the tale about "the Sultan of Ormus" alluded to above. Later on, too, there is abundant evidence that the Persian merchant remained his companion in his travels in India and further east. On the whole, the safest assumption would appear to be that he took the journeys on the Persian mainland from and back to Hormûz as above described, crossing the Bendemîr River, so called from the Band-i-Amîr or barrage across it, built in the eleventh century, which is some distance from Shîrâz and is a famous sight. At Shîrâz he met his Persian friend and learnt from him all he could of Herât, did not write his notes for some time afterwards, and then mixed up Herât with Herât-i-Khâra.

¶ The journeys above conjectured and a story related by Varthema connected with them fit within the time table made obligatory to him with reference to the South-west Monsoon in the Indian Ocean. It would not have been possible for him to go straight on to India during the summer of 1504, as the South-west Monsoon bursts on the Persian coast by the beginning of June and no *nâkhudâ* or native skipper would have ventured to face the Indian Ocean while it lasted, *i.e.* say before October. How, then, did Varthema spend his time? Khwâja Junair was a wealthy man and had a niece "called Samis [Shams], that is, the Sun," or, as would be said in English, "Sunbeam," and he took Varthema to his house at Herât-i-Khâra and offered her to him. No doubt Varthema lived with her there, and as every Persian merchant of standing has to own land to maintain his status, it is quite reasonable to suppose that Khwâja Junair had property in fertile Herât-i-Khâra, and moreover would wish to be there during the harvest season. Here, no doubt, Varthema stayed with his temporary wife till the South-west Monsoon was over, and then started for India in October 1504. That he did not remain in Persia longer can be estimated from the fact, to be observed later on, that he was at Anjedîva Island off the south-west coast of India before it was taken by the Portuguese in 1505.

IN INDIA: CAMBAY TO CALICUT

¶ Varthema gives no reliable account of time while in Persia, but assuming the above description of his doings there to be right, it seems that he sailed from Hormûz to Jûâ or Kau, which he calls Cheo, on a mouth of the Indus in India. The season is now favourable for further journeys by sea down the west coast. He gives no account of Jûâ and goes on to Cambay, which he misplaces as "near to Indus," following an ancient error which lasted even beyond his time. Otherwise he correctly describes the entrance to the town, and briefly notices the celebrated bore in the Gulf of Cambay. He is correct also in his mention of the local products—turbith (jalap), arrowroot, spikenard, assafoetida and lac, and also carnelians from the Râjpîpla Hills. The diamonds he mentions came from afar—from the distant mart of Golconda in the Deccan. It may be assumed that he reached Cambay about 10 October, 1504.

¶ The habits of "the Sultan of Cambay" are next described. He was the well-known Mahmûd Baigâra of Gujarât, and the great length of his moustaches is duly noted. They are described as curling round his ears, in the Sikh fashion of to-day as regards their beards, which by the followers of that faith are never cut. Varthema then tells a story which was current in his day and afterwards, and even in Mahmûd's lifetime, as to his being "a poison man." This story is really a *réchauffé* of the old folktale of "the Poison Damsel," and Barbosa, in his *Book*, repeats it in such fashion as to lead to the supposition that the basis of the story's popularity was observation of the manner and effect of taking opium and hemp drugs, although Varthema's account clearly attributes the poison to the very common habit of chewing betel. We have also a description of "a certain race," who are "neither Moors nor heathens," *i.e.* neither Muslims nor Hindus, and from the account of them Jains are clearly indicated. They have long abounded in that part of India.

¶ Varthema then talks of "the King of the Ioghe," by which last term he means the *jôgîs* or *yôgîs*, *i.e.* Hindu ascetics. His account reads like a garbled story of the pilgrimage of some wealthy native to a Hindu shrine, and hearsay tales told him at different times of Hindu ascetics of many kinds, combined with personal observations of the appearance of such people on various occasions. In the course of his account he uses the expression *all'apostolica* to describe their dress. This expression he employs more than once to describe Oriental costume, and by it refers to the Roman *toga* used by Italian painters to represent the dress of the Apostles, and in this book it is used to represent roughly the method of wearing the *langôtî* or loin-cloth in India, or indeed any loose robe worn in Eastern fashion.

¶ Varthema is still keeping no kind of diary or time table, but from his statements it is pretty evident that he travelled southwards from Cambay by sea, and it may be assumed that he left it during October. His brief account of the place is explained by his opening statement in his chapter "Concerning Cambay to Calicut in India," which runs thus: "Having promised at the commencement, if I remember rightly, to treat all subjects with brevity, in order that my narrative may not be wearisome, I will continue to relate concisely those things, which appeared to me the most worthy to be known, and the most interesting."

¶ He next says: "Departing from the said city of Combeia, I travelled on until I arrived at another city named Cevul [Châul], which is distant from the above-mentioned city twelve days' journey, and the country between the one and the other of these cities is called Guzerati." Châul is, however, much lower down the west coast than Gujarât extends and lies south of Bombay, then of course only a fisherman's island and a place of no importance whatever. Leaving Châul, at which he arrived about 25 October, and continuing down the coast, he touches at Dabul or Dâbhôl and goes on to Goa, which he calls Goga. He probably reached it about 1 November. The Portuguese did not occupy Goa until 1510, and so Varthema finds it a fortress, "in which there is sometimes a captain who is called Savain, who has 400 Mamelukes, he himself being a Mameluke." Here he is very interesting, as he is unconsciously mentioning Yûsuf 'Adil Shâh of Bîjâpur by a common Portuguese title of the Sabayo or Çabaym, *i.e.* Sâvai, which he obtained from his original home at Sâva in Northern Persia, whence he came to India as an 'Usmânî Turkish *mamlûk*.

¶ Here, too, Varthema quaintly remarks: "This captain, with 400 Mamelukes, wages a great war with the King of Narsinga," thus incidentally introducing the great Vijayanagar Empire of Southern India. Here also he makes acquaintance with the *pardau* or pagoda, which he thus describes: "These golden ducats are called by them *pardai*, and are smaller than the seraphim of Cairo, but thicker, and have two devils [Shiva and Pârbatî] stamped upon one side of them, and certain letters on the other." From Goa, "travelling for seven days on the mainland, I arrived at a city which is called Decan," *i.e.* at Bîjâpur, which he presumably reached about 10 November. Here he is using, after a fashion which he follows on several occasions, the name of a country or kingdom for its capital. In his day, Bîjâpur was the capital of the Deccan.

¶ Varthema has but little to say of Bîjâpur and its sovereign, though the king in his day was the great Yûsuf 'Adil Shâh, who had founded the dynasty named after him in 1489, and had been unquestionably a *mamlûk* of the Bâhmanî kingdom that once had covered the whole Deccan from sea to sea. He had been governor of Bîjâpur and took the opportunity of the break up of the Bâhmanîs to seize the western portion of their dominion down to the west coast, which he ruled from Châul to Bhatkal. Varthema notices that he was "a great enemy to the Christians," referring no doubt to the difficulties raised by 'Adil Shâh being first a somewhat fanatical Shî'a and then a Sunnî Muslim for political reasons, and he tells a fanciful tale about the mines in Karnûl, which supplied the great diamond market at Golconda.

¶ After leaving Bîjâpur, Varthema journeys in five days to the coast at "Bathacala," reaching it, say, 16 November, 1504. This "Bathacala" Badger identified, not with Bhatkal, but with Sadâsivagarh, called by Hamilton Batcoal, within Kârwâr Head, close to Anjedîva or Anchedîva Island, also mentioned by Varthema, on the ground that the place he means must have been north of Honâwar or Onore, as he passed on by that town after visiting "Bathacala," whereas Bhatkal is to the south of Honâwar. Dames, in editing Barbosa, says that it was close to Cintacora, a name that has puzzled enquirers, and is no doubt the Centacola that Varthema says he visited after going to Anjedîva Island. "Bathacala" is fairly described as a typical town of the west coast. Anjedîva was not captured by the Portuguese till 1505, so when Varthema saw it in 1504, the island was still in native hands, and he gives a reasonably correct account of it.

¶ He next crosses back to the mainland, touches at Centacola, and goes on to Honâwar or Onore, reaching it probably by 18 November. Thence he passes on to the neighbouring Mangalore, and so on to Cannanore, arriving at that place, say, by 21 November. He gives a fair description of the west coast, considering that he was a pioneer traveller. Cannanore, he informs us, is "a fine and large city in which the King of Portugal has a strong castle [of St Angelo]." By this expression he means presumably that there was a strong stockade round the Portuguese factory established at that place, as the Portuguese under Pedro Alvarez Cabral and João de Nueva first appeared at Cannanore in 1501, and Vasco da Gama erected the factory there in 1502, but the fort was not completed till 1507 under Francisco d'Almeida. He is right in saying that the native ruler was very friendly towards the Portuguese, and generally in his description of the town, especially as to its being a port for the import of horses from Persia. He winds up his story by saying: "The king of this place [Cannanore] has 50,000 Naeri, that is, gentlemen who fight with swords, shields, lances and bows and with artillery"—a shrewd description of the military caste of the Nairs.

¶ From Cannanore Varthema goes to Vijayanagar, which he reaches in fifteen days, say, about 6 December, 1504. He calls it "the city of Bisinegar" in the kingdom of Narsinga. Vijayanagar, which is south of the Deccan, was the last Hindu empire in India, and was founded about 1336, lasting till 1563. It had a splendid capital, the ruins of which still exist at Hampê. It was called Bisinagar by Varthema, usually Bisnaga by the Portuguese, and Bîjanagar by English travellers, and was the great stronghold of Hinduism in the south. It kept back the Muslim aggressors from the Deccan for over two centuries and eventually prevented Islâm from overrunning South India. Varthema saw it towards its close, though it was still in full vigour in his day, as one of the greatest of its rulers, Krishnadeva Râya, did not ascend the throne till 1509, after the time of his visit. The ruler of his day was Narsingha Râya, hence his name became also the ordinary contemporary Portuguese name for the kingdom—Narsinga.

¶ His very brief description of Vijayanagar is borne out by other accounts of his day, but he confines himself mainly to describing the elephant, which animal had evidently impressed him. His account is clear and he was obviously familiar with the elephant. However, he, perhaps naturally, mixes up tigers and lions, which he heard of but apparently did not see. As regards the King of Vijayanagar he shrewdly remarks: "This king is a very great friend of the Christians, especially of the King of Portugal, because he does not know much of any other Christians." His account of Vijayanagar winds up with a good description of the currency then obtaining there.

¶ From Vijayanagar he returned to Cannanore, reaching it, say, about 21 December, and goes thence to some insignificant places: twelve miles by land to Dharmapatam near Tellicherry, where he mentions there were "15,000 Moors," no doubt meaning thereby the Moplahs. Thence he goes a day's journey to Pantalâyinî and Kappata, small places of no consequence. After this he goes to "the very noble city of Calicut," where he introduces us to the Zamorin—a much discussed name for the monarch thereof. It may be assumed that he reached Calicut about 1 January, 1505.

IN CALICUT

¶ Varthema devotes more space to Calicut than to any other place in his itinerary, though he did not stay there long on his first visit in 1505, giving as his reason for a speedy departure that his commercial companion, the Persian merchant Khwâja Junair, was obliged to go on quickly for reasons of his trade. But in 1506 and 1507 he was for about eighteen months a factor there for the Portuguese Viceroy Francisco d'Almeida, and so had every opportunity of learning all about the town. He evidently thought that his description of his first visit was the right place for a long account of it.

¶ To Varthema, Calicut was the chief town in all India: "Having nearly arrived at the head of India, that is to say, at the place in which the greatest dignity of India is centred." Here he gives the Portuguese sense to the word "India," which at that time meant the little areas they controlled and the country round them in South India. He describes the town as he saw it—a poor sort of place—and goes on to be extremely discursive in relating what struck his imagination. In fact, his "chapters" here dance in a bewildering manner from subject to subject just as various points of interest occur to him, and he is consequently not easy to follow: but he was evidently not much impressed with the buildings on the west coast. Even the palace of the Zamorin, described as of great extent and full of wonderful things, he only values as "worth 200 ducats or thereabouts." He notices that "the floor of the house is all adorned with cow-dung." This plastering with liquified cow-dung was performed—as it always is in India—as a purifying preservative for cleanliness. He also notices that the Zamorin was afflicted with "the French disease and had it in the throat." "French" here is a translation of the Arabic Farang or Frank, and means that the Arabs attributed an European origin to venereal disease, but the description seems to imply that the Zamorin had something the matter with his throat, perhaps cancer. Varthema was also evidently greatly exercised about the lighting of the Zamorin's palace, and gives an interesting version of the custom of feeding Brâhmans in crowds on the death of a Zamorin, hinting also at a custom of public abstention from shaving on the third day after such a death.

¶ Varthema passes on to a quaint account of the religion of the people: "The King of Calicut is a pagan, and worships the devil in the manner you shall hear." He must have observed various ceremonies at Hindu temples and mixed them up with recollections of conversations with educated people—European languages, especially Spanish, were known to many *mamlûk* slaves in India at that period. "They acknowledge that there is a God who has created the heaven and the earth and all the world." This he learnt from educated Hindus, and then he passes on to the belief in the godling or *dêvatâ*, who does good and evil to mankind, and so is much propitiated: "Which devil they call Deumo and God they call Tamerani," *i.e.* the name for the godling is *dêvan* and for the Supreme God is Tamburân, Lord or Master. Under the title of Sathanas (Satan) he describes the images of Narsingh and the goddess Kâlî, and as to his account of her worship he must have looked on at some ceremonies of the lower orders, nowadays classed together as "devil-worship" and far removed from the religious observances of the philosophic and thoughtful Hindu. There is, however, evidence to show that he applied the term Sathanas to any prominent Hindu image. Varthema also notices the "devil-dancing" ceremonies used at the planting of a rice-field and on exorcising the evil spirit supposed to possess those who are seriously ill.

¶ In his discursive way Varthema has a chapter, "showing how a great number of people came to Calicut on the 25th of December to receive their pardon." Incidentally this statement goes to show that he was in Calicut on Christmas Day 1504 and later, so that it may be assumed that he did not leave for his further journey eastwards till January 1505. The "pardon" was probably in reality the Navarâtra Festival at the Hindu New Year—a festival which he says he saw in the neighbourhood of Calicut, or it may have been one of the festivals held on Srîvalayanâd Hill outside Calicut. Badger suggests that the temple he describes as the scene of the festivities was that in which Vasco da Gama made his historic mistake of taking a Hindu service for a Christian one, though it is more likely to have been the Great Tâli Temple in the heart of the town.

¶ The story is, however, worth repeating here from Greene's *Collection of Voyages*, i, 51 f.: "The temple was as large as a great monastery. It was built of freestone and covered with tiles. Over the front door there hung seven balls, and before it stood a pillar as high as the mast of a ship, made of wire [? iron], with a weathercock of the same at the top. Within, it was full of images. This made da Gama and the rest take it for a Christian church. Entering it, they were met by certain men, naked from the waist upwards, and from thence to the knees covered with calico. They wore pieces of calico also under the armpits, with certain threads, which were hung over their left shoulder, and passed under the right arm (just as the Romish priests used to wear their stoles formerly). These men with a sponge dipped in a fountain, sprinkled their visitants, and then gave each of them some sanders [sandal-wood] pulverized to strew upon their heads, as the Papists do ashes, and on their arms. The Portuguese did the one, but not the other, because their clothes were on. On the walls of the temple were many images painted, some with great teeth sticking above an inch out of their mouths: others with four arms and such frightful faces that the Portuguese began to doubt whether it was a Christian church or not. Upon the top of the chapel, which stood in the middle of the temple, was a fort, or freestone tower, with a little wire [? iron] door and stone stairs on the outside. In the wall of this tower was an image, on sight whereof the Malabars called out 'Mary' [Mari-amma, goddess of smallpox]. Whereupon da Gama and the rest, taking it for an image of the Virgin, fell on their knees and prayed. Only one, Juam de Sala, who had some doubt of the matter, in making his genuflections, said: 'If this be the devil, I worship God,' which made da Gama smile."

¶ From religion Varthema naturally passes to the Brâhmans—in this case the Nambûdrîs of the south-west coast—telling us an unsavoury tale of their share in the selection of a wife by the Zamorin on the matriarchal system, and describing with some accuracy the manner in which a strict Brâhman takes his food, though he attributes the habits he notices to the Zamorin himself at his meals. After dealing with the Brâhmans, he passes on to the other castes of the west coast, giving a remarkable account of them considering his very early date and that he could hardly have had a predecessor. The Portuguese Barbosa, who was a contemporary, is quite as elaborate and much more accurate, but then he learnt Malayâlam, the language of the country. It is, however, quite possible that Varthema obtained his information from the same sources as Barbosa. He notices also the haughty aloofness of both Brâhmans and Nairs from the "untouchable" lower classes of society, and the general abstinence from "cow beef," and from flesh altogether by the Brâhmans, together with the indiscriminate diet of the lowest classes, which includes mice and "fish dried in the sun." With regard to these last he draws a lurid, but not too exaggerated, picture of their method of rearing children.

¶ He further notes the well-known matriarchal system of inheritance prevalent in that part of India, by which "the heir of the King is the son of one of his sisters," though he gives a garbled reason for it, and makes some exaggerated observations on social customs generally, but he is correct as to the use of betel. He then returns to the inheritance laws, and gives a vague explanation of the real reason for them in a chapter which is quaint indeed, and bears an equally quaint title in his book: "How the Pagans sometimes exchange their wives." In this account—in which his attempts to reproduce the Malayâlam language are beyond correction—he is really trying to describe the system under which a woman, though nominally married, cohabits, legitimately according to her custom, with any man other than her husband whom she desires, and therefore any child she has is hers and not her husband's, and is the heir of her brother—as Varthema says: "The children go according to the word of the woman," though here he is not quite correct.

¶ He then describes the usual mode of eating and repeats an old tale as to the recovery of debts by making surreptitiously a magic circle round the debtor, and has an amusing, though incorrect, account of Hindu bathing customs and the "manner of saying their prayers." His account of the mode "of fighting of these people of Calicut" is even more amusing, and he notices that the Nairs "have black teeth on account of the leaves [betel] which I have already told you they eat." They do not, however, eat the leaves, but chew them and spit them out. He notices, too, correctly that many of the lower orders do not burn but bury their dead. Lastly, he observes the large number of "Moors," *i.e.* foreign Asiatic merchants, flocking to Calicut and creating the Moplah population. Foreign merchants of all classes would naturally interest Varthema and his companion, the Persian merchant Khwâja Junair, and we have accordingly a good account of the "bankers and money-changers" of Calicut, and their methods of dealing, weighing goods and testing the fineness of gold by the touchstone. There is also a description of the custom of secretly settling bargains by the touch of hands and fingers under a cloth, which is current among the Eastern peoples from the Arabs and Abyssinians to the natives of India and the Further East.

¶ From places and people Varthema passes on to plants and animals, and gives a good description of the "money of Malabar." He then describes the pepper plant and its products, and also ginger, and mentions the myrobalan tree. Under the name of *ciccara* he tells us about the jack-fruit, and gives also a rough description of the mango, "which is called *amba*, the stem of which is called *manga*," though *ambâ* is Indian vernacular and *mangga* is Malay for the fruit. Several other fruits which he mentions both by name and description are difficult to identify, and then he has a long account of "the most fruitful tree in the world," *i.e.* the coconut, which he correctly names by the Malayâlam term for it, *tenga*. He gives practically every use of both the tree and its products in an entertaining manner, and then he winds up his account of the produce of the south-western Indian soil by the remark: "In this country of Calicut there is found a great quantity of *zerzalino*, from which they make excellent [gingelly] oil," and to which there has already been a reference.

¶ Of the animals, he mentions many kinds, remarking, wrongly however, that elephants are not found in south-western India. He mentions also peacocks, parrots and mainas, these last under the Persian name of *sâr*, probably learnt from his companion, Khwâja Junair. He has, too, a very garbled account of the crocodile as a "serpent." Incidentally, he here mentions the Jains, under the strange title of "the King of Calicut," on whom apparently everything unusual is fastened. He notices also the Jain habit, inculcated by their religion, of killing nothing and cherishing all living things, even snakes of all descriptions.

¶ The last subject for discussion as to Calicut now, though not the latest in order in Varthema's pages, is his account of the "manner of navigation." On this point he makes an important set of observations, at any rate so far as regards his further journey. He first tells us that their vessels are "of 300 or 400 butts," showing thus in an interesting way that the "tonnage" of ships was based, as now in England, on their assumed capacity to carry "tons" or "casks" of cargo. He then gives a fairly accurate account of the "ships" of the southern coast of India, and becomes unusually interesting as to navigation. He tells us that Cape Comorin is eight days' journey from Calicut, that the sailing season is from September to April, and that from 1 May to 15 August the sea routes are closed by the South-west Monsoon. He then makes the interesting observation: "At the end of April they depart from the coast of Calicut, and pass the Cape of Cumerin, and enter into another course of navigation, which is safe during these four months [May, June, July, August] and go for small spices." That is to say, that about 20 April at the latest vessels coasted down to Cape Comorin, and went round it to the east coast, where they were sheltered from the Monsoon, if they kept close to land. He calls the great cape Cape Cumerin, which is nearer to the vernacular name Kumarî than the modern form. Lastly, he describes the various kinds of boats he saw about Calicut by names in various languages other than the local vernacular, Malayâlạm.

ROUND CAPE COMORIN TO CEYLON AND THE COROMANDEL COAST

¶ It may be assumed, then, that Varthema left Calicut soon after he arrived, giving as the reason—as already noted—that his friend, Khwâja Junair, found it necessary to leave that place because it had been "ruined by the King of Portugal, for the merchants who used to come there were not there, neither did they come. And the reason why they did not come was that the [King of Calicut] consented that the Moors should kill forty-eight Portuguese, whom I saw put to death. And on this account the King of Portugal is always at war, and he has killed, and every day kills, great numbers." Varthema is here recounting historical facts. Vasco da Gama began in 1498 by having friendly relations with the Zamorin, but after Cabral settled a factory at Calicut in 1500 there was trouble between him and the Portuguese, and Vasco da Gama again appeared before the town in 1502. There was then much further hostility and cruelty on both sides, and when, about 1505, Lopo Suarez d'Albergaria came with a fleet and demanded Portuguese prisoners from the Zamorin, some were kept back—the 48 whom Varthema says he saw killed. In revenge for this Suarez bombarded the town and did great damage.

¶ He leaves by the Backwater of Cochin, which he describes as "a river, which is the most beautiful I ever saw" and goes to Kâyankullam, where he finds "Christians of those of St Thomas"—an ancient body, as to whose origin there is still much controversy. He stays three days and reaches Quilon, say about the middle of January, 1505. He describes it as "extremely powerful," and gives a most interesting reference to the never-ending struggles between the little states along the south-west coast, which prevented Malabar from becoming a land of any political importance. "At that time the king of this city [Quilon] was the friend of the King of Portugal, but being at war with others, it did not appear to us well to remain here." It was this very playing fast and loose with the Portuguese by the petty states of Malabar out of enmity to each other that gave the Portuguese the chance of establishing themselves along the west coast. From Quilon Varthema takes to the sea, and doubling Cape Comorin reaches Kâyal on the east coast of India. He correctly remarks on the pearl fishery on that coast, probably at Tuticorin, though he does not say that he put in there.

¶ After leaving Quilon Varthema is brief and vague, but clear enough until he leaves Kâyal, when he becomes difficult. From Kâyal, he says, "we then passed further onwards and arrived at a city which is called Cioromandel, which is a marine district, and distant from Colon [Quilon] seven days' journey by sea, more or less, according to the wind"; and he clearly infers that he went all the way by sea, reaching "Cioromandel," it may be presumed, about 20 January. The journey thither implies, however, going through the Palk Strait between India and Ceylon, though he makes no mention of this difficult passage on his northward voyage up the eastern coast of India. His "city called Cioromandel" is apparently Negapatam, as no town on the east or Coromandel coast has ever been called Coromandel, that term, really Chôlamandala, meaning the Country of the Chôlas. Negapatam, however, though not far from, is not "situated opposite to the island of Zeilon [Ceylon]," as Varthema puts it. But he is right otherwise in describing Negapatam as subject to the Vijayanagar Empire and as "the route to many large countries." At this place he hears tales from Christians that the "body of St Thomas was twelve miles distant." This, no doubt, refers to the reputed tomb of St Thomas at San Thomé not far from Madras, which is of course much more than twelve miles north of Negapatam.

¶ Here the Persian, Khwâja Junair, disposes of his merchandise, but the companions do not stay long, because "they were at war with the King of Tarnassari" (*i.e.* Tenasserim across the Bay of Bengal) which is quite likely, as there was constant friction between the Tamils of the Coromandel coast of India and the Talaings (Peguans or Môns) of what is now the coast of Burma across the Bay. Varthema, however, does not

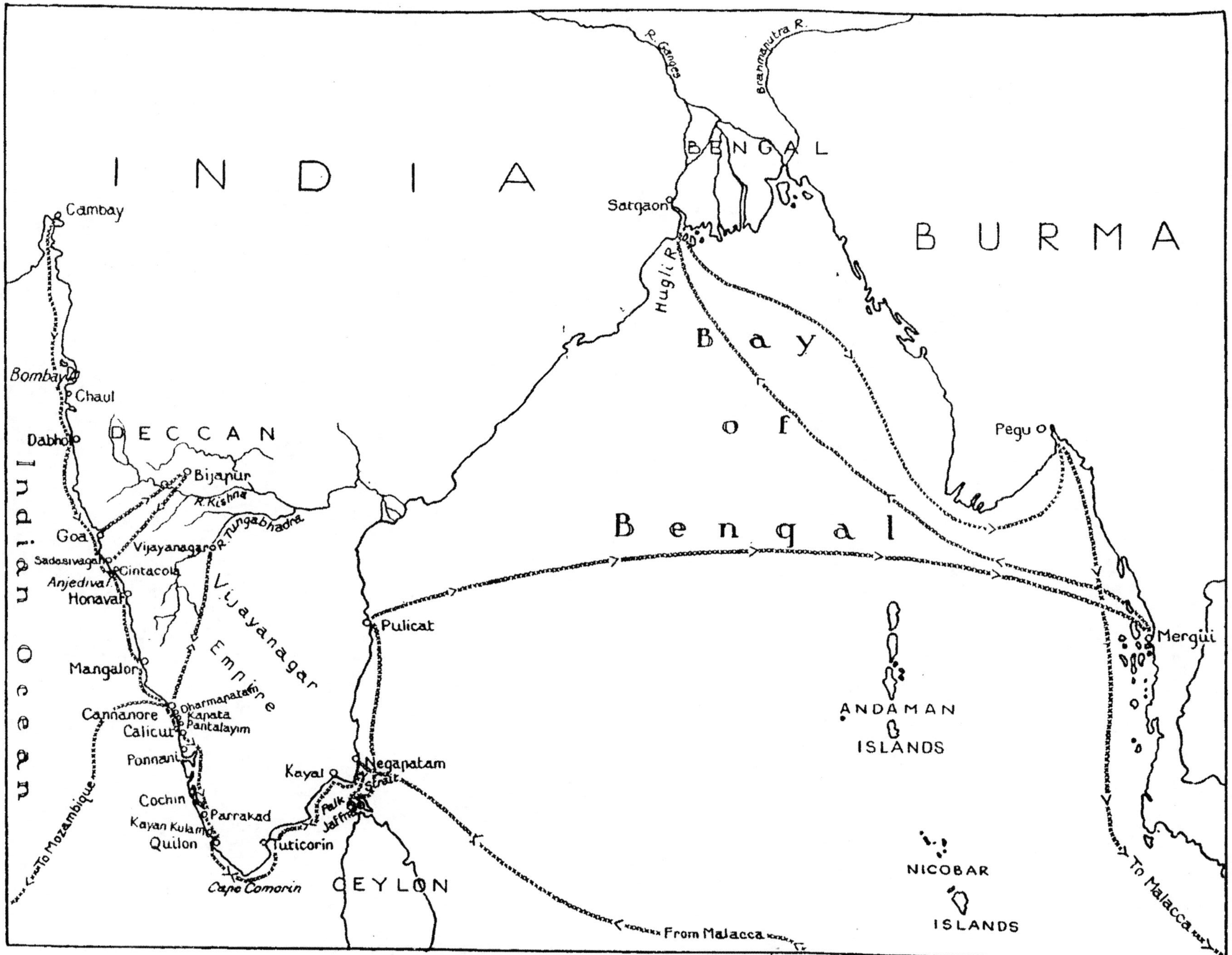

VARTHEMA'S ITINERARY IN THE BAY OF BENGAL

at once go further onwards on his journey, but retraces his steps, and goes backwards to Ceylon with a convoy. He is, nevertheless, very far from being clear here: "we took a ship with some other merchants, which ships are called *ciampane*, for they are flat-bottomed, and require little water and carry much goods." By *ciampane*, an Italian plural form, he clearly means *sampans*, open flat-bottomed boats of Further Indian origin, hardly fit for the sea unless it be very still. However, the weather in January is hereabouts usually quite calm, and the journey to Ceylon from Negapatam in a *sampan* is not by any means impossible, but it should be noticed here that later on Varthema seems to mean a larger vessel than the ordinary *sampan* by the term *ciampana*. He then goes on to say: "We passed a gulf of twelve or fifteen leagues where we had incurred great peril because there are many shoals and rocks there." This is clearly the Palk Strait.

¶ He does not mention any place in Ceylon at which he landed, but as he was very quickly back from this expedition at Pulicat, north of Madras, which last did not then exist, it is pretty certain that he touched at Jaffna in the north of the island, especially as it is the chief point of communication with India, reaching it about 25 January. His general description of Ceylon and its jewels are fairly accurate, though they contain several serious errors, but these are not unnatural. The *carzofoli* he mentions were more likely custard apples than artichokes, and his *melangoli* were probably sweet limes, not oranges. He gives also a rough account of the method of preparing cinnamon bark for trade. He repeats, too, a story about Adam's Peak, the great prominent mountain of Ceylon which "A Moorish merchant told me" was a place of pilgrimage "because, as they say, Adam was up there praying and doing penance, and that the impressions of his feet are seen to this day, and that they are about two spans long." Dames, in his edition of Barbosa's *Book*, however, shows that the shrine on the top of Adam's Peak is really of Buddhist origin and that the legend thereof concerning Buddha has been foisted on to Adam by Arab sailors. Lastly, Varthema has a story which runs thus: "Being in our ship one evening, a man came on the part of the king to my companion, and told him that he should carry to him his corals and saffron; for he had a great quantity of both. A merchant of the said island, who was a Moor [probably a Labbâi], hearing these words, said to him secretly: 'Do not go to the king, for he will pay for your goods after his own fashion.' And this he said out of cunning, in order that my companion might go away, because he himself had the same kind of merchandise. However, answer was given to the message of the king, that on the following day he would go to his lord. And when morning came, he took a vessel and rowed over to the mainland." This story makes one think that Varthema and his companion never really landed on Ceylon at all, but did what business they had off Jaffna in their ship.

¶ It must by this time have been about 3 February, 1505, when "we arrived [from Ceylon] in the course of three days at a place which is called Paleachet, which is subject to the King of Narsinga," *i.e.* Pulicat to the north of Madras, then in the Vijayanagar dominions. But three days is much too short a time for the journey, as, if there was any wind to speak of at all, it would have been from the north-east and in their teeth. He describes Pulicat as a place of great traffic, "especially in jewels, for they come here from Zailon and from Pego," a very interesting form of Pegu, which the English nowadays pronounce as Peegyoo, both vowels long, but which the natives thereof call Pagô, accent on the *ô*. "As this country [Pulicat] was at fierce war with the King of Tarnassari, we could not remain here a very long time. But after remaining here a few days we took our route towards the city of Tarnassari, which is distant a thousand miles from here. At which city we arrived in fourteen days by sea." Varthema must have sailed round the north of the Andaman Islands and reached Tenasserim about 1 March, 1505, at the finest time of the year for a sea voyage in the Bay of Bengal.

IN TENASSERIM

¶ We are now presented with a long account of the place so called by Varthema on the eastern shores of the Bay of Bengal, which then belonged to the kingdom of Siam and is now part of the British province of Burma. It is a true pioneer account and is quite wrong in some of the observations made, but on the whole it is remarkably shrewd. He unquestionably visited "Tenasserim," which he should have called Mergui, as he mistakes the name of the province for its capital, just as he has already done in the case of "Cioromandel" and other places. And in regard to certain other mistakes of the like nature to be found in his account, it must be remembered that, like all Europeans of his time and much later, he had no suspicion of the true form of the religion of this country—Buddhism—and that, so far as he knew, no visitors who could write had preceded him. Tenasserim as a town was superseded by Mergui before Varthema's time, which was, as he says, the mart for trade in the Bay of Bengal for the Siamese government. He describes the country "as constantly fighting with the King of Narsinga and the King of Banghella [Bengal]," and as possessing a large army. He also describes the plants and fauna, not always accurately but fairly well, notes the "white parrots," or cockatoos, and "other kinds which are of seven very beautiful colours." By these last he means lories, a name which in the Malayan vernacular is *nûrî*, but means, however, five, not seven, remarkably brilliant colours. He remarks also the game cocks and hens, which are indigenous, and on the national love of cock-fighting, but what he says of goats and sheep is rather wild, though he is right as to the huge size of the buffaloes. He notices also correctly the great quantities of fish, and a bone which may have belonged to one of the whales that frequent the Bay of Bengal.

¶ As regards the people, he is only fairly right as to their appearance, costumes and feeding, but he mistakes the upper classes for Brâhmans, though there can be no such people in a Buddhist country like Tenasserim. Then he has a circumstantial account of the deflouring of brides before marriage, which is nevertheless apocryphal, unless the perpetrators thereof were foreign merchants. He next gives a fair account of the common custom in these lands of burning the bodies of the more highly esteemed Buddhist monks, whom he miscalls Brâhmans, and says that on these occasions "his wife is always present, making exceedingly great lamentations, and no other woman." Buddhist monks have, of course, no wives, but in Tenasserim the custom of burning the dead was much extended among the lay population. He also tells us of suitors proving their love for their ladies by burning "the naked flesh" of their arms, which must be a hearsay account of the well-known Siamese custom of ordeal by fire. Lastly, he interpolates here an account of *sati* or burning of widows, which clearly belongs to something he saw in Calicut, as he speaks, in connection with it, of "the Deumo," a form representing *dêvan*, a Hindu name for a god. There could, however, be no custom of *sati* or anything approaching it in a Buddhist country such as Tenasserim. It is possible, nevertheless, though hardly likely, that Varthema saw such a ceremony among some of the many Hindus resident in the place. His account of the bridal customs, like some of the others mentioned above, savour also of recollections of stories heard at Calicut.

¶ Among other customs, Varthema correctly notices that "their writing is on paper like ours, not on the leaves of a tree like that of Calicut." The Far Eastern peoples have long made a coarse paper by hammering, and the use of palm leaves for writing was long enough continued in Calicut for the present writer to have had his washing bills so prepared there in 1873. He is also shrewd in his observations as to the wide spread of the knowledge of reading and writing, which prevailed, in consequence, though he did not know it, of the schools for the lay people kept up in

Buddhist monasteries. He is further generally correct in his remarks on the laws of inheritance, and finally he writes with knowledge as to the shipping employed on the coast of the Malay Peninsula. Here his account of a "kind of large ship which is called *giunchi*" is valuable for the history of the Malay *jong* being applied, in various forms of the term *junk*, to Far Eastern ships of all sizes. He further makes a most interesting statement that on these *giunchi* "they carry some little vessels [*prahu*, *prow*] to a city called Melacha [Malacca], and from thence they go with these little vessels for small spices to a place which you shall know when the proper time comes."

IN BENGAL

¶ From Tenasserim Varthema goes to Bengal, reaching his destination about the middle of March. He says frankly that this journey was undertaken out of curiosity: "Let us return to my companion, for he and I had a desire to see farther on." Then he tells us that "having sold some of our merchandise we took the route towards the city of Banghella" as merchants. This term—the city of Banghella—has long been and still is, a source of trouble to scholars: where was it? This question greatly exercised Badger in 1863, it sorely troubled Dames when editing the contemporary *Book of Duarte Barbosa* in 1921, and it has been the cause of many researches by Indian scholars in Bengal itself. Varthema, however, evidently repeats his former practice and calls the town he visited after the province in which it was situated—Bengal. The actual site is hardly yet settled, but it may be taken, for the purpose of defining Varthema's journey, to be Satgâon on an old bed of the Hûglî River. On this assumption he is right in saying that "the sultan of this place is a Moor," and that the people "are all Mahommedans," as Bengal at that time was under the Husain Shâhî Dynasty; but that it was "constantly at war with the King of Narsingha" is an exaggeration, though no doubt other Hindus gave continual trouble. Barbosa makes the same mistake, and no doubt the Portuguese in Varthema's time thought that the Vijayanagar Empire extended throughout India to Bengal. It is correctly noted, however, that the trade was largely in cotton and silk stuffs, which went all over Asia and Europe.

¶ Varthema next tells a curious story of meeting certain Asiatic Christians at "Banghella," with whom he and his Persian comrade, Khwâja Junair, eventually travelled further east: "We also found some Christian merchants here. They said that they were from a city called Sarnau, and had brought for sale silken stuffs, and aloes-wood, and benzoin, and musk. Which

Christians said that in their country there were many lords also Christians, but they are subject to the great Khan [of] Cathai [China]." This part of the account reads as if Varthema had met merchants, who were Mongolians of some kind and were Nestorian Christians. Such an idea is confirmed by a statement that "they write in the contrary way to us, that is, after the manner of Armenia." But Armenians—always mixed up with Nestorians in Varthema's time—write as Europeans do, and so these Christians were not strictly Armenians. Varthema then writes: "These same men are as white as we are," and "as to the dress of these Christians," he says, "they were clothed in a *xebec* [jerkin] made with folds, and the sleeves were quilted with cotton. And on their heads they wore a cap a palm and a half long, made of red cloth. . . . . These Christians do not wear shoes, but they wear a kind of breeches made of silk, similar to those worn by mariners. . . . And they eat at a table after our fashion, and they eat every kind of flesh." The inference here is that they were of a Chinese or Far Eastern race.

¶ So it may be assumed that the Christians whom Varthema met in Bengal were Nestorian merchants from some part of the Far East. The term "city of Sarnau," however, raises a difficulty, whether it represents a "city" or a "country" after Varthema's fashion. According to him, it was subject to the "Khan of Cathai," *i.e.* to the Mongol Emperor of China. It contained Nestorian Christians, as it is known that the Far East did from before the days of Marco Polo in the thirteenth century. It produced silk, aloes-wood (eagle-wood), benzoin and musk. It will be seen also later on that these Christians of Sarnau travelled with Varthema and Khwâja Junair, as their guides, to Pegu, Malacca, Sumâtra and the Spice Islands of the Malay Archipelago, which they evidently knew well, and in the language of which, say Malay, they could apparently act as interpreters. They must also have known Arabic as a *lingua franca* to be able to talk freely with Varthema and his companion. They were finally parted with at Malacca, when Varthema and his companion were on their way back to India, so that they might return to Sarnau. But no such name as Sarnau is now known as the equivalent for any place or country as part of China or the Far East, and there is an apparently obvious derivation for it in Shahr-i-Nau or "the New City," a town in the northern part of Persia, where in Varthema's day and before it Nestorian Christians abounded, and it would not have been difficult physically for his Christian friends to have wandered thence as merchants to Bengal. But the other conditions make it impossible to identify it with the Sarnau of the text, and this derivation must therefore be rejected.

¶ The correct situation of Sarnau, however, is, as Mr F. W. Lucas has pointed out to the present writer, to be found in Yule's *Marco Polo*, ed. 1875, Book III, chap. VII, pp. 594 ff: "For some centuries Siam was generally known to traders by the Persian name Shahr-i-nao or New City. This seems to be the name generally applied to it by the *Shijârat Malâyu* (or *Malay Chronicle*), and it is used by 'Abdu'r-Razzâk. It appears among the early navigators of the sixteenth century, as da Gama, Varthema, Giovanni d'Empoli and Mendez Pinto, in the shape of Sarnau, Xarnau [Sharnau]. Whether this name was applied to [the then] new city of Ayuthia, or was a translation of the older Lophaburî (which appears to be the Sanskrit or Pali Navapura = New City), I do not know."

¶ Mr J. M. Kindersley has looked up the passage in the *Shijârat Malâyu* (ed. 'Abdu'llâh *bin* 'Abdu'lkâdir Manohi; Leiden, Büll, 1884) and writes as follows: "Chapter viii runs as follows: 'Says the Chronicler, To continue, the King of Shahar-annûi was monarch of a very large kingdom, and his officers and men were so numerous that they could not be numbered any longer. Now it was told to the king of Shahar-annûi that the country of Samadrâ [Sumâtra] was full of all kinds of traders and merchants, and its king was a very great one.'" The chapter then goes on, somewhat apocryphally, to describe the King of Shahar-annûi's plot for kidnapping the King of Sumâtra, which succeeds, and the release of the said king after he had been made into "a keeper of chickens." Mr Kindersley is inclined to think that Shahar-annûi of the Malay annals has nothing to do with the Sarnau of Varthema, but writing on the above quotation from the *Shijârat Malâyu*, Mr Otto Blagden remarks that in Chapter viii "Shahar-annûi is either Lophburî or Ayuthia (both in Siam)."

¶ Mr Lucas has also found the following references to Sarnau in his splendid collection of maps. On Diego Homem's, *Karton der Aussereuropäischen Erdteile*, 1568, on the west side of the head of the Gulf of Siam is found Sorna. In a corresponding position in two maps in Linschoten's *Voyages into the East and West Indies* (English text), 1599, are found respectively Sornam and Sornan, and on a map in the Latin edition, 1599, is found Sornam. Both Manrique in his *Travels* and Fernão Mendez Pinto, in his *Peregrinação*, write the name as Sornau.

¶ It is clear, therefore, on the whole that by Sarnau Varthema's Christian friends meant a region at the head of the Gulf of Siam, though by the sixteenth century the modern kingdom of Siam had been long founded and was not subject to "the Khan of Cathai." It answers, however, to the other conditions, except that it is news to hear that the Nestorian faith had found its way even there.

¶ It is agreed between "the Christians," Varthema and Khwâja Junair that they should in future travel together, and they commence their journey by going to "Pego." So "we passed a gulf [Martaban] towards the south, and so arrived at the city of Pego," apparently about the beginning of April, 1505, though the Gulf of Martaban is, strictly speaking, just to the east of the entrance to the Pegu River.

IN PEGU

¶ Varthema correctly describes Pegu as "on the mainland and near to the sea." In his day it was still not fully developed and was under its indigenous Talaing kings of a dynasty that lasted from 1287 to 1540, and the reigning king was the locally famous Binyâ Rân, who ruled from 1481 to 1526. This accounts for his not being so enthusiastic in describing the town as were some of his successors, who saw it as an imperial city later on. The king is described as being at war with the King of Ava, that is, of Burma proper: who was this King of Ava? In the beginning of the sixteenth century there was a time of great political confusion in the country now known as Burma and it was divided between small principalities of differing nationalities. So, though an old Shân dynasty had been ruling at Ava since 1298, there was also ruling in the petty kingdom of Taungnû (Tonghoo) a dynasty of mixed Burmese and Shân descent, which was much more likely to have been the enemy of Pegu than the King of Ava itself, especially as in the next generation a great king of Taungnû, Tabin Shwêdî, took Pegu in 1540 and founded there what was subsequently known as the Talaing Empire. With the help of his successors, Bayin Naung and Nàndâ Bayin, he gave a capital to Pegu in the form of a city that greatly excited the admiration of European travellers. It was not till 1613 that the Burmans ruled in Pegu, to be ousted later on by the Talaings, and not till 1757 that Alompra (Alaungphayâ) established Burmese rule over all Burma.

¶ In one of his remarks Varthema shows signs of having recognized that the religion of this region was peculiar: "Their faith, customs, manner of living and dress, are after the manner of Tarnassari." This is probably the earliest hint we have of a European dimly recognizing the existence of Buddhism as apart from Hinduism. Then he goes on to say that the king "has with him more than a thousand Christians of the country which has been above mentioned to you," that is, Nestorians from Sarnau. Here he is premature, as there is no evidence of the existence of Christians of any kind, employed in Pegu before the Portuguese a few years after

Varthema's visit. Sir Henry Yule has, however, pointed out that he may have mistaken Buddhists for Christians from hearing incorrectly that the soldiers worshipped Buddha, Dharma and Sangha (Buddha, the Law and the Assembly or Church), and assumed that this was their Trinity and thence that the soldiers were Christians.

¶ From his various statements, it is pretty clear that Varthema spent some days in Pegu and thereabouts, and he gives a longish account of his proceedings in consequence. His descriptions of the place and country are good, considering his opportunities, and there are some remarks which show that he writes from personal observation. For instance, he observes: "In like manner I do not know if there can be found in the world such thick canes as I found here, of which I saw some which were really as thick as a barrel." This is the giant bamboo, a peculiarity of the Lower Burma region. He also notes: "You must know that in the said city, a large pearl and diamond are worth more here than with us, and also an emerald." This is right, as precious stones, if good, were, even in the time of the present writer, more valuable in Burma than in England. He says besides that such stones came from Capellan, a name that still requires explanation, but it means the Ruby Mines, a district of Upper Burma. Again he says: "And so we departed thence in a ship made all of one piece, and more than fifteen or sixteen paces long"—a fair description of the great river boats of Burma. Next he gives a long account of a visit to the king, and a typical description of the polite conversation, which took place on such occasions between a king of the type of Binyâ Rân of Pegu and an important Oriental merchant of the class to which Khwâja Junair belonged. His last remark is important: "The next day we saw two women burnt alive voluntarily, in the manner as I have described it in Tarnassari." Here again he must have witnessed a *sati* of some Hindu immigrants, unless he mistook one of the barbarous punishments then common in Burma for a case of *sati*. Perhaps he even mistook the burning of the body of a venerated Buddhist monk for a case of *sati*.

IN MALACCA AND SUMÂTRA

¶ On leaving Pegu Varthema sailed to Malacca, arriving, it may be assumed, about 21 April. "Near to the said city we found an extremely great *fiumara*, as large as any we had ever seen, which they call Gaza, which is evidently more than twenty-five miles wide." By *fiumara* and Gaza he seems to mean the Straits of Singapore, if we take Gaza to represent the Arabic *bughâz*, a strait. But he goes on to call the *fiumara* a river, clearly by mistake: "And opposite to the said river there is a very large island, which is called Sumatra." In this last remark we are presented incidentally with the name of Sumâtra for the first time in history in that form. Oddly enough, Varthema here shows the vagueness of his geographical notions by remarking "the river Gaza, otherwise Gange, as I think." His next statement is important for history: "When we had arrived at the city of Melacha, we were immediately presented to the Sultan, who is a Moor, as is also all his kingdom. The said city is on the mainland and pays tribute to the King of Cini [here meaning Siam], who caused this place to be built about eighty years ago, because there is a good port there, which is the principal port of the main ocean." As a matter of historical fact Malacca, as a State, is older at any rate than the thirteenth century, but in the early part of the fifteenth century it had become a well-established Muslim State, and was in arms against its then suzerain, Siam, when China intervened on receiving the nominal submission of the Muhammadan ruler. It is to this, no doubt, that Varthema is referring in the statement above quoted.

¶ The general description of infertility, which he gives to Malacca, is correct. Also when the Portuguese attacked Malacca soon after Varthema's visit, they observed that it was, as he says, in a very flourishing condition and that tin was obtainable there. He next says that the dress of the people was "after the fashion of Cairo," and on this observation Badger notes: "I had frequent opportunities, during my long residence at Aden, of seeing many Malay merchants on their way to Meccah, who generally dressed like the same class in Syria and Egypt." One cannot help observing here that Varthema is unlikely to have made such a remark if he was only reporting about Malacca from hearsay. The people he considers to be fair in complexion, being "of the nation of Giavai [Java]," *i.e.* Malays. Other remarks about them also show close observation: *e.g.* "Those of the country take the law into their own hands, and they are the worst race that was ever created on earth." Here we have a reference to the well-known Malay custom of "running amuck." Another statement also, "When the king wishes to interfere with them, they say that they will disinhabit the land, because they are men of the sea," is a neat reference to that class of Malays which impresses itself on foreigners, and is known in their own country as the Orang Laut or Sea People. Varthema was, however, afraid to stay long in such a place and made across the strait to Pedîr on the north-east coast of Sumâtra, then subject to the King of Achîn. It should be remembered that here he was past the action of the monsoons, which do not blow so close to the

Equator, and was therefore free to sail at any season of the year. He probably reached Pedîr by 28 April.

¶ Varthema makes the mistake of taking Pedîr to be the chief port in Sumâtra—it was the great port for pepper in the early Portuguese times—and in recording his visit there takes the opportunity of describing the island generally from hearsay. He begins by perpetuating an old error: "I think that it is Taprobana." This shows he had been reading, especially as he goes on: "In which there are three crowned kings who are pagans, and their faith, their manner of living, dress and customs, are the same as in Tarnassari, and the wives also are burnt alive." Though the people of Tenasserim are Buddhists, the reference is obviously to the old Hindu occupation of Sumâtra, before it became Muhammadan, the conversion having taken place some time before the date of Varthema's visit. Otherwise his description of the island is much that of other writers of his time or soon after it, such as Barbosa, de Barros, etc. Two remarks, however, show personal observation: "Hēre justice is strictly administered, as in Calicut," and "their money is gold, and silver, and tin." At Pedîr the coined money of Achîn, which was gold, would be found in the bazaars, while currency in silver and tin was in common use along the shores of the Malay Peninsula and Archipelago long before Varthema's time. Besides this native Malay currency, money from China and India circulated on the sea coast at that date, and Varthema notices the number of money-changers. Remarks about the severity of punishments under the Achîn administration, such as he makes, are to be found in the accounts of many early travellers.

¶ He also descants at length on such products as long pepper and eagle-wood or wood-aloes: "The first and most perfect sort [of the latter] is called *calampat* [*kalambak*] and which does not grow in this island, but comes from a city called Sarnau, which (as the Christians our companions said) is near to their city, and here this first sort grows. The second sort is called *loban* [*lubân*], which comes from a river. The name of the third sort is called *bochor* [*bakh-khûr*]." In this description he is both vague and difficult, even though he proceeds to tell us that his "Christian" companions asserted that "the reason the said *calampat* does not come to us [in Europe and Asia Minor] is this, that in Gran Cathai, and in the kingdom of Cini and Macini, and Sarnau and Giava, they have a much greater abundance of gold than we have." The terms Gran Cathai, Cini and Macini, all vaguely represent the Chinese Empire, and are differentiated in the text from Sarnau, of which we have already heard in connection with Varthema's Christian friends. In the above quoted passages *lubân* and *bakh-khûr*

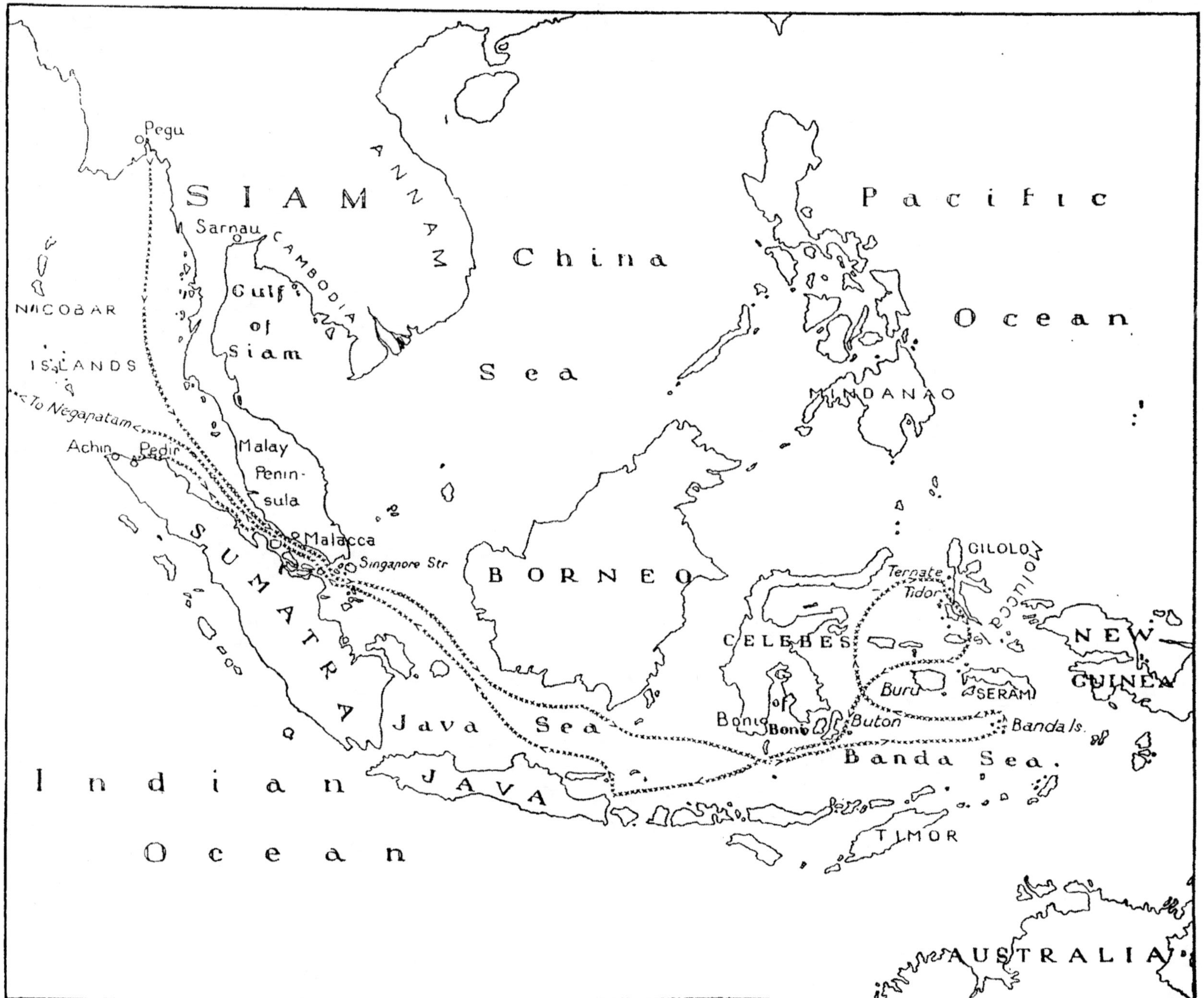

VARTHEMA'S ITINERARY IN THE MALAY ARCHIPELAGO (SPICE ISLANDS)

are Arabic terms respectively for frankincense and incense generally, and the whole statement seems, as already pointed out, to fix the Sarnau from which the "Christians" came as in the south-eastern part of the Asiatic continent. After treating his readers to a traveller's tale or two about the houses of the people, the size of turtles and elephants' tusks and serpents, he tells us a long and characteristic story as to how he and his companions came to sail about 15 May to the Banda or "Nutmeg" Islands in a *ciampana*, by which he must mean a species of Malay junk.

IN THE SPICE ISLANDS

¶ Varthema now makes a journey which is practically unique, for he is the first European visitor to Banda and the Moluccas, who, at any rate, has left a record behind him. He must have reached Banda about 18 May, sailing through the Java and Banda Seas inside the Malay Archipelago, or as he puts it, among "about twenty islands, part inhabited and part not." He has but a small opinion of the people he met with, and with some reason, but at Banda he correctly notices the nutmeg tree. He then sails for the Moluccas "where the cloves grow," reaching those islands about 21 May. Varthema applies the term Monoch, *i.e.* Molucca, to one small island of the group so called, after the fashion already noticed. From his description he probably means Ternâte. He and his companions soon tire of the place, and after correctly describing the clove tree, he explains how he went on to see the "island which is called Bornei" (apparently referring to Borneo); but his description is too brief and too uncertain to make it possible to say exactly at what point he landed, except that it must have been on the south-west coast—assuming that it was to Borneo that he went. It is possible that Varthema landed on Buton, as did Dampier long afterwards, on his way from Ternâte to Java, and that he meant that island when he wrote "Bornei." It is also possible that the name "Bornei" arose by a confusion of the name of Borneo with that of Boni, a well-known town at the south of Celebes which has given its name to the great gulf between the southern branches of that erratic island, though it is not likely that Varthema actually touched at Boni itself or went anywhere near it. But it is much more likely that, as Mr Lucas has pointed out to me, he really landed at one of the towns on the coast of Buru, finding his way there among the islands to the south of the Moluccas. Buru, or by Dutch spelling, Boero, is still the name of the island. Mr Lucas has searched some thirty maps between 1529 and 1660, and finds the name to consist of variants of

Buru and Boero. In fact the name has never changed, and Buru was an island visited in the early days of European navigation. It seems to have been on the main trade route of the time: *e.g.* Antonio de Breu was there on behalf of Afonso d'Albuquerque in 1511, and about the same time one of Serrão's ships was burnt there, when it was old and rotten; afterwards del Cano of Magellan's fleet visited it in 1621.

¶ It is, however, certain that the region of the Moluccas was the furthest point of his voyages, and thence he began to retrace his steps and to journey westwards. From "Bornei" he goes to Java, arriving about 1 June. It was wrongly described to him by his Christian friends as "the largest island in the world, and the most rich."

¶ On his way to Java, he has a striking conversation with "the captain of the said ship," a "chartered vessel." That is, the conversation was with an Arab *nâkhudâ* or skipper, who "carried the compass with the magnet after our manner." This "captain" told Varthema and his companions that "on the other side of the said island [Java], towards the south, there are some other races, who navigate by the said four or five stars opposite to ours; and, moreover, they gave us to understand that beyond the said island the day does not last more than four hours, and that there it was colder than in any other part of the world." On this Badger, Sir Clements Markham, and H. C. Major long ago remarked that such a statement is of "very great importance." "The said four or five stars" are the Southern Cross, and the whole statement shows acquaintance with navigation in the southern seas below Australia and even Tasmania long before they were discovered by Europeans. This is not the place to discuss such a question, and it must be left where Varthema has put it.

¶ Java is described as of "many kingdoms, the kings of which are pagans." There is nothing to show at what part of the island he landed, except that he describes some of the people as cannibals, referring, no doubt, to the notorious Battas. Ceremonial cannibalism existed beyond dispute in the Malay Archipelago long after Varthema's time, and Crawfurd, who is a high authority, is too sweeping in his condemnation of him, when he says that "his account is obviously false or worthless, for he describes parents as selling their children to be eaten by the purchasers, and himself as quitting the island in haste for fear of being made a meal of." But Varthema probably only repeated the exaggerated stories he was likely to hear of the Battas. Badger assumes that his landing was on some obscure point near the north-east corner of the island, and his guess is as good as any that might be offered.

¶ Varthema in the course of his remarks notices the religion of the people he saw and his description is that of a pure Hinduism, though Islâm had been established in the island, as it were officially, for about half a century before his visit, but it could not have become prevalent everywhere. Incidentally he notes a superstition widely spread in India: "A great many worship the first thing they meet in the morning." He mentions, too, inaccurately that "the island produces an immense quantity of silk, part in our manner and part wild"; meaning that he found much silk there that was the highly finished product of China, as well as the rougher product of Bengal (*tasar*). Also, according to the report of his contemporary Barbosa, he is wrong in saying: "No artillery of any kind is used here, nor do they know at all how to make it." But it is quite possible that the use of artillery in the modern sense, which was then comparatively new in Asia generally, had not reached the point in Java at which Varthema landed.

¶ Otherwise his brief general account is accurate so far as it goes. He speaks of the people thus: "I believe that these inhabitants are the most trustworthy men in the world." This remark is supported by Crawfurd, writing three centuries later from a complete knowledge of the people. He also describes the blow-pipe (*sumpîtan*) and the use of poisoned arrows, and lastly we are told that Khwâja Junair bought two little eunuch boys, to be sold later on, no doubt, in Persia to some rich harem. Varthema and his friends, however, did not want to stay long in what they thought was a very dangerous place and left Java on a journey homewards to Malacca. Here incidentally we get a touch, in the *Itinerary*, in the neighbourhood of Java, which goes to show that Varthema wrote from personal experience: "According to what my companion said, I think that this was the month of June; for I had lost our months, and sometimes the name of the day." And according to the rough time-table made out independently in this *Discourse* so far, from Varthema's statements extending over a long period, it must have been during June, 1505, that he was in Java. But there is a still further point here to show that he is stating actual facts in his account, as he shows unconsciously that when he was in Java he was across the Equator, by stating as a remarkable fact that, when turning our "eyes towards where the sun sets . . . the sun [at midday] cast a shadow to the left."

ON THE RETURN HOMEWARDS TO CALICUT

¶ Varthema's geographical knowledge was necessarily vague in the extreme and he evidently thought, on going to "Bornei" and Java from the Moluccas, that he was going onwards. The feeling is quite intelligible, as anyone who travels in the circular underground railway in London can realize: there is always a sense of going onwards. It is not till he leaves Java that he feels he is retracing his steps homewards: "Having remained in this island of Giava altogether fourteen days, we determined to return back...partly through the fear of their cruelty in eating men, partly also through the extreme cold, we did not dare to proceed farther, and also because there was hardly any other place known to them [the Christians]." Here we have all the reasons for the return homewards, of which the extremity of cold is clearly a mistake in a place on the sea near the Equator, unless Varthema is referring to the scanty clothing that he says elsewhere he wore in the tropics. The present writer knows from personal experience how cold the body can feel in the heart of the tropics when scantily clad. So they charter "a large vessel, that is, a *giunco* [junk]," and reach Malacca apparently without touching at any port *en route*, and arrive there about 21 June. Here Varthema and Khwâja Junair part with the Christians amid "bewailings and lamentations it would be impossible shortly to describe," and make for Cioromandel (Negapatam on the south-east coast of India) in the "large junk," arriving there about 18 July. The South-west Monsoon would then be at its height, but the journey would be quite possible for a large junk if they kept well to the south and watched the weather. Here the junk is discharged and Varthema and his companion take a *ciampana* (*sampan*), clearly here a native ship of some size, through the Palk Strait between India and Ceylon and round Cape Comorin to Quilon on the south-west coast of India, where he must have arrived about 10 August. Here Varthema finds "twenty-two Portuguese Christians," which makes him eager for the first time to escape from his Oriental companion. But he is afraid, and so he goes on to Calicut with him "by the river," *i.e.* by the same route as on his outward journey, arriving about 27 August, 1505. August, though a South-west Monsoon month, is often not unfavourable for sailing in this latitude.

AGAIN IN CALICUT

¶ With his mind full of some means to escape, Varthema meets two jewellers, named in Portuguese João Maria and Pero Antonio, who really are Milanese, *i.e.* Italians like himself. They had arrived in Cochin with the Portuguese fleet and had run away to Calicut. He here shows us that he and other Europeans in similar case in the East adopted the "Eastern" mode of life: "They and I went naked after the manner of the country," *i.e.* except as to loin cloths. With the Milanese he makes friends and finds that they are employed by the Zamorin to make guns. Varthema now proceeds to deceive his Persian friend and kindly benefactor, Khwâja Junair, in order to get away from him. The story is not very pleasant reading. So that he might be by himself he persuades the poor Persian that he must "sleep in the mosque, and that I did not want any goods, but that I wished always to be poor." And then he says: "The Moors are the most stupid people in the world, so that he was satisfied.... I began to put my hypocrisy in practice, and pretended to be a Moorish saint,...and happy was he who could kiss my hand and some my knees." He next tells us a rather ludicrous tale of how he played at being a physician and cured "a Moorish merchant," a friend of Khwâja Junair, who had fallen "sick of a very great malady." This feat added to his character for sanctity and gained "great credit for my hypocrisy. They said that I was the friend of God. This merchant wished to give me ten ducats, but I would not receive anything. I even gave three ducats which I had to the poor, and this I did publicly in order that they might know that I did not want any property or money." This and the previous statement to the same effect seem to show that Varthema made no money out of his travels with the Persian merchant.

¶ While he is still seeking a way to cut himself adrift from the Muhammadans, some of Francisco d'Almeida's ships arrive from Portugal at Cannanore, showing that the date is now about September, 1505. "Two Persian merchants of Canonor arrived, whom he [Khwâja Junair] immediately called to eat with him. They answered: 'We have no wish to eat and bring bad news,'" *i.e.* news of the arrival of the Portuguese fleet. This passage neatly brings out the fact that bringers of bad news were in Varthema's time liable to punishment in India, as they were in Europe, just as a bringer of good news expected a reward. The narrative of Varthema's deception then proceeds: "On the following day all the Moors, having heard the news, went to the mosque to say their prayers," and here Varthema takes the opportunity to explain the *mu'azzin's* call and the *fâtiha*, the opening verses of the *Korân*, used in the daily prayers. Indeed, he seems to have led the prayers as an *imâm*: "They set me publicly to make the prayer"; quite a possible act, as we read in Slatin Pasha's wonderful *Life*, that he was made to lead them while a prisoner of the Mahdî. The Arabic forms were so impressed on his memory that he could repeat them readily years after his escape.

¶ After the prayers Varthema returns to Khwâja Junair's house and pretends to be very ill, saying that the air of Calicut is "not good for me." So his kindly friend, who "for the singular affection which he bore me, would have done everything to please me," suggests that he should go to a friend he had in Cannanore. Then comes the climax: "Finally, having well seen...all the artillery, and the army which had been raised against the Christians, I set out on my journey to give them notice of it, and to save myself from the hands of dogs." So Varthema proceeded to play the spy, and apart from this the last words quoted are particularly callous, considering what Khwâja Junair had done for him, but it seems to have been in Varthema's nature to be careless of others where his personal interest clashed with theirs. He deserted the commander of the *hajj* caravan at Mecca; he left his Arab escort in the lurch at Aden to face the wrath of a mistress deserted at Radâ'a al-'Arab; he left a young "wife" behind in Persia without compunction; and now he escapes by gross deception from a companion who had more than befriended him for about a year and a half with only words of abuse. He does not show himself as a man of any real kindness of character.

¶ Varthema now gives us another of his few dates: "On Thursday morning, the third of September [1505], I set out with the two Persians by sea." The "two Persians" were friends of Khwâja Junair, whom he insisted on sending with Varthema to take him to his friend at Cannanore. He feels that his position is a dangerous one and he had reason, for some Nair guards saw him making off and forced him to come back to shore. But while they are going to report the matter he escapes with his two new Persian companions by walking along the shore for twelve miles until they found a *parao*, or prow, to take them to Cannanore, which they reach on Saturday, 5 September. They are most hospitably received by Khwâja Junair's friend. Next morning, Sunday, Varthema gives this friend the slip, and goes to the Portuguese factory, where he asks for Dom Lourenço, the son of Francisco d'Almeida, the Viceroy. He is then sent, on 9 September, to Cochin to the Viceroy himself in a galley commanded by João Serrão, a noted captain of the time. He is well received on account of the information he could give about Calicut.

¶ He now tries to do his best for his friends the two Milanese jewellers at Calicut, and gets a safe conduct for them from the Viceroy. This he forwards by a "pagan" slave, but it is of no use, for the slave stirred up against them the "King of the Gioghi" recluses, at that time in Calicut "with 3000 Gioghi," and the result was that they were murdered by the *jôgîs*. It is interesting to note that these *jôgîs* used quoits in the attack, which gives a verisimilitude to the story: "These Gioghi cast at them certain pieces of iron which are made round like a wheel, and they threw them with a sling, and struck Ioan-Maria on the head and Pietro Antonio on the head, so that they fell to the ground." Afterwards Varthema says, probably with truth, that "the wife of Ioan-Maria escaped with her son to Canonor, and I purchased the son for eight ducats of gold, and had him baptised on St Lawrence's day, and gave him the name of Lorenzo, because I baptised him on that same day." But the boy died of the "French disease" at the end of 1506. In giving the account of this murder Varthema gives also one of his rare dates, for he says that the news of it reached Cannanore on 12 March, 1506.

¶ He then gives us another date and says that he witnessed the attack of the Portuguese fleet at Cannanore on a large threatening fleet "of Moors" belonging to the Zamorin of Calicut and the Sultân Kânsûh al-Ghôrî of Cairo, which had arrived off the west coast of India with the object of preventing the Portuguese from interfering with the Arab trade to India. The fight, he says, took place on 16 March, 1506, the Portuguese commander being Dom Lourenço d'Almeida, and was successful. Varthema also mentions the gallantry of João Serrão and "Simon Martin," possibly Andres de São Martim, on this occasion, and lastly he remarks: "I leave you to imagine how great was the joy of the Viceroy and of the King of Cuccin [Cochin], who is a true friend of the King of Portugal, on seeing us return victorious."

A FACTOR IN CALICUT AND COCHIN

¶ As soon as he came under Portuguese protection, Varthema dropped his Muhammadan religion and habits, and no doubt costume also, and about the middle of 1506 the Viceroy gave him "of his favour, a certain office, which was that of the factorship of these parts, and I remained in this office about a year and a half [till about November, 1507]." There were two classes of *feitor* or factor at this period: the Feitor proper, Factor or Agent of the Government, and the *feitor* or trade agent of a great personage. It was no doubt in the latter capacity on behalf of the Viceroy, Dom Francisco d'Almeida, that Varthema served. He was sent as such again to Cannanore to enquire into certain frauds, and once more he gives dates by saying that "a very great war" with the Zamorin of Calicut "lasted from 27th April to 17th [or 27th] August 1507." This war broke out because the old friendly "King of Canonor" had died and was succeeded by "a great enemy of ours" and an ally of an inimical Zamorin. On the first of the above dates the Portuguese in the fort at Cannanore were going to get water when they were attacked by "the Moors." The captain of the fort at that time was Lourenço de Brito, and he, with help sent by Dom Lourenço, the son of the Viceroy, from Cochin, defended the fortress, until the opportune arrival of Tristan da Cunha (Tristão d'Acunha) with a Portuguese fleet put the enemy to rout. Varthema here notes that after the siege "an ambassador, who was named Mamal Maricar, who was the richest man in the country, came to demand peace." This is a most interesting reference to the Mârakkâr family, who were the sea-captains of the Zamorin at that period, though they were mere pirates in the eyes of the Portuguese. According to Logan's fine monograph, *Malabar* (I, 332, footnote), Mamâle Mârakkâr's son-in-law was killed in the fight with de Brito, and he went there afterwards to upbraid him, not to sue for peace. Varthema must have distinguished himself in this siege, as when it was over the Viceroy conferred knighthood on him—"the most valiant Captain Tristan da Cugna was my sponsor." This dignity was subsequently confirmed by the King of Portugal.

¶ In November, 1507, Varthema desired to go home, but was detained as the Viceroy was about to make an attack on the port of Ponnani some 34 miles south-east of Calicut. The attack took place on 24 November, the Viceroy and Tristan da Cunha each taking a personal share in it and sending a son to the assault, which was successful. Varthema gives a lively account of this fight, the last act he records of his sojourn in the East. On 6 December, 1507, he leaves India for Europe.

THE VOYAGE HOME

¶ On his homeward voyage Varthema is very brief, and describes the east coast of Africa as "Ethiopia," giving a general description of it and the war waged on it by Tristan da Cunha. The first place he mentions is Mozambique, giving a quaint account of its inhabitants. Thence he passes on towards the Cape of Good Hope inside the Island of San Lorenzo (São Lourenço), *i.e.* Madagascar. The fleet is driven back to Madagascar by bad weather, and then after "a very great storm" his ship—the *Santo Vicentio*, belonging to Bartholomeo Marchioni of Florence, dwelling in the city of Lisbon—gets separated from the rest, and goes on homewards alone. She passes St Helena, on the way to which some whales are encountered to the terror of the sailors. She also passes Ascension, off which some boobies are met with, and then she touches at the Azores, which are described. Finally she arrives at "the noble city of Lisbon," whence Varthema goes to see the King of Portugal at his palace of Almeirim. After securing his "patent of knighthood," he at last reaches Rome.

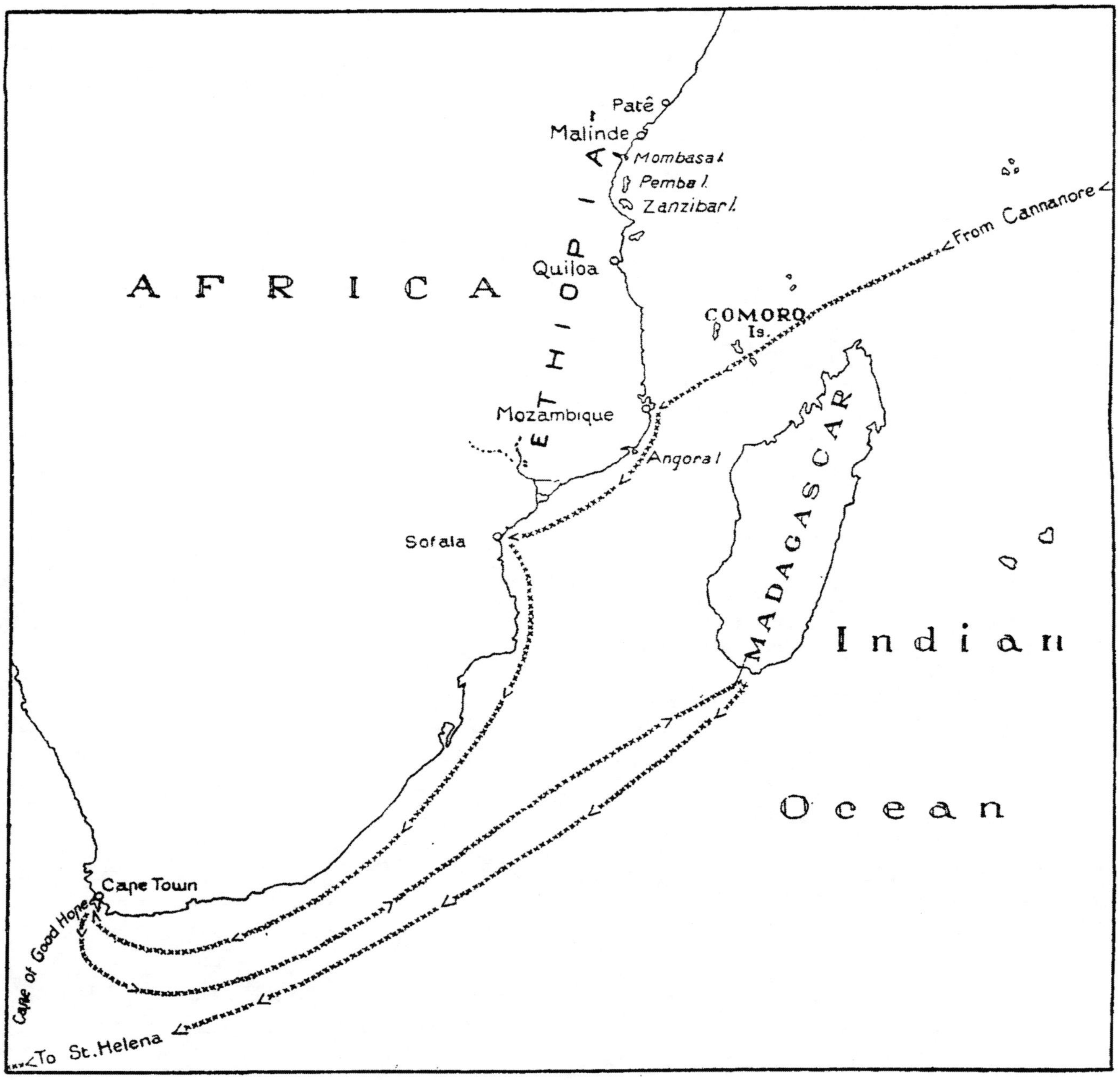

VARTHEMA'S ITINERARY HOMEWARDS

¶ There is a difficulty in reconciling the dates of the return journey. It commenced on 6 December, 1507, and the route taken involved a journey across the Indian Ocean from Cochin to Mozambique, where a stay of 15 days was made. Afterwards there was another stay of two days at the Azores. Besides these delays 12 days were lost in storms off the Cape of Good Hope. Then the journey was continued past St Helena, Ascension and the Azores to Lisbon. It is not easy to see how Varthema in these circumstances could have reached Lisbon before the autumn of 1508. He had then to see the King of Portugal and find his way to Rome. Further, in the "privilege" for publishing his book, it is stated that he was seven years absent from Italy, and he also says so himself in the course of his record, reckoning time in medieval European, as well as Indian, fashion by current days, weeks, months or years, and meaning thereby that he was absent from about the end of 1502 to about the end of 1508. At the same time it is to be inferred from the dedication of his book to Agnesina Colonna that her brother Giudobaldo, Duke of Urbino, was alive when it was written, but he died on 11 April, 1508, months before it seems possible for Varthema to have reached Italy. Unless, therefore, it can be assumed—as Badger does—that he purposely antedated his dedication, it does not seem possible that he could have been back in Italy in time to write it before April, 1508. He did not get permission to print his book of travels till 17 November, 1510, and that date allows him plenty of time to have composed his *Itinerary* by the time he asked for permission to publish it.

ITINERARIO
de Ludouico de Varthema Bolognese
nello Egypto/ nella Surria/ nella Arabia deser-
ta & felice/ nella Persia/ nella India/ & nel
la Ethiopia. La fede/ el uiuere/ & co
stumi de tutte le prefate Pro-
uincie con Gratia & Pri
uilegio infra nota
to.

¶ Stampato in Roma per maestro Stephano guilli
reti de Loreno/ & maestro Hercule de Nani
Bolognese/ ad instātia de maestro Lo
douico de Henricis da Corneto
Vicētino. Nel Anno. M.
D. X. a di. vi. de De
cembrio.

FACSIMILE OF THE TEXT OF THE TITLE-PAGE AND COLOPHON OF VARTHEMA'S ORIGINAL BOOK, 1510

THE ITINERARY OF LUDOVICO DI VARTHEMA OF BOLOGNA

[PRIVILEGE]

[TRANSLATED *from the original* LATIN *by* G. P. BADGER]

RAPHAEL, by Divine grace, Bishop of Portueri, Cardinal of Saint George, Chamberlain of our Most Holy Lord the Pope, and of the Holy Roman Church, to all and singular, by whatsoever name called, and with whatsoever dignity or office invested, and to all others whom it does or may concern, to whom these our letters may come,—Peace in the Lord for ever.

¶ Whereas among other subjects and sciences which, as well by the inspiration of genius as by art and experience, promote the benefit, usefulness, and enjoyment of mankind, and by transmission from hand to hand are enlarged and illustrated, the description and measurement of the world and of parts of the earth, which the Greeks call Cosmography, Geography, Topography, Geometry, and other like names, do not hold the last place, and yield no less pleasure than profit; on which account those who have devoted themselves to such studies have always been held in the highest honour, and have been abundantly rewarded.—Therefore, whereas our well-beloved friend Ludovico Vartomanus of Bologna, who (as we are assured) has for the space of seven years travelled over the most remote and hardly-known regions of Asia and Africa, and has largely written in the vernacular tongue of their sites, seas, rivers, pools, lakes, forests, mountains, cities, lands, people, and their established manners, rites, laws, and other memorable things, and has corrected many places, (as one may well do who sees all with his own eyes, and has not merely heard thereof or received it from others,) in Ptolemy, Strabo, Pliny, and other most famous writers, and has also added much to what others have written thereon up to this time.—It is our pleasure, being moreover advised thereto by many other Most Reverend Cardinals of the Apostolic See, that what he has committed to writing and collected into a volume, should be printed for the public use and study of the things therein contained, and that it should be held worthy, not only of praise and commendation, but of ample reward. We, being desirous (as is meet) to assist him as far as we are able, and to recompense his industry with all due favours, do, by these presents, proclaim, decree, and inhibit, in virtue of a mandate from our Most Holy Lord the Pope in person, communicated to us by word of mouth to that effect, and by the authority of our Chamberlain's office, that all Printers who shall be applied to by the said Ludovico, that they print his writings on his own request or that of any of his heirs; and that all other Printers abstain from printing them, and that no Printers or persons of any other condition whatsoever, either of themselves, or through any other or others, shall dare or presume to sell the printed books or volumes of the said Ludovico, without the consent of the said Ludovico or of his acknowledged heirs, for the space of ten years to come, to be reckoned from the date of their first impression; and, further, that they lend no aid, counsel or countenance, to either Printers or Venders of the same, against the wishes of the said Ludovico and his heirs, under the penalty of one hundred ducats of gold to be exacted for every counterfeit and from every one so counterfeiting, without any other declaration of the fact, through the medium of the Apostolic Chamber, to be applied to the use of the said Ludovico or his heirs. We further command and inhibit, under the same penalty, all those whom it may concern, that this our edict, decree, and will, be executed in like manner at the instance of the said Ludovico, or of his successors and heirs, for the space of the aforesaid ten years, against all and every one who, in any manner, or under any pretext, shall be guilty of counterfeit,—the Apostolical constitutions, ordinances, statutes, and customs, even when confirmed by oath, also the privileges and licenses granted to any persons whatsoever, under any words or form of words, notwithstanding.

¶ Given at Rome, at our Palace of Saint Laurence in Damaso, the xviith day of November M.D.X., with the usual seal of our Chamberlain's office appended.

MATTHEUS BONFINIS
Secretarius

THE ITINERARY OF LUDOVICO DI VARTHEMA OF BOLOGNA

[DEDICATION]

To

THE MOST ILLUSTRIOUS AND MOST EXCELLENT LADY THE COUNTESS OF ALBI AND DUCHESS OF TAGLIACOZZO, MADAME AGNESINA FELTRIA COLONNA, LUDOVICO DI VARTHEMA OF BOLOGNA WISHES HEALTH

THERE have been many men who have devoted themselves to the investigation of the things of this world, and by the aid of divers studies, journeys, and very exact relations, have endeavoured to accomplish their desire. Others, again, of more perspicacious understandings, to whom the earth has not sufficed, such as the Chaldeans and Phœnicians, have begun to traverse the highest regions of Heaven with careful observations and watchings; from all which I know that each has gained most deserved and high praise from others and abundant satisfaction to themselves. Wherefore I, feeling a very great desire for similar results, and leaving alone the Heavens as a burthen more suitable for the shoulders of Atlas and of Hercules, determined to investigate some small portion of this our terrestrial globe; and not having any inclination (knowing myself to be of very slender understanding) to arrive at my desire by study or conjectures, I determined, personally, and with my own eyes, to endeavour to ascertain the situations of places, the qualities of peoples, the diversities of animals, the varieties of the fruit-bearing and odoriferous trees of Egypt, Syria, Arabia Deserta and Felix, Persia, India and Ethiopia, remembering well that the testimony of one eye-witness is worth more than ten heard-says. Having then, by Divine assistance, in part accomplished my object and examined various provinces and foreign nations, it appeared to me that I had done nothing if I kept hidden within myself the things I had witnessed and experienced, instead of communicating them to other studious men. Wherefore I bethought myself to give a very faithful description of this my voyage, according to my humble abilities, thinking thereby to do an action which would be agreeable to my readers; for that, whereas I procured the pleasure of seeing new manners and customs by very great dangers and insupportable fatigue, they will enjoy the same advantage and pleasure, without discomfort or danger, by merely reading. Reflecting, then, to whom I might best address this my laborious little work, you, Most Illustrious and Most Excellent Lady, occurred to me as being a special observer of noteworthy things, and a lover of every virtue. Nor did my judgment appear to me vain, considering the infused learning transferred by the radiant light of that Most Illustrious and Excellent Lord the Duke of Urbino your Father, being as it were to us a sun of arms and of science. I do not speak of the very Excellent Lord your Brother, who (although still a young man) has so distinguished himself in his Latin and Greek studies as to be spoken of as almost a Demosthenes and a Cicero. Wherefore, having derived every virtue from such broad and clear streams, you cannot do other than take pleasure in honourable works and entertain a great desire for them. He who can justly appreciate them, would willingly go with his corporeal feet where he flies with the wings of his mind, remembering that one of the praises awarded to the most wise and eloquent Ulysses was, that he had seen many customs of men and many countries. But as your Ladyship is occupied with the affairs of your Most Illustrious Lord and Consort (whom, like another Artemisia, you love and respect), and about the distinguished family which, with admirable rule, you adorn by your graces, I say it will suffice if amongst your other good works you will feed your mind with this fruitful, although, perhaps, unpolished reading, not acting like many other ladies who lend their ears to light songs and vain words, taking no account of time, unlike the angelic mind of your Ladyship, which allows no moment to pass without some good fruit. Your kindness will easily supply all want of skill in the connection of the narrative, grasping only the truth of the facts. And if these, my labours, should prove agreeable to you and meet with your approbation, I shall consider that I have received sufficient praise and satisfaction for my long wanderings, my rather fearful exile, during which I have endured, innumerable times, hunger and thirst, cold and heat, war, imprisonment, and an infinite number of other dangerous inconveniences, and shall gain fresh courage for that other journey which I hope to undertake in a short time; for having examined some parts of the countries and islands of the east, south, and west, I am resolved, if it please God, to investigate those of the north. And thus, as I do not see that I am fit for any other pursuit, to spend in this praiseworthy exercise the remainder of my fleeting days.

THE ITINERARY OF LUDOVICO DI VARTHEMA

CHAPTER I

CONCERNING EGYPT AND SYRIA

THE same desire to behold the various kingdoms of the world which has urged on others, excited me also to a similar enterprise; and inasmuch as all countries have been very much laid open by our people, I deliberated in my own mind that I would see those which had been the least frequented by the Venetians. Wherefore spreading our sails to a favourable wind, and having implored the Divine aid, we committed ourselves to the sea. When we came to Alexandria, a city of Egypt, I, longing for novelty (as a thirsty man longs for fresh water) departed from these places as being well known to all, and, entering the Nile, arrived at Cairo.

¶ On my arrival in Cairo I, who had been previously much astonished at the account of its size, came to the conclusion that it was not so large as it had been reported to be. But its size in circumference is about equal to that of Rome. It is true, however, that it contains very many more habitations than there are in Rome, and that the population is larger. The mistake which many have made is this, that there are several hamlets outside the walls of Cairo which some believed to be within the circuit of Cairo itself; this, however, cannot be the case, for they are distant some two or three miles, and are distinct villages. I shall not enter into any long account of their faith and manners, because everyone knows that they are inhabited by Moors [Muhammadans] and Mamelukes [*mamlûks*]. The lord over them is the Grand Sultan [Kânsûh al-Ghôrî], who is served by the Mamelukes, and the Mamelukes are lords over the Moors.

¶ I say nothing about the riches and beauty of the aforesaid Cairo and of the pride of the Mamelukes, because they are well known to all our countrymen. I sailed thence into Syria; and first to Baruti [Beyrout], the distance from the one place to the other by sea is 500 miles. In that Baruti I remained several days. It is a country thickly inhabited by the Moors, and is well supplied with everything. The sea breaks against the walls, and you must know that the district is not entirely surrounded by walls, but only in some parts, that is to say, towards the west and towards the sea. I did not see anything there worthy to be recorded, excepting an ancient building, which, they say, was inhabited by the daughter of the king when the dragon wanted to devour her, and where St. George killed the said dragon. This ancient building is all in ruins; and I departed thence, and proceeded in the direction of Tripoli in Syria, which is two days' journey towards the east. This Tripoli is subject to the Grand Sultan [Kânsûh al-Ghôrî], and all are Mahommedans, and the said city abounds in everything. And I departed thence and went to Aleppo, which is eight days' journey inland, which said Aleppo is a very beautiful city, and is under the Grand Sultan of Cairo, and is the mart [*scala*] of Turkey and Syria, and they are all Mahommedans. It is a country of very great traffic in merchandise, and particularly with the Persians and Azamini ['Ajamî, Persian subjects], who come as far as there. This is the route which is taken to go into Turkey and Syria by those who come from Azemia ['Ajam, Persia].

¶ And I departed thence and went towards Damascus, which is distant ten short days' journey. Midway there is a city which is called Aman [Hamâ], in which there grows a vast quantity of cotton, and very good fruit. And near to Damascus, sixteen miles distant from it, I found another district called Menin [Menîn], which is situated on the summit of a mountain, and is inhabited by Christians of the Greek Church, who are subjects of the lord of Damascus. In this place there are two very beautiful churches, which are said to have been erected by Helena, the mother of Constantine. Very excellent fruits grow there, and most especially good grapes; and here also there are very beautiful gardens and fountains. I departed thence, and went to the most noble city of Damascus.

¶ Truly it would not be possible to describe the beauty and the excellence of this Damascus, in which I resided some months in order to learn the Moorish [Arabic] language, because this city is entirely inhabited by Moors and Mamelukes and many Greek Christians. Here I must give an account of the government of the lord of the said city, which lord is subject to the Great Sultan of Cairo. You must know that in the said city of Damascus there is a very beautiful and strong castle, which is said to have been built by a Florentine Mameluke at his own expense, he being lord of the said city. And, moreover, in each angle of the said castle, the arms of Florence are sculptured in marble. It is surrounded by very wide fosses, and has four extremely strong towers and drawbridges, and powerful and excellent artillery are constantly mounted there. Fifty Mamelukes, in the service of the Grand Sultan, are constantly quartered with the governor of the castle. This Florentine was a Mameluke of the Grand Sultan; and it is reported that in his time the Sultan was poisoned, and could find no one who could relieve him of the said poison, when it pleased God that this Florentine should cure him.

For this service he gave him the said city of Damascus, and thus he came to build the castle. Afterwards he died in Damascus; and the people held him in great veneration as a holy man, possessing great knowledge, and from that time forward the castle has always been in the possession of the Sultan. When a new Sultan succeeds to the throne, one of his lords, who are called Amirra [Amîr, Emir], says to him: "Lord, I have been for so long a time your slave, give me Damascus, and I will give you one hundred thousand, or two hundred thousand, teraphim [seraphim, *ashrafî*, ducat] of gold." Then the lord grants him this favour. But you must know, that if in the course of two years the said lord does not send him 25,000 teraphim, he seeks to kill him by force of arms, or in some other manner; but if he makes him the said present, he remains in the government. The said lord has always ten or twelve lords and barons of the said city with him, and when the Sultan wants two or three hundred thousand teraphim from the lords or merchants of the said city, who are not treated with justice, but whom they vie with each other in oppressing by robbery and assassination (for the Moors live under the Mamelukes like the lamb under the wolf), the said Sultan sends two letters to the governor of the said castle, one of which simply enjoins him to bring together in the castle such lords or merchants as he may think proper. And when they are assembled, the second letter is read, the object of which is immediately carried out, whether for good or for evil. And in this manner the said lord seeks to obtain money. Sometimes the said lord becomes so powerful that he will not go into the castle; whereat many barons and merchants, feeling themselves in danger, mount their horses and retire towards Turkey. We will say no more upon this subject, excepting that the men of the guard of the said castle, in each of the four great towers, are always on the watch. They make no cry during the night, but each has a drum, made in the shape of a half-box, upon which they beat vigorously with a stick, and each answers the other with these said drums. He who delays answering for the space of a *pater noster*, is imprisoned for a year.

¶ Now that we have seen the customs of the Lord of Damascus, it is necessary that I should make mention of some circumstances relating to the city, which is extremely populous and very rich. It is impossible to imagine the richness and elegance of the workmanship there. Here you have a great abundance of grain and of meat, and the most prolific country for fruits that was ever seen, and especially for fresh grapes, during all seasons. I will mention the good and the bad fruits which grow there. Pomegranates and quinces, good: almonds and large olives, extremely good. The most beautiful white and red roses that were ever seen. There are also good apples and pears and peaches, but with a very bad taste, the reason of which is that Damascus abounds much in water. A stream runs through the city, and the greater number of the houses have very beautiful fountains of mosaic work. The houses are dirty externally, but within they are very beautiful, adorned with many works of marble and porphyry.

¶ In this city there are many mosques. One, which is the principal, is as large as St. Peter's at Rome. It has no roof in the centre, but the surrounding parts are covered in. It is reported that they keep there the body of St. Zachariah the prophet, and they pay him very great honour. In the said mosque there are four principal doors of metal, and within there are many fountains. Again, we see where the canonica stood, which belonged formerly to the Christians, in which canonica there are many ancient works in mosaic. Again, I saw the place where they report that Christ said to St. Paul, "*Saule, Saule, cur me persequeris?*" which is without the city, about a mile from one of the gates thereof. They bury there all the Christians who die in the said city. Again, there is that tower in the wall of the district where (as they say) St. Paul was imprisoned. The Moors have many times rebuilt it, but in the morning it is found broken and thrown down, as the angel broke it when he drew St. Paul out of the said tower. I also saw the house where (as they say) Cain slew Abel his brother, which is a mile without the city in the opposite direction, on the side of a hill in a large deep valley. We will now turn to the liberty which the said Mamelukes enjoy in the said city of Damascus.

¶ The Mamelukes are renegade Christians, who have been purchased by the said lord. Certain it is that the said Mamelukes never lose any time, but are constantly exercising themselves either in arms or in letters, in order that they may acquire excellence. And you must know that every Mameluke, great or little, has for his pay six saraphi per month, and his expenses for himself, his horse, and a family; and they have as much more when they are engaged on any warlike expedition. The said Mamelukes, when they go about the city, are always in companies of two or three, as it would be a great disgrace if they went alone. If they accidentally meet two or three ladies, they possess this privilege, or if they do not possess it they take it: they go to lay in wait for these ladies in certain places like great inns, which are called chano [*khân*], and as the said ladies pass before the door each Mameluke takes his lady by the hand, draws her in, and does what he will with her. But the lady resists being known, because they all wear the face covered, so that they know us, but we do not know them. The Mameluke says to her, that he wishes to know who she is, and she replies: "Brother, is it not enough that you do with me what you will, without desiring to know who I am?" and she entreats him so much that he lets her go. And sometimes they think that they take the daughter of the lord, when in fact they take their own wives; and this has happened while I was there. These ladies go very well clad in silk, and over it they wear certain white garments of wool, thin and bright like silk, and they all wear white buskins and red or purple shoes, and many jewels around their heads, and in their ears, and on their hands. These ladies when they are married, at their own will and pleasure, that is, when they do not wish to remain with their husbands any longer, go to the cadi of their faith and cause themselves to be *talacare* [*talak*, divorce], that is, to be separated from their husband; and then they take another, and he takes another wife. Although they say that the Moors have five or six wives, I for my part have never seen any who had more than two or three at the most. These Moors for the greater part eat in the streets, that is, where the clothes are sold; they have their food cooked and eat it there, and there are very many horses, camels, and buffalo[e]s, and sheep and goats. There is here an abundance of good fresh cheese; and if you wish to purchase milk, there are forty or fifty goats, which go every day through the district, and which have ears more than a span in length. The master of these goats takes them up into your chamber, even if your house have three stories, and there in your presence he milks as much as you please into a handsome tin vessel. And there are many milch goats. Here, again, is sold a great quantity of truffles: sometimes twenty-five or thirty camels arrive laden with them, and in three or four days they are sold. They come from the mountains of Armenia and Turkey. The said Moors go clothed in certain long and wide garments, without girdles, made of silk or cloth, and the greater number wear breeches of wool and white shoes. When a Moor meets a Mameluke, although he may be the principal merchant of the place, he is obliged to do honour and give place to the Mameluke, and if he do not so he is bastinadoed. The Christians have there many warehouses, which contain cloths, and silk and satin, velvets, and brass, and all merchandise that is required; but they are ill treated.

CHAPTER II

CONCERNING ARABIA DESERTA

THE matters relating to Damascus having been here described perhaps more diffusely than was necessary, opportunity invites me to resume my journey. In 1503, on the 8th day of April, the caravan being set in order to go to Mecca, and I being desirous of beholding various scenes and not knowing how to set about it, formed a great friendship with the captain of the said Mamelukes of the caravan, who was a Christian renegade, so that he clothed me like a Mameluke and gave me a good horse, and placed me in company with the other Mamelukes, and this was accomplished by means of the money and other things which I gave him; and in this manner we set ourselves on the way, and travelled three days to a place which is called Mezeribe [al-Mazarîb], and there we remained three days, in order that the merchants might provide themselves, by purchase, with as many horses as they required. In this Mezeribe there is a lord who is named Zambei [az-Za'abî], and he is lord of the country, that is to say, of the Arabians; which Zambei has three brothers and four male children, and he has 40,000 horses, and for his court he has 10,000 mares. And he has here 300,000 camels, for his pasture-ground extends two days' journey. And this lord Zambei, when he thinks proper, wages war with the Sultan of Cairo, and the Lord of Damascus and of Jerusalem, and sometimes, in harvest time, when they think that he is a hundred miles distant, he plans some morning a great incursion to the granaries of the said city, and finds the grain and the barley nicely packed up in sacks, and carries it off. Sometimes he runs a whole day and night with his said mares without stopping, and when they have arrived at the end of their journey they give them camels' milk to drink, because it is very refreshing. Truly it appears to me that they do not run but that they fly like falcons; for I have been with them, and you must know that they ride, for the most part, without saddles, and in their shirts, excepting some of their principal men. Their arms consist of a lance of Indian cane ten or twelve cubits in length with a piece of iron at the end, and when they go on any expedition they keep as close together as starlings. The said Arabians are very small men, and are of a dark tawny colour, and they have a feminine voice, and long, stiff, and black hair. And truly these Arabs are in such vast numbers that they cannot be counted, and they are constantly fighting amongst themselves. They inhabit the mountain and come down at the time when the caravan passes through to go to Mecca, in order to lie in wait at the passes for the purpose of robbing the said caravan. They carry their wives, children, and all their furniture, and also their houses, upon camels, which houses are like the tents of soldiers, and are of black wool and of a sad appearance.

¶ On the 11th of April, the said caravan departed from Mezeribe; there were 35,000 camels, about 40,000 persons, and we were sixty Mamelukes in guard of the said caravan. One third of the Mamelukes went in advance of the caravan with the standard, another third in the centre, and the other third marched in the rear. You must understand that we performed our journey in this wise. From Damascus to Mecca is a journey of forty days and forty nights: thus, we set out from Mezeribe in the morning and travelled for twenty hours. At that point certain signals made by the captain were passed from band to band that the whole company should stop where they then found themselves, and they pass twenty-four hours in unloading, and feeding themselves and their camels. And then they make signals, and the camels are immediately laden again. And you must know that they give the said camels for food only five loaves of barley-meal, uncooked, and each of about the size of a pomegranate, and then they mount their horses and journey all night and all the following day for the said twenty-two [*sic*] hours, and then for twenty-four hours do as before. And every eight days they find water, that is, by digging in the earth or sand; also, certain wells and cisterns are found, and at the end of the eight days they stop for one or two days, because the said camels carry as great a burthen as two mules, and they only give the poor animals drink once in every three days. When we halted at the said waters we always had to fight with a vast number of Arabs, but they never killed more than one man and one lady, for such is the baseness of their minds, that we sixty Mamelukes were sufficient defence against forty or fifty thousand Arabs; for pagans, there are no better people with arms in their hands than are the Mamelukes. You must know that I had excellent experiences of these Mamelukes during the journey. Amongst others, I saw a Mameluke take one of his slaves and place a pomegranate on his head, and make him stand twelve or fifteen paces distant from him, and at the second trial strike off the pomegranate by a shot from a bow. Again, I saw another Mameluke, running at full gallop, take off his saddle and place it upon his head, and afterwards return it to its original place without falling, and always at full gallop. Their saddles are made according to our usage.

¶ And when we had travelled twelve days we found the valley of Sodom and Gomorrah. Verily the Scriptures do not lie, for one sees how they were destroyed by a miracle of God; and I say that there are three cities which were on the top of three mountains, and around them to the height of three or four cubits is still seen what appears to be blood, like red wax mixed with earth. Of a truth, I believe, upon what I have seen, that they were a wicked people, for all around the entire country is desert and barren. The earth produces no one thing, nor water; and they lived upon manna and were punished, for not acknowledging the benefits they received; and by a miracle everything is still seen in ruin. Then we passed that valley, which was at least twenty miles, and there died there from thirst thirty-three persons, and many were buried in the sand who were not quite dead, and they left only their faces uncovered. Afterwards we found a little mountain, near which was a well, whereat we were well pleased. We halted upon the said mountain. The next day, early in the morning, there came 24,000 Arabs, who said that we must pay for their water. We answered that we could not pay, for the water was given by God. They began to fight with us, saying that we had taken their water. We fortified ourselves, and made a wall of our camels, and the merchants stood within the said camels, and we were constantly skirmishing, so that they kept us besieged two days and two nights, and things came at last to that state, that neither we nor they had any more water to drink. They had completely surrounded the mountain with people, saying that they would break through the caravan. Not being able to continue the fighting, our captain consulted with the Moorish merchants and we gave them (the Arabs) 1200 ducats of gold. They took the money, and then said that 10,000 ducats of gold would not pay for their water, and we knew that they wanted something else besides money. So our prudent captain arranged with the caravan, that all those men who were capable of bearing arms should not ride on the camels, and that each should prepare his arms. The morning having come, we put forward all the caravan, and we Mamelukes remained behind. We were in all three hundred persons, and we soon began to fight. One man and one lady were killed by bows on our side, and they did us no further harm. We killed of them 1600 persons. Nor is it to be wondered at that we killed so many of them: the cause was, that they were all naked and on horseback, without saddles, so that they had a difficulty in turning on their way.

¶ At the end of eight days we found a mountain [Khaibar] which appeared to be ten or twelve miles in circumference, in which mountain there dwell four or five thousand Jews, who go naked, and are in height five or six spans, and have a feminine voice, and are more black than any other colour. They live entirely upon the flesh of sheep, and eat nothing else. They are circumcised, and confess that they are Jews; and if they can get a Moor into their hands, they skin him alive. At the foot of the said mountain we found a tank of water, which is water that falls in the rainy season. We loaded with the said water 16,000 camels, whereat the Jews were ill-pleased; and they went about that mountain like wild goats, and on no account would they descend into the plain, because they are mortal enemies of the Moors. At the foot of the mountain, by the said water, there were six or eight feet of beautiful thornbushes, in which we found two turtledoves, which circumstance appeared to us like a miracle, inasmuch as we had travelled fifteen days and nights and had not met with a single animal or bird. The next day we resumed our journey, and in two days' time arrived at a city which is called Medinathalnabi [Medina: Medînatu'n-Nabi, the City of the Prophet]. Near that city, at a distance of four miles, we found a well, by which the caravan halted for a day, and at this well each person washed himself, and put on clean linen to go into the said city, which contains about three hundred hearths, and is surrounded by walls made of earth. The houses within are constructed with stone walls. The country around the said city lies under the curse of God, for the land is barren, with the exception that about two stones' cast, outside the city, there are about fifty or sixty feet of palmtrees in a garden, at the end of which there is a certain conduit of water, which descends at least twenty-four steps, of which water the caravan takes possession when it arrives there. Now, some who say that the body of Mahomet is suspended in the air at Mecca must be reproved; I say that it is not true. I have seen his sepulchre in this city, Medinathalnabi, in which we remained three days, and wished to see everything. The first day we went into the city, at the entrance by the door of their mosque, and each of us, small or great, was obliged to be accompanied by some person, who took us by the hand, and led us where Mahomet was buried.

¶ The mosque is made square in this manner: being about one hundred paces long, and eighty wide, and it has around it two doors on three sides, and the roof made arched, and there are more than 400 columns made of burnt stone, all whitened, and there are about 3,000 lighted lamps burning on one side of the arches. On the right hand, at the head of the mosque, there is a square tower, about five paces on every side, which tower has a cloth of silk around it. At the distance of two paces from the said tower there is a very beautiful grating of metal, where persons stand to see the said tower; and at one side, on the left, there is a little door which leads you to the said tower, and in the said tower there is another little door, and by one of the doors there are about twenty books, and on the other side there are twenty-five books, which are those of Mahomet and of his Companions, which books declare his life and the commandments of his sect. Within the said door there is a sepulchre, that is, a pit under ground, wherein was placed Mahomet, also Haly, and Babacher, and Othman, and Aumar, and Fatoma [Muhammad, 'Alî, Abubakr, 'Uthmân, Umr, Fâtima]. Mahomet was captain, and he was an Arab. Haly was son-in-law of Mahomet, that is, he was the husband of Fatoma, who was the daughter of Mahomet. Babacher was he of whom we should say that he was cardinal, and wanted to be pope. Othman was one of his captains. Aumar was another of his captains. And these said books treat about each of his people, that is, of the said captains; and on this account it is that this *canaille* cut each other to pieces, for some wish to act according to the commandments of one, and some of another, and thus they do not know how to make up their minds; and they kill each other like beasts about these heresies, for they are all false.

¶ In order to explain the sect of Mahomet, you must know that over the said tower there is a cupola, in which you can walk round the top, that is, outside. You must understand the trick they played off upon the whole caravan the first evening we arrived at the tomb of Mahomet. Our captain sent for the superior of the said mosque, to whom he said: that he should show him the body of Nabi—this Nabi means the Prophet Mahomet—that he would give him three thousand seraphim of gold; and that he had neither father nor mother, nor brothers nor sisters, nor wife nor children, neither had he come to purchase spices or jewels, but that he had come to save his soul, and to see the body of the Prophet. Then the superior answered him with great violence, and rage, and pride, saying: "How do those eyes of yours, which have done so much evil in the world, desire to see him for whom God has created the heavens and the earth?" Then answered our captain: "*Sidi intecate el melie,*" that is to say, "Sir, you say true; but do me a favour, let me see the body of the Prophet, and immediately that I have seen it, I will pull out my eyes for the love of him." And Sidi [for Sherîf or head of the mosque] answered: "O Sir, I will tell you the truth. It is true that our Prophet wished to die here, in order to set us a good example; for he could well have died at Mecca had he so willed, but he desired to exercise poverty for our instruction; and as soon as he was dead, he was carried at once into heaven by the angels, and he says that he is equal with God." Our captain said to him: "*Eise Hebene Marian phion?*" that is, "Jesus Christ the son of Mary, where is he?" The Sidi answered: "*Azafel al Nabi,*" that is, "at the feet of

Mahomet." Our captain answered: "*Besbes, hiosi,*" that is, "enough, enough! I will not know more." Then the captain came out and said to us: "See where I wanted to throw away three thousand seraphim!" In the night time, at three o'clock, there came into the camp about ten or twelve of those old men of that sect, for the caravan was encamped near the gate, two stones' cast off, and these old men began to cry out, some in one part and some in another: "*Leilla illala, Mahometh resullala; lam Nabi, hia la, hia resullala, stasforla,*" that is, "God pardon me." "*Leilla illala,*" means, "God was, God will be"; and "*Mahometh resullala*" is, "Mahomet, the messenger of God, will rise again"; "*lam Nabi*" signifies, "O Prophet! O God!" "*Hia resullala*" means, "Mahomet will rise again." "*Stasforla*" signifies, "God pardon me." Our captain and we, hearing this noise, immediately ran with our arms in our hands, thinking they were Arabs who wanted to rob the caravan, saying to them: "What is this you are crying out?" for they made just such a noise as is heard amongst us Christians when a saint performs a miracle. These old men answered: "*Inte mar abser miri igimen elbeit el Naby uramen il sama?*"[1] that is, "Do you not see the brilliant light which comes out of the sepulchre of the Prophet?" Our captain said: "I do not see anything"; and he asked all of us if we had seen anything, and we answered: "No." One of the old men replied: "Are you slaves?" that is, Mamelukes. The captain said: "Yes, they were slaves." The old man answered: "Oh, sirs! you cannot see these celestial things because you are not well confirmed in our faith." Our captain replied: "*Lami ianon ancati telethe elphi seraphi: vualla anemaiati chelp menel-chelp,*" which means, "Oh, fools, I was willing to give you three thousand ducats, by God, but I won't give you them now, you dogs, sons of dogs." You must know that these lights were certain artificial fires which they had cunningly lighted on the top of the said tower to make us believe that they were lights which issued from the sepulchre of Mahomet; wherefore our captain ordered that none of us should on any account enter the said mosque. And you must know (I tell it you for a truth) there is no coffin of iron or steel, nor loadstone, nor any mountain within four miles. We remained there three days in order to give rest to the camels. The people of the said city supply themselves with the provisions which come from Arabia Felix, and from Cairo, and from Ethiopia [African coast] by sea, for from thence to the sea is four days' journey.

¶ Now we being tired of these things and vanities of Mahomet, prepared ourselves to pass onwards, and with our pilots, great observers of their compasses and charts, necessary when traversing the sea, began the journey southwards, and we found a very fine well in which there was a great quantity of water, which well, the Moors say, was made by St. Mark the Evangelist, by a miracle of God, on account of the want of water which prevails in that country. This well was dry at our departure. (I must not forget to mention our meeting with the sea of sand, which we left before we found the mountain of the Jews, and through which we travelled five days and five nights. Now you must understand all about this. This is a very large level plain, which is full of white sand as fine as meal, where, if unfortunately the wind should blow from the south as you come from the north, all would be dead men, and although we had the wind with us we could not see each other at a distance of ten paces. The men ride on camels in certain wooden boxes, in which they sleep and eat, and the pilots go in advance with their compasses as they do at sea. And here many died from thirst, and a great many died because when they dug and found water they drank so much that they burst; and here mummies are made. When the wind blows from the north this sand collects against a very large mountain [Mt. Athâlith], which is a spur of Mount Sinai. When we were at the top of the said mountain we found a door [or doorway] of the said mountain made by the hand of man. On the left side upon the top of the said mountain there is a grotto to which there is a door of iron. Some say that Mahomet stopped there to pray. At this door a very great noise is heard. We passed this said mountain with great danger, so much so that we thought we should never arrive at this place.) Then we departed from the said well and travelled for ten days, and twice we fought with 50,000 Arabs, till at length we arrived at Mecca, and there was a very great war, one brother with another, for there are four brothers, and they fought to be Lords of Mecca.

¶ We will now speak of the very noble city of Mecca, what it is, its state, and who governs it. The city is most beautiful, and is very well inhabited, and contains about 6,000 families. The houses are extremely good, like our own, and there are houses worth three or four thousand ducats each. This city is not surrounded by walls. A quarter of a mile distant from the city we found a mountain where there was a road cut by human labour. And then we descended into the plain. The walls of the said city are the mountains, and it has four entrances. The governor of this city is a Sultan, that is, one of the four brothers, and is of the race of Mahomet [*i.e.* a Sherîf], and is subject to the Grand Sultan of Cairo. His three brothers are always at war with him. On the 18th of May we entered into the said city of Mecca; we entered from the north, and afterwards we descended into the plain. On the side towards the south there are two mountains which almost touch each other, where is the pass to go to the gate of

Mecca. On the other side, where the sun rises, there is another mountain pass, like a valley, through which is the road to the mountain where they celebrate the sacrifice of Abraham and Isaac, which mountain is distant from the said city about eight or ten miles. The height of this mountain is two or three casts of a stone by hand, and it is of some kind of stone, not marble, but of another colour. On the top of this said mountain there is a mosque according to their custom, which has three doors. At the foot of the said mountain there are two very beautiful reservoirs of water. One is for the caravan from Cairo, and the other for the caravan from Damascus; which water is collected there from the rain and comes from a great distance. Now, let us return to the city. At the proper time we will speak of the sacrifice which they make at the foot of the said mountain. When we entered into the said city we found the caravan from Cairo, which had arrived eight days before us, because they had not travelled by the same route as ourselves. In the said caravan there were sixty-four thousand camels and one hundred Mamelukes. You must know that, in my opinion, the curse of God has been laid upon the said city, for the country produces neither grass nor trees, nor any one thing. And they suffer from so great a dearth of water, that if every one were to drink as much as he might wish, four *quattrini* worth of water daily would not suffice them. I will tell you in what manner they live. A great part of their provisions comes from Cairo, that is, from the Red Sea. There is a port called Zida [Jedda], which is distant from the said city forty miles. A great quantity of food also comes there from Arabia Felix, and also a great part comes from Ethiopia. We found a great number of pilgrims, of whom some came from Ethiopia, some from India Major, some from India Minor, some from Persia, and some from Syria. Truly I never saw so many people collected in one spot as during the twenty days I remained there. Of these people some had come for the purposes of trade, and some on pilgrimage for their pardon, in which pardon you shall understand what they do.

¶ First we will speak of the merchandise, which comes from many parts. From India Major there come a great many jewels and all sorts of spices, and part comes from Ethiopia [African coast]; and there also comes from India Major, from a city called Bangchella [Bengal], a very large quantity of stuffs of cotton and of silk, so that in this city there is carried on a very extensive traffic of merchandise, that is, of jewels, spices of every kind in abundance, cotton in large quantities, wax and odoriferous substances in the greatest abundance.

¶ Now let us turn to the pardoning of the said pilgrims. In the midst of the said city there is a very beautiful temple, similar to the Colosseum of

Rome, but not made of such large stones, but of burnt bricks, and it is round in the same manner; it has ninety or one hundred doors around it, and is arched, and has many of these doors. On entering the said temple you descend ten or twelve steps of marble, and here and there about the said entrance there stand men who sell jewels, and nothing else. And when you have descended the said steps you find the said temple all around, and everything, that is, the walls, covered with gold. And under the said arches there stand about 4,000 or 5,000 persons, men and women, which persons sell all kinds of odoriferous things; the greater part are powders for preserving human bodies, because pagans come there from all parts of the world. Truly, it would not be possible to describe the sweetness and the odours which are smelt within this temple. It appears like a spicery full of musk, and of other most delicious odours. On the 23rd of May the said pardon commences in the above-mentioned temple. The pardon is this: Within the said temple, and uncovered, and in the centre, there is a tower, the size of which is about five or six paces on every side, around which tower there is a cloth of black silk. And there is a door all of silver, of the height of a man, by which you enter into the said tower. On each side of the door there is a jar, which they say is full of balsam, and which is shown on the day of Pentecost. And they say that that balsam is part of the treasures of the Sultan. On each side of the said tower there is a large ring at the corner. On the 24th of May all the people begin, before day, to go seven times around the said tower, always touching and kissing each corner. And at about ten or twelve paces distant from the said tower there is another tower, like one of your chapels, with three or four doors. In the centre of the said tower there is a very beautiful well, which is seventy fathoms deep, and the water is brackish. At this well there stand six or eight men appointed to draw water for the people. And when the said people have gone seven times around the first tower, they go to this well, and place themselves with their backs towards the brink of the well, saying: "*Bizmilei erachman erachin stoforla aladin*," which means, "In the name of God, God pardon me my sins." And those who draw the water throw three bucketsful over each person, from the crown of their heads to their feet, and all bathe, even though their dress be made of silk. And they say in this wise, that all their sins remain there after this washing. And they say that the first tower which they walked round was the first house that Abraham built. And all having thus bathed, they go by way of the valley to the said mountain of which we have before spoken, and remain there two days and one night. And when they are all at the foot of the said mountain, they make the sacrifice there.

¶ Every generous mind is the most readily delighted and incited to great deeds by novel events. Wherefore, in order to satisfy many of this disposition, I will add concisely the custom which is observed in their sacrifices. Every man and woman kills at least two or three, and some four and some six sheep; so that I really believe that on the first day more than 30,000 sheep are killed by cutting their throats, facing the east. Each person gives them to the poor for the love of God, for there were about 30,000 poor people there, who made a very large hole in the earth, and then put in it camels' dung, and thus they made a little fire, and warmed the flesh a little, and then ate it. And truly, it is my opinion, that these poor men came more on account of their hunger than for the sake of the pardon; and as a proof that it was so, we had a great number of cucumbers, which came from Arabia Felix, and we ate them all but the rind, which we afterwards threw away outside our tent. And about forty or fifty of the said poor people stood before our tent, and made a great scrambling among themselves, in order to pick up the said rinds, which were full of sand. By this it appeared to us that they came rather to satisfy their hunger than to wash away their sins. On the second day a cadi of their faith, like one of our preachers, ascended to the top of the said mountain and made a discourse to all the people, which discourse lasted for about an hour; and he made in their language a sort of lamentation, and besought the people that they should weep for their sins. And he said to them in a loud voice: "Oh, Abraham, well-wished for and well-loved of God!" And then he said: "Oh, Isaac, chosen of God, friend of God, beseech God for the people of Naby!" and then were heard very great lamentations. And when he had finished his sermon, the whole caravan rushed back into Mecca with the greatest haste, for at the distance of six miles there were more than 20,000 Arabs, who wanted to rob the caravan, and we arrived for the defence of Mecca. But when we had gone half way, that is, between Mecca and the mountain where the sacrifice is made, we found a certain little wall four fathoms high, and at the foot of the said wall a very great quantity of small stones, which stones are thrown there by all the people when they pass that way, for the objects which you shall hear. They say that when God commanded Abraham that he should go and sacrifice his son, he went before him, and he said to his son that he must follow after him, because it was necessary to fulfil the commandments of God. The son answered him: "I am well pleased to fulfil the commandment of God." And when Isaac arrived at the abovementioned little wall, they say that the devil appeared to him in the form of one of his friends and said to him: "My friend Isaac, where art thou going?" He answered him: "I am going to my father, who is waiting for me in such a place." The devil answered him: "Do not go, my son, for thy father will sacrifice thee to God and will put thee to death." And Isaac replied: "Let it be so; if such be the will of God, so let it be." The devil then disappeared, and a little farther on he appeared in the form of another dear friend of Isaac, and said to him the above-mentioned words. They relate that Isaac answered with anger: "Let it be so;" and took a stone and threw it in the devil's face: and for this reason, when the people arrive at the said place, each one throws a stone at the said wall, and then they go to the city. We found in the street of the said city 15,000 or 20,000 doves, which they say are of the stock of that dove which spoke to Mahomet in the form of the Holy Spirit, which doves fly about the whole district at their pleasure, that is, in the shops where they sell grain, millet, rice, and other vegetable productions. And the owners of the said articles are not at liberty to kill them or catch them. And if anyone were to strike any of those doves, they would fear that the country would be ruined. And you must know that they cause very great expense within the temple.

¶ In another part of the said temple is an enclosed place in which there are two live unicorns, and these are shown as very remarkable objects, which they certainly are. I will tell you how they are made. The elder is formed like a colt of thirty months old, and he has a horn in the forehead, which horn is about three *braccia* in length. The other unicorn is like a colt of one year old, and he has a horn of about four *palmi* long. The colour of the said animal resembles that of a dark bay horse, and his head resembles that of a stag; his neck is not very long, and he has some thin and short hair which hangs on one side; his legs are slender and lean like those of a goat; the foot is a little cloven in the fore part, and long and goat-like, and there are some hairs on the hind part of the said legs. Truly this monster must be a very fierce and solitary animal. These two animals were presented to the Sultan of Mecca as the finest things that could be found in the world at the present day, and as the richest treasure ever sent by a king of Ethiopia, that is, by a Moorish king [of Zeila]. He made this present in order to secure an alliance with the said Sultan of Mecca.

¶ I must here show how the human intellect manifests itself under certain circumstances, in so far as it became necessary for me to exercise it in order to escape from the caravan of Mecca. Having gone to make some purchases for my captain, I was recognized by a Moor who looked me in the face and said to me: "*In te menaine?*" that is, "Where are you from?" I answered: "I am a Moor." He replied: "*In te chedeab,*" that is, "You are not telling the truth." I said to him: "*Orazalnabi Aneymuz lemma,*" that is, "By the head of Mahomet, I am a Moor." He answered: "*Thale beithane,*" that is, "Come to my house;" and I went with him. When I had arrived at his house, he spoke to me in Italian, and told me where I had come from, and that he knew that I was not a Moor, and he told me that he had been in Genoa and in Venice, and gave me proofs of it. When I heard this, I told him that I was a Roman, and that I had become a Mameluke at Cairo. When he heard this he was much pleased, and treated me with very great honour, and as it was my intention to proceed further, I began to say to him, if this was the city of Mecca which was so renowned through all the world, where were the jewels and spices, and where were all the various kinds of merchandise which it was reported were brought there. I asked him this only that he might tell me why they had not arrived as usual, and in order not to ask him if the King of Portugal was the cause, he being Lord of the Mare Oceano [the Atlantic] and of the Persian and Arabian Gulfs. Then he began to tell me by degrees why the said articles had not come as they were accustomed to do. And when he told me that the King of Portugal was the cause, I pretended to be much grieved, and spoke great ill of the said king, merely that he might not think that I was pleased that the Christians should make such a journey. When he saw that I displayed hostility to the Christians, he showed me yet greater honour, and told me everything point by point. And when I was well informed, I said to him: "O, friend, I beg you, *Menahamena lhabi*, to tell me some mode or way by which I may escape from the caravan, because my intention is to go to find those beings who are hostile to the Christians; for I assure you that, if they knew what I am capable of, they would send to find me even to Mecca." He answered me: "By the faith of our prophet what can you do?" I answered him that I was the most skilful maker of large mortars in the world. Hearing this he said: "Mahomet be ever praised, who has sent us such a man to serve the Moors and God." So he concealed me in his house with his wife. And he begged me that I would induce our captain to drive out from Mecca fifteen camels laden with spices, and this he did in order not to pay thirty seraphim to the Sultan for the toll. I replied that if he would save me in this house, I would enable him to carry off a hundred camels if he had so many, for the Mamelukes have this privilege. And when he heard this he was much pleased. Afterwards, he instructed me in the manner in which I should conduct myself, and directed me to a king who is in the parts of India Major, and who is called the King of Deccan [Yûsuf 'Adil Shâh of Bîjâpur]. When the time comes we will speak of that king. The day before the caravan set out he concealed me in his house in a secret place. In the morning, two hours before day, there went through the city a great quantity of instruments and trumpets, sounding according to their custom, and making proclamation that all the Mamelukes, under pain of death, should mount their horses and commence their journey towards Syria. Whereupon, my heart was seized with a great perturbation when I heard this proclamation, and I earnestly recommended myself with tears to the wife of the said merchant, and besought God that he would save me from such violence. On Tuesday morning the said caravan departed, and the merchant left me in his house with his wife; and he went with the caravan, and told his wife, that on the following Friday, she must send me away in company with the caravan of India which was going to Zida [Jedda], which is a port of Mecca, forty miles distant. I cannot express the kindness I received from this lady, and especially from her niece of fifteen years old, they promising me that, if I would remain there, they would make me rich. But I declined all their offers on account of the present danger. When Friday came, I set out with the caravan at noon, to the no small regret of the said ladies, who made great lamentations, and at midnight we arrived at a certain city of Arabia [Hudda], and remained there all night and until noon of the following day. On Saturday we departed and travelled until midnight, when we entered into the said port of the city of Zida.

¶ This city is not surrounded by walls, but by very beautiful houses, as is the custom in Italy; we will, therefore, not dwell long on a description of it. It is a city of very extensive traffic, because a great number of the pagan people come here; the reason being that neither Christians nor Jews are admitted. When I had arrived at the said city I immediately entered into a mosque, that is, a temple, where there were at least 25,000 poor people, and I hid myself in a corner of the said temple, and remained there for fourteen days. All day long I remained stretched upon the ground covered up with my garments, and keeping up a constant groaning as though I were suffering intense pain in my stomach and body. The merchants said: "Who is that who is lamenting so?" The poor people who were near me said: "It is a poor Moor, who is dying." Every evening when night came I quitted the mosque and went to buy food. I leave you to judge whether or no I had an appetite, eating only once a day, and that very badly. This city is governed by the lord of Cairo. The lord of it is one who is a brother of Barachet [Barakât], that is, of the Sultan of Mecca. They are subject to the Grand Sultan of Cairo. There does not occur to me much to say here, for they are Moors. The land does not produce one single thing, and there is a great scarcity of water, that is to say, of fresh water. The sea beats against the walls of the houses. All sorts of necessaries are found here, but they come from Cairo, from Arabia Felix, and from other places. In this city there are always a great number of sick people, and they say that this is in consequence of the bad air of the place. It contains about five hundred families. At the end of fourteen days I made an agreement with the master of a vessel which was going towards Persia, for in the said port there were about one hundred ships great and small. Three days afterwards we set sail, and began to navigate the Red Sea.

¶ It will be understood that this sea is not red, but that the water is like that of any other sea. In this sea we sailed one day until the setting of the sun, because it is not possible to navigate it during the night time. And every day they proceeded in this manner until they arrived at an island called Chamaram [Kamarân]. After this island you can proceed in safety. The reason why it is not possible to sail during night is, that there are many islands and many rocks, and it is necessary that a man should always be stationed on the top of the mast of the ship in order to see the route, which cannot be done during the night-time, and therefore they can only navigate during the day.

CHAPTER III

CONCERNING ARABIA FELIX

HAVING discoursed of the places, cities, and customs of the people of Arabia Deserta, as far as it was permitted me to see them, it appears to me that it will be proper, with brevity and more happily, to enter upon Arabia Felix. At the end of six days we arrived at a city which is called Gezan [Jîzân], which city has a very fine port; and we found there forty-five vessels belonging to different countries. This city is situated on the sea shore, and is subject to a Moorish lord, and is a district very fruitful and good, like Christian countries. Here there are very good grapes and peaches, quinces, pomegranates, very strong garlic, tolerable onions, excellent nuts, melons, roses, flowers, nectarines, figs, gourds, citrons, lemons, and sour oranges, so that it is a paradise. The inhabitants of this city go almost naked, and live after the manner of the Moors. There is here abundance of flesh, grain, barley, and white millet, which they call *dora*, and which makes good bread. We remained here three days in order to lay in provisions.

¶ Departing from the said city Gezan, we went for five days always in sight of land, that is to say, the land was on our left hand; and seeing some habitations on the sea shore, we disembarked fourteen of our people to ask for some provisions in exchange for our money. They answered our request by beginning to throw stones at us with slings, and these were certain people who are called Baduin [Bedouîn, al-Badawî]: they were in number more than one hundred, and we were only fourteen. We fought with them for about an hour, so that twenty-four of them remained dead on the field, and all the others took to flight; for they were naked, and had no other arms than these slings. We took all that we could, namely, fowls, calves, oxen, and other things fit to eat. In the course of two or three hours the disturbance began to increase, as did also the inhabitants of the said land, so that they were more than six hundred, and we were obliged to withdraw to our ship.

¶ On that same day we took our course towards an island called Chamaram [Kamarân], which island appears to be ten or twelve miles in circumference, where there is a place containing about two hundred families, which is inhabited by Moors. In this said island there is sweet fresh water and flesh, and the best salt I ever saw is made there. It has a port towards the mainland, from which it is distant about eight miles. This island is subject to the Sultan of the Amanni [Yamanî, Yemenî], that is, the Sultan of Arabia Felix [Imâm of Sanâ'a], and we remained there two days. We then steered towards the mouth of the Red Sea, and for two days you can navigate in safety night and day, but from the island to Zida [Jedda] you cannot navigate by night. And when we had arrived at the said mouth, it really appeared as though we were within a hemmed-in house; for that embouchure is about two or three miles wide, and on the right hand thereof there is land about ten paces high and uninhabited, so far as we could perceive from a distance. On the left hand of the said embouchure there is a very high mountain, and it is of stone; and in the middle of the said embouchure there is a certain little uninhabited island which is called Bebmendo [Babelmandeb, Babu'l-Mandab]. Those who wish to go to Zeilla take the route on the right hand, and those who want to go to Aden take that on the left hand; and this we did in order to go to Aden, and we always sailed in sight of land. From the said Bebmendo we arrived at the city of Aden in a little less than two days and a half.

¶ Aden is the strongest city that was ever seen on level ground. It has walls on two sides, and on the other sides there are very large mountains. On these mountains there are five castles, and the land is level, and contains about five thousand or six thousand families. The market is held at two o'clock in the night, on account of the intense heat in the city during the day. At a stone's cast from this city there is a mountain, upon which stands a castle, and at the foot of this mountain the ships cast anchor. This city is extremely beautiful, and the capital of Arabia Felix. It is the rendezvous for all the ships which come from India Major and Minor, from Ethiopia and from Persia. All the ships which are bound for Mecca put in here. As soon as a ship comes into port, the officers of the Sultan of the said city board it, and desire to know whence it comes, the nature of its cargo, and when it left its own country, and how many persons there are on board. And when they have obtained all this information, they remove from the said ship the masts, sails, rudder, and anchors, and carry them all into the said city; and this they do in order that the said persons may not depart without paying the dues to the Sultan. The second day after my arrival in the said city I was taken and put in irons, and this occurred through one of my companions, who said to me: "Christian dog, son of a dog." Some Moors heard this speech, and through this I was taken with great violence to the palace of the Vice-Sultan, and they immediately consulted whether they should at once put me to death, because the Sultan was not in the city. They said that I was a spy of the Christians. But as the Sultan of this country never puts anyone to death, these people respected my life, and kept me sixty-five days with eighteen pounds' weight of iron on my feet. On the third day after we had been taken, there ran to the palace forty or sixty Moors, belonging to two or three ships which had been captured by the Portuguese, and who had escaped by swimming, and they said that we belonged to these Portuguese ships, and that we had come there as spies. For this fancy of theirs they ran to the palace in the greatest fury, with arms in their hands to slay us; but through the merciful intervention of God, those who guarded us fastened the door on the inner side. At this report the district rose in arms, and some desired that we should die and some not. At last the Vice-Sultan obtained that we should be spared. At the end of sixty-five days the Sultan sent for us, and we were both taken on a camel, still, however, with the said irons on our feet. We were eight days on the road, and were then presented to the Sultan at a city called Rhada [Radâ'a al-'Arab]. At the time when we arrived at the city the Sultan was reviewing eighty thousand men, because he was about to go to war with another Sultan of a city called Sana [Sanâ'a], which is distant from Rhada three days' journey. This city lies partly on an acclivity and partly on the plain, and it is very beautiful and ancient, populous and rich. When we were presented before the Sultan he asked me whence I came. I answered: "*Anabletrom iasidi anaigi assalem menel Cayro anegi Medinathalnaby & Mecca & badanigi bledech cul ragel calem inte sidi seich hiasidi ane abdech Inte maarf sidi ane musolimim.*" That is, the Sultan said: "Whence are you and what do you purpose doing?" I answered: "that I was a Roman, that I had become a Mameluke at Cairo, that I had been to Medina, to Naby, where Mahomet is buried, and to Mecca, and that then I had come to see his Highness; because through all Syria, and at Mecca, and at Medina, it was said that he was a saint, and if he was a saint, (as I believed), he must know that I was not a spy of the Christians, and that I was a good Moor and his slave." Then said the Sultan: "Say, *Leilla illala Mahometh resullala*" [the Muslim Creed]. But I could not pronounce the words at all, whether such were the will of God, or through the fear which had seized me. The Sultan, seeing that I could not pronounce these words, commanded that I should be thrown into prison and kept with the greatest strictness by the men of eighteen castles, that is, four for each castle. They remained four days, and then were changed for four others from four other castles. And in this order they guarded me for three months, with a loaf of millet in the morning and one in the evening, although six of these loaves would not have sufficed me for one day, and sometimes I should have been well pleased if I could have had enough water.

¶ Two days afterwards, the Sultan took the field, and marched to the said city Sana [Sanâ'a] with his army, in which there were three thousand horsemen, sons of Christians, as black as Moors. They were of those of Prester John, whom they purchased at the age of eight or nine years, and had them trained to arms. These constituted his own guard, because they were worth more than all the rest of the eighty thousand. The others were all naked, with the exception of a piece of linen worn like a mantle. When they enter into battle they use a kind of round shield, made of two pieces of cow hide or ox hide fastened together. In the centre of the said round shields there are four rods, which keep them straight. These shields are painted, so that they appear to those who see them to be the handsomest and best that could be made. They are about as large as the bottom of a tub, and the handle consists of a piece of wood of a size that can be grasped by the hand, fastened by two nails. They also carry in their hand a dart and a short and broad sword, and wear a cloth vest of red or some other colour stuffed with cotton, which protects them from the cold and also from their enemies. They make use of this when they go out to fight. They all also generally carry a sling for the purpose of throwing stones wound round their heads, and under this sling they carry a piece of wood, a span in length, which is called *mesuech* [*miswâk*], with which they clean their teeth, and generally from forty or fifty years downwards they wear two horns made of their own hair, so that they look like young kids. The said Sultan also takes with his army five thousand camels laden with tents, all of cotton, and also ropes of cotton.

¶ Having seen this army depart, let us return to my prison. In the said palace of the city there was one of the three wives of the Sultan, who remained there with twelve or thirteen very beautiful damsels, whose colour was more near to black than otherwise. This queen was very kind to me. I and my companion and a Moor, being all three in prison here, we arranged that one of us should pretend to be mad, in order the better to assist one another. Finally, the lot fell upon me to be mad. Having then taken this enterprise upon myself, it behoved me to do such things as were natural to madmen. Truly, I never found myself so wearied or so exhausted as during the first three days that I feigned madness. The reason was that I had constantly behind me fifty or sixty little children, who threw stones at me, and I threw stones at them. They cried out: "*Iami iasion Iami ianun*"; that is to say: "Madman [*majnûn*]." And I had my shirt constantly full of stones, and acted like a madman. The queen was always at her window with her damsels, and remained there from morning till evening to see me and talk with me; and I, being mocked by many men and merchants, taking off my shirt, went, quite naked as I was, before the queen, who took the greatest delight in seeing me, and would not let me leave her, and gave me good and sound food to eat, so that I gained my point. She also said to me: "Give it to those beasts, for if you kill them it will be their own fault." A sheep was passing through the king's court, the tail of which weighed forty pounds. I seized it and demanded of it if it was a Moor, or a Christian, or, in truth, a Jew; and repeating these words to it and many others I said: "Prove yourself a Moor and say: *Leilla illala Mahometh resullala*"; and he, standing like a patient animal which could not speak, I took a stick and broke all its four legs. The queen stood there laughing, and afterwards fed me for three days on the flesh of it, than which I do not know that I ever ate better. Three days afterwards I killed, in the same manner as I had killed the sheep, an ass which was carrying water to the palace, because he would not become a Moor. Acting in the same manner by a Jew, I cudgelled him to such an extent that I left him for dead. But one day, being about to act in my usual manner, I came across one of those who had me in custody, and who was more mad than I was, who said to me: "Christian dog, son of a dog." I threw a good many stones at him, and he began to turn towards me with all the children, and struck me with a stone in the breast which did me an ill service. I, not being able to follow him on account of the irons on my feet, took the way to my prison; but before I reached it he struck me with another stone in the side, which gave me much more pain than the first. I could easily have avoided both if I had chosen to do so, but I chose to receive them to give colour to my madness. And therefore I immediately entered my prison and blocked myself in with very large stones, and remained there two days and two nights without eating or drinking. The queen and the others feared that I might be dead, and caused the door to be broken open, and these dogs brought me some pieces of marble, saying: "Eat, this is sugar"; and some others gave me grapes filled with earth, and said that it was salt, and I eat the marble and the grapes and everything, all together. On that same day, some merchants belonging to the city brought two men who were esteemed amongst them as two hermits would be amongst us, and who dwelt in certain mountains. I was shown to them, and the merchants asked these men: "Whether did it appear to them that I was holy or mad?" One of them said: "It appears to me that he is holy"; the other said it appeared to him that I was mad. In this way they kept disputing for more than an hour, and I, in order to get rid of them, raised my shirt and pissed over them both; whereupon they began to run away crying out: "*Migenon migenon suffi maffis,*" that is, "He is mad, he is mad, he is not holy." The queen was at her window with her maidens, and seeing this they all began to laugh, saying: "*O achala o raza al Naby ade ragel maphe donia methalon*"; that is, "By the good God, by the head of Mahomet, this is the most capital fellow in the world." The next morning I found asleep him who had given me the two blows with the stones. I seized him by the horns [tufts of hair], and putting my knees upon the pit of his stomach, gave him so many blows upon the face that he was covered with blood, and I left him for dead. The queen remained standing at her window, exclaiming: "Kill those beasts." The governor of that city, discovering through many circumstances that my companions treacherously wished to escape, and had made a hole in their prison and removed their irons, and that I had not done so, and as he knew that the queen took great pleasure in me, he would not do me any injury until he had spoken with her; who, when she had heard everything, considered me in her own mind to be rational, and sent for me, and had me placed in a lower chamber in the palace without any door, but still with the irons on my feet.

¶ The first night ensuing, the queen came to visit me with five or six of her damsels, and began to examine me, and I began to give her to understand by degrees that I was not mad. She, being a clever woman, saw that I was not at all mad, and began to make much of me; ordered a good bed after their fashion to be given me, and sent me plenty of good food. The following day she had prepared for me a bath according to their custom, with many perfumes, and continued these caresses for twelve days. Afterwards, she began to come down to visit me every night at three or four o'clock, and always brought me good things to eat. Entering where I was, she called me "*Iunus tale inte iohan,*" that is, "Lodovico, come here, are you hungry?" And I replied: "*E vualla,*" that is, "Yes," for the hunger which was to come; and I rose on my feet and went to her in my shirt. And she said: "*Leis leis camis foch,*" that is, "Not in that manner, take off your shirt." I replied: "*Iaseti ane maomigenon de lain,*" which is, "O, madam, I am not mad now." She answered me: "*Vualla ane arf in te habedenin te migenon inte mafdunia metalon,*" that is, "By God, I know well that thou never wast mad, on the contrary, that thou art the best witted man that ever was seen." In order to please her I took off my shirt, and held it before me for modesty's sake, and thus she kept me before her for two hours, contemplating me as though I had been a nymph, and uttering a lamentation to God in this manner: "*Ialla in te sta cal ade abiat me telsamps Inte stacal ane auset; Ialla Ianaby iosane assiet: Villet ane asuet ade ragel abiath Insalla ade ragel Iosane Insalla oel binth mit lade,*" that is, "O God, thou hast created this man white like the sun, thou has created my husband black, my son also is black, and I am black. Would to God that this man were my husband. Would to God that I might have a son like this man." And saying these words she wept continually and sighed, passing her hands over me all the while, and promising me that, as soon as the Sultan returned, she would make him take off my irons. On the next night the queen came to me with two of her damsels and brought me some good food to eat, and said to me: "*Tale Iunus,*" that is, "Come here, Lodovico"; "*Ane igi andech,*" I replied. "*Leis setti ane mochaet ich fio,*" that is, said the queen, "Lodovico, would you like that I should come and stay a little while with you." I answered: "No; that it was quite enough that I was in chains, without her causing me to have my head cut off." Then said she: "*Let caffane darchi alarazane,*" that is, "Do not be afraid, for I will stake my own head for your safety." "*In cane in te mayrith ane Gazella in sich: olla Tegia in sich ollè Galzerana insich,*" that is, "If you do not wish me to come, shall Gazella, or Tegia, or Galzerana [women's names] come?" She only said this because she wished to come herself and remain with me in the place of one of these three. But I never would consent, because I thought of this from the time when she began to show me so many kindnesses.

Considering also, that as soon as she had had her wish she would have given me gold and silver, horses and slaves, and whatever I had desired. And then she would have given me ten black slaves, who would have been a guard upon me, so that I should never have been able to escape from the country, for all Arabia Felix was informed of me, that is to say, at the passes. And if I had once ran away, I could not have escaped death, or chains for life. For this reason, therefore, I never would yield to her, and also because I did not wish to lose both my soul and body. I wept all night, recommending myself to God. Three days from that time the Sultan returned, and the queen immediately sent to inform me that if I would remain with her she would make me rich. I replied: "That if she would cause my chains to be taken off, and perform the promise she made to God and Mahomet I would then do whatever her highness wished. She immediately had me taken before the Sultan, who asked me where I wished to go when he had taken off my chains. I answered him: "*Iasidi habu mafis una mafis, meret mafis uuellet mafis, ochu mafis octa mafis alla al naby Intebes sidi in te iati iaculane abdech*," that is, "O lord, I have no father, no mother, no wife. I have no children, I have neither brothers nor sisters, I have only God, and the Prophet, and you, O lord: will it please you to give me food, for I wish to be your slave all my life?" And I wept constantly. The queen was present all the time, and said to the Sultan: "Thou wilt have to render an account to God of this poor man, whom without any cause thou hast kept so long in chains. Beware of the anger of God." Said the Sultan: "Well, go where thou wilt, I give thee thy liberty." And immediately he had my chains taken off, and I knelt before him and kissed his feet, and then I kissed the queen's hand, who took me also by the hand saying: "Come with me, poor fellow, for I know that thou art dying of hunger." When I was in her chamber she kissed me more than a hundred times, and then she gave me many good things to eat. But I did not feel any inclination to eat, for I had seen the queen speak privately to the Sultan, and I thought that she had asked me of the Sultan for a slave. Wherefore I said to the queen: "I will not eat unless you promise to give me my liberty." She replied: "*Scut mi Ianu inte maarfesiati alla*," that is, "Hold thy peace, madman, thou dost not know what God has ordained for thee." "*Incane inte milie inte amirra*," that is, "If thou wilt be good thou shalt be a lord." Now, I knew the kind of lordship she wished to confer upon me; but I answered her that she should let me get a little fatter, and get back my blood, for the great fear I was in filled my breast with other thoughts than those of love. She answered: "*Vuulla inte calem milie ane iaticullion beit e digege e amam e filfil e cherfa e gronfili e iosindi*," that is, "By God, thou art right, but I will give thee every day eggs, hens, pigeons, pepper, cinnamon, cloves, and nutmegs [properly coconuts]." Then I recovered my spirits somewhat at the good words and promises she gave me. In order the better to restore me, I remained fifteen or twenty days in her palace. One day she sent for me and asked me if I would go hunting with her. I replied in the affirmative and went with her. On our return I pretended to fall sick from weakness, and remained in this feigned state eight days, while she continually sent persons to visit me. One day I sent to inform her that I had made a promise to God and to Mahomet that I would visit a holy man who was in Aden, and who, they said, performed miracles; and I maintained that it was true in order to accomplish my object. She sent to tell me that she was well pleased, and ordered a camel and twenty-five seraphim [ducats] of gold to be given to me, whereat I was much rejoiced. The following day I mounted and went to Aden in eight days, and immediately visited the holy man, who was worshipped because he always lived in poverty and chastity, and spent his life like a hermit. And, truly, there are many in that country who pass this kind of life, but they are deceived from not having been baptised. When I had performed my devotions on the second day, I pretended to be cured by virtue of that holy man. Afterwards I wrote to the queen, that by the virtue of God and of that holy man I was cured, and since God had been so merciful to me I wished to go and see the whole of her kingdom. This I did because the fleet was in that place, and could not depart for a month. I spoke secretly with the captain of a ship, and told him that I wished to go to India, and if he would take me I would give him a handsome present. He replied: "That before he went to India he wished to touch at Persia." With that I was satisfied, and so we agreed.

¶ The following day I rode for fifteen miles, and found a city which is called Lagi [Lâhaj]; the place is level and very populous. A vast number of date-trees grow here, there is also plenty of animal food and grain as with us. But there are no grapes here, and a great scarcity of firewood. This city is uncivilized, and the inhabitants are Arabs, who are not very rich. I departed thence and went to another city, which is one day's journey from the first mentioned, and is called Aiaz ['Az'az]. It stands upon two mountains, between which there is a very beautiful valley and a beautiful fountain, in which valley the market is held to which the men come from both the mountains. And very few of those markets are held without quarrels taking place. The reason is this: those who inhabit the mountain towards the north wish that those who inhabit the mountain towards the south should believe with them in Mahomet with all his companions; while these will only believe in Mahomet and Ali, and say that the other captains are false. For this reason they kill each other like dogs. Let us return to the market, to which are brought many kinds of small spices, and a great quantity of stuffs, of wool, and of silk, and very excellent fruits, such as peaches, pomegranates, and quinces, figs, nuts, and good grapes. You must know that on each of these mountains there is a very strong fortress. Having beheld these things I departed thence and went to another city, which is distant from this two days' journey and is called Dante [Damt], and is an extremely strong city, situated on the top of a very great mountain, and is inhabited by Arabs, who are poor, because the country is very barren.

¶ In order to follow out the desires after novel things already conceived in our minds we departed from that place, taking our way towards another city, distant two days' journey, which is called Almacarana [al-Makrâna], and is situated on the top of a mountain, the ascent to which is seven miles, and to which only two persons can go abreast on account of the narrowness of the path. The city is level on the top of the mountain, and is very beautiful and good. Food enough for the whole city is collected here, and for this reason it appears to me to be the strongest city in the world. There is no want of water there nor of any other necessary of life, and above all, there is a cistern there which would supply water for 100,000 persons. The Sultan keeps all his treasure in this city, because he derives his origin and descent from it. For this reason the Sultan always keeps one of his wives here. You must know that articles of every possible kind are brought here, and it has the best air of any place in the world. The inhabitants are more white than any other colour. In this city the Sultan keeps more gold than a hundred camels could carry, and I say this because I have seen it.

¶ When I had rambled about the above-mentioned city, on parting thence I went to another place, distant from this one day's journey, which is called Reame [Yârim], and is for the most part inhabited by black people, who are very great merchants. This country is extremely fertile, excepting in firewood, and the city contains about two thousand families. On one side of this city there is a mountain, upon which stands a very strong castle. And here there is a kind of sheep, some of which I have seen, whose tails alone weigh forty-four pounds. They have no horns, and cannot walk on account of their size. Here also is found a kind of white grape, which has no seeds within, than which I never tasted better. Here also I found all kinds of fruit as I said above. The climate here is most perfect and singular. In this place I conversed with many persons who were more than one hundred and twenty-five years old, and were still very healthy. The people here go more naked than otherwise, but the men of good condition wear a shirt. The lower orders wear half a sheet crosswise, after the fashion of prelates. Through the whole of this Arabia Felix the men wear horns made of their own hair, and the women wear loose trowsers, after the fashion of seamen.

¶ Then I departed and took to a city named Sana, which is distant from the said city Reame three days' journey. It is situated on the top of a very large mountain, and is extremely strong. The Sultan encamped before with 80,000 men for eight months in order to capture it, but could only gain it by capitulation. The walls of this city are of earth, of the height of ten *braza*, and twenty *braza* wide. Think, that eight horses can go abreast on the top of it. In this place many fruits grow the same as in our country, and there are many fountains. In this Sana there is a Sultan who has twelve sons, one of whom is called Mahometh. He is like a madman: he bites people and kills them, and then eats their flesh until his appetite is satisfied. He is four *braza* high, well proportioned, and of a dark brown colour. In this city there are found some kinds of small spices which grow in the neighbourhood. This place contains about 4,000 hearths. The houses are very handsome and resemble ours. Within the city there are many vines and gardens as with us.

¶ After seeing Sana I resumed my journey and went to another city called Taesa [Ta'iz], which is distant three days' journey from Sana aforesaid, and is situated in a mountain. This city is very beautiful, and abounds in all kinds of elegancies, and, above all, in a vast quantity of rose water, which is distilled here. It is reported of this city that it is extremely ancient: there is a temple there built like the Santa Maria Rotonda of Rome, and many other very ancient palaces. There are very great merchants here. These people dress like those above mentioned. They are olive coloured. Departing thence I went to another city, distant from this three days' journey, which is called Zibit [Zabîd]; a large and very excellent city, situated near the Red Sea, at half a day's journey. It is a place of very considerable extent by the Red Sea, and is supplied with an immense quantity of sugar, and has most excellent fruits; is situated on a plain between two mountains, and has no walls around it. A very great traffic is carried on here in spices of all kinds, which are brought from other countries. The dress and colour of these people is the same as of those before mentioned. Then I departed from this place and went to another city, distant one day's journey, called

Damar [Dharnâr], inhabited by Moors, who are very great merchants. The said city is very fertile, and the manner of living and customs of the inhabitants are the same as of those before mentioned.

¶ All these above-named cities are subject to the Sultan of the Amanni [Yemenî], that is, the Sultan of Arabia Felix, who is called Sechamir [Shêkh 'Amir]. *Secho* is the same as saint, *amir*, lord, and the reason why they call him holy is this, that he never put any one to death excepting in war. You must know that in my time he had 15,000 or 16,000 men in chains, and to all he gave two *quattrini* per man for their expenses daily, and thus he left them to die in prison when they deserved death. He also has 16,000 slaves whom he maintains, and they are all black.

¶ Departing from this place I went to the above-mentioned city of Aden for five days. In the middle of the route I found a most terrible mountain, in which we saw more than 10,000 apes, amongst which were certain animals like lions [hyaenas], which do great injury to man when in their power to do so. On their account it is not possible to pass by that route excepting in companies of at least one hundred persons. We passed in very great danger, and with no little hunting of the said animals. However, we killed a great number of them with bows and slings and dogs, so that we passed in safety. As soon as I had arrived in Aden, I placed myself in the mosque pretending to be ill, and remained there all day. In the evening I went to find the captain of the ship, so that he put me on board secretly.

CHAPTER IV

CONCERNING "ETHIOPIA"

HAVING determined to see other countries we put to sea according to our intention; but as fortune is accustomed to exercise her unstable will on the water, equally unstable, we were turned somewhat from our design; for, six days from that time we took the route to Persia, sailing for seven days, and then an accident occurred which made us run as far as Ethiopia [Somâlî coast], together with twenty-five ships laden with madder to dye clothes; for every year they lade as many as twenty-five ships in Aden with it. This madder grows in Arabia Felix. With extreme labour we entered into the port of a city named Zeila, and remained there five days, in order to see it and wait for favourable weather.

¶ The beforenamed city of Zeila is a place of immense traffic, especially in gold and elephants' teeth. Here also are sold a very great number of slaves, which are those people of Prester John whom the Moors take in battle, and from this place they are carried into Persia, Arabia Felix, and to Mecca, Cairo, and into India. In this city people live extremely well, and justice is excellently administered. Much grain grows here and much animal food, oil in great quantity, made not from olives but from *zerzalino* [*juljulân*, gingelly], honey and wax in great abundance. Here is found a kind of sheep, the tail of which weighs fifteen or sixteen pounds, and with the head and neck quite black, but the whole of the rest of the body white. There are also some other sheep, which have tails a *brazzo* long and twisted like vines, and they have the dewlap like that of a bull, which almost touches the ground. Also in this place I found a certain kind of cows, which had horns like a stag and were wild, which had been presented to the Sultan of the said city. I also saw here other cows, which had a single horn in the forehead, which horn is a *palmo* and a half in length, and turns more towards the back of the cow than forwards. The colour of these is red; that of the former is black. There is an abundance of provisions in this city, and there are many merchants here. The place has poor walls and a bad port, nevertheless it is situated on level ground and the mainland. The king of this Zeila is a Moor, and has many soldiers, both foot and horse. The people are warlike. Their dress consists of a shirt. They are olive-coloured. They go badly armed, and are all Mahommedans.

¶ As soon as the weather became favourable, we set sail and arrived at an island which is called Barbara [Berbera], the lord of which with all the inhabitants are Moors. This island is small but good and very well peopled, and contains many animals of every kind. The people are for the most part black, and their wealth consists more in animals than in other things. We remained here one day, and then set sail and took the route towards Persia.

CHAPTER V

CONCERNING PERSIA

WHEN we had sailed about twelve days we arrived at a city [in India] which is called Diuobandierrumi, that is, "Diu, the port of the Turks," which city is situated a short distance from the mainland. When the tide rises it is an island, and when it falls you can pass over on foot. This city is subject to the Sultan of Combeia, and the captain of this Diuo is one named Menacheaz [Malik 'Aiyâz]. We remained here two days.

There is an immense trade in this city. Four hundred Turkish merchants reside here constantly. This city is surrounded by walls and contains much artillery within it. They have certain vessels which are called *thalae* [*at-talâyî*, *atalaya*], which are [shore-boats] somewhat less than galleys. We departed thence and went to a city which is called Goa [Gôghâ, Gogo], distant from the above about three days' journey. This Goa is a district of large extent and great traffic, and is fat and wealthy. The inhabitants, however, are all Mahommedans. We quitted Goa and went to another district called Guilfar [Giulfar, Zuffâr, Dhofâr], which is most excellent and abounding in everything. There is a good seaport there, from which port setting sail with propitious winds we arrived at another port which is called Meschet [Maskat, Muscat].

¶ Pursuing our journey, we departed from Meschet and went to the noble city of Ormus [Hormûz], which is extremely beautiful. It is an island, and is the chief, that is, as a maritime place, and for merchandise. It is distant from the mainland ten or twelve miles. In this said island there is not sufficient water or food, but all comes from the mainland. Near this island, at a distance of three days' journey, they fish up the largest pearls which are found in the world, and the manner of fishing for them is as you shall hear. There are certain fishers with some little boats, who throw out a large stone attached to a thick rope, one from the stern and one from the prow, in order that the said boats may remain firm: they throw down another rope, also with a stone, to the bottom. In the middle of the boat is one of these fishers, who hangs a couple of bags round his neck, and ties a large stone to his feet, and goes fifteen paces under water, and remains there as long as he is able, in order to find the oysters in which are pearls. As he finds them he puts them into the bags, and then leaves the stone which he had at his feet, and comes up by one of the said ropes. Sometimes, as many as three hundred vessels belonging to different countries are assembled at the said city, the Sultan of which is a Mahommedan.

¶ At the time when I visited this country there happened that which you shall hear. The Sultan of Ormus had eleven male children. The youngest was considered to be simple, that is, half a fool: the eldest was looked upon as a devil unchained. Also the said Sultan had brought up two slaves, the sons of Christians, that is, of those of Prester John, whom he had purchased when quite young, and he loved them like his own children. They were gallant cavaliers and lords of castles. One night, the eldest son of the Sultan put out the eyes of his father, mother, and all his brothers, excepting the half-witted one; then he carried them into the chamber of his father and mother, and put fire in the midst, and burnt the chamber with the bodies and all that was therein. Early in the morning what had taken place became known, and the city arose at the rumour, and he fortified himself in the palace, and proclaimed himself Sultan. The younger brother, who was considered a fool, did not, however, show himself to be such a fool as he was supposed to be; for, hearing what had taken place, he took refuge in a Moorish mosque, saying: "*Vualla occuane saithan uchatelabu eculo cuane*," that is, "O God, my brother is a devil; he has killed my father, my mother, and all my brothers, and after having killed them he has burnt them." At the expiration of fifteen days the city became tranquil. The Sultan sent for one of the slaves above mentioned and said to him: "*Thale inte Mahometh*." The slave, who was named Mahometh, answered: "*Escult iasidi*," that is, "What dost thou say, lord?" Said the Sultan: "*An ne Soldan?*" that is, "Am I Sultan?" Mahometh replied: "*Heu valla siti inte Soldan*," that is, "Yes, by God, thou art Sultan." Then the Sultan took him by the hand and made much of him, and said to him: "*Roa chatel zaibei anneiati arba ochan sechala*," that is, "Go and kill thy companion, and I will give thee five castles." Mahometh replied: "*Iasidi anue iacul menau men saibi theletin sane vualla sidi ancasent*," that is, "O lord, I have eaten with my companion thirty years and acted with him, I cannot bring my mind to do such a thing." Then said the Sultan: "Well, let it alone." Four days afterwards, the said Sultan sent for the other slave, who was named Caim, and made the same speech to him that he had made to his companion, that is, that he should go and kill. "*Bizemele*," Caim said at once, "*erechman erachin Iasidi*," that is, "So be it, lord, in the name of God"; and then he armed himself secretly and went immediately to find Mahometh his companion. When Mahometh saw him, he looked him fixedly in the face, and said to him: "O traitor, thou canst not deny it, for I detect thee by thy countenance; but look now, for I will slay thee sooner than that thou slay me." Caim, who saw himself discovered and known, drew forth his dagger, and threw it at the feet of Mahometh, and falling on his knees before him said: "O, my lord, pardon me although I deserve death, and if it seem good to thee take these arms and kill me, for I came to kill thee." Mahometh replied: "It may be well said that thou art a traitor, having been with me, and acted with me, and eaten together with me for thirty years, and then at last to wish to put me to death in so vile a manner. Thou poor creature, dost thou not see that this man is a devil. Rise, however, for I pardon thee. But in order that thou mayest understand, know that this man urged me, three days ago, to kill thee, but I would not in any way consent. Now, leave all to God, but go and do as I shall tell thee. Go to the Sultan, and tell him that thou hast slain me." Caim replied: "I am content," and immediately went to the Sultan. When the Sultan saw him he said to him: "Well, hast thou slain thy friend?" Caim answered: "Yes, sir, by God." Said the Sultan: "Come here," and he went close to the Sultan, who seized him by the breast and killed him by blows of his dagger. Three days afterwards Mahometh armed himself secretly and went to the Sultan's chamber, who, when he saw him, was disturbed and exclaimed: "O dog, son of a dog, art thou still alive?" Said Mahometh: "I am alive, in spite of thee, and I will kill thee, for thou art worse than a dog or a devil"; and in this way, with their arms in their hands, they fought awhile. At length Mahometh killed the Sultan, and then fortified himself in the palace. And because he was so much beloved in the city, the people all ran to the palace crying out: "Long live Mahometh the Sultan!" and he continued Sultan about twenty days. When these twenty days were passed, he sent for all the lords and merchants of the city, and spoke to them in this wise: "That that which he had done he had been obliged to do; that he well knew that he had no right to the supreme power, and he entreated all the people that they would allow him to make king that son who was considered crazy"; and thus he was made king. It is true, however, that Mahometh governs everything. All the city said: "Surely this man must be the friend of God." Wherefore he was made governor of the city and of the Sultan, the Sultan being of the condition above mentioned. You must know that there are generally in this city four hundred foreign merchants, who traffic in silks, pearls, jewels, and spices. The common food of this city consists more of rice than of bread, because corn does not grow in this place.

¶ Having heard this lamentable event, and seen the customs of the above-named city and island of Ormus, departing thence I passed into Persia, and travelling for twelve days I found a city called Eri [Herât-i-Khâra], and the country is called Corazani [Khurâsân], which would be the same as to say "The Romagna." The King of Corazani dwells in this city, where there is great plenty, and an abundance of stuffs, and especially of silk, so that in one day you can purchase here three thousand or four thousand camel loads of silk. The district is most abundant in articles of food, and there is also a great market for rhubarb. I have seen it purchased at six pounds for the ducat, according to our use, that is, twelve ounces to the pound. This city contains about 6,000 or 7,000 hearths. The inhabitants are all Mahommedans. I quitted this place and travelled twenty days on the mainland, finding cities and castles very well peopled.

Photo: Sir Percy Sykes

THE BARRAGE (11TH CENTURY) OF THE RIVER BENDEMIR, MISTAKEN BY VARTHEMA FOR THE EUPHRATES (EUFRA), *see p.* 43.

¶ I arrived at a large and fine river, which is called by the people there Eufra [Ufrât: Band-i-Amîr, Bendemir], but, so far as I can judge, I believe that it is the Euphrates, on account of its great size. Travelling onwards for three days to the left hand, but following the river, I found a city which is named Schirazo [Shîrâz], and this city receives its lord, who is a Persian and a Mahommedan, from the Persians. In this city there is a great abundance of jewels, that is, of turquoises, and an infinite quantity of Balass rubies. It is true that they are not produced here, but come (as is reported) from a city which is called Balachsam [Badakhshân]. And in the said city there is a very large quantity of ultra marine, and much *tucia* [*tutiâ*, antimony] and musk. You must know that musk is rarely met with in our parts which is not adulterated. The fact is this, for I have seen some experiments on this wise. Take a bladder of musk in the morning, fasting, and break it, and let three or four men in file smell it, and it will immediately make blood flow from the nose, and this happens because it is real musk and not adulterated. I asked how long its goodness continued. Some merchants answered me: "That if it were not adulterated it lasted ten years." Upon this it occurred to me that that which comes to our part is adulterated by the hands of these Persians, who are the most cunning men in intellect, and at falsifying things, of any nation in the world. And I likewise will say of them, that they are the best companions and the most liberal of any men who inhabit the earth. I say this because I have experienced it with a Persian merchant whom I met in this city of Schirazo. However, he was of the city of Eri above mentioned, in Corazani. This same merchant knew me two years previously in Mecca, and he said to me: "Iunus, what are you doing here? Are you not he who some time ago went to Mecca?" I answered that I was, and that I was going about exploring the world. He answered me: "God be praised! for I shall have a companion who will explore the world with me." We remained fifteen days in the same city of Schirazo. And this merchant, who was called Cazazionor [Khwâja Junair], said: "Do not leave me, for we will explore a good part of the world." And thus we set ourselves together *en route* to go towards Sambragante [Samarkand].

¶ The merchants say that the present Sambragante is a city as large as Cairo. The king of the said city is a Mahommedan. Some merchants say that he has sixty thousand horsemen, and they are all white people and warlike. We did not proceed farther; and the reason was, that the Soffi [Shâh 'Abbâs Safavî, the Sophie] was going through this country putting everything to fire and flame; and especially he put to the sword all those who believed in Bubachar and Othman and Aumar [Abubakr, 'Uthmân,

'Umr], who are all companions of Mahomet; but he leaves unmolested those who believe in Mahomet and Ali, and protects them. Then my companion said to me: "Come here, Iunus: in order that you may be certain that I wish you well, and that you may have reason to know that I mean to exercise good fellowship towards you, I will give you a niece of mine who is called Samis [Shams], that is, the Sun. And truly she had a name which suited her, for she was extremely beautiful. And he said to me further: "You must know now that I do not travel about the world because I am in want of wealth; but I go for my pleasure, and in order to see and to know many things." And with this we set ourselves on our way, and returned towards Eri [Herât-i-Khâra]. When we had arrived at his house, he immediately shewed me his said niece, with whom I pretended to be greatly pleased, although my mind was intent on other things. We returned to the city of Ormus at the end of eight days, and embarked on board ship, and steered towards India, and arrived at a port which is called Cheo [Jûâ].

CHAPTER VI

CONCERNING CAMBAY TO CALICUT IN INDIA

HAVING promised at the commencement, if I remember rightly, to treat all subjects with brevity, in order that my narrative might not be wearisome, I will continue to relate concisely those things which appeared to me the most worthy to be known, and the most interesting.

¶ We entered India where, near to the said port [Cheo], there is a very large river called the Indus, which Indus is near to a city called Combeia [Cambay]. This city is situated three miles inland, and to the south of the said Indus. You must know that you cannot go to the said city either with large or middling-sized ships, excepting at high water. There is a river which goes to the said city, and the tide flows up three or four miles. You must know that the waters rise in the reverse way to ours; for with us they rise when the moon is at the full, but they increase here when the moon is on the wane. This city of Combeia is walled, after our fashion; and truly it is a most excellent city, abounding in grain and very good fruits. In this district there are eight or nine kinds of small spices, that is to say, *turbidi*, *gallanga*, *spiconardo*, *saphetica*, and *lacra* [jalap, arrowroot, spikenard, assafœtida and lac], with other spices, the names of which I do not remember. An immense quantity of cotton is produced here, so that every year forty or fifty vessels are laden with cotton and silk stuffs, which stuffs are carried into different countries. In this kingdom of Combeia also, about six days' journey, there is the mountain whence cornelians are extracted, and the mountain of chalcedonies. Nine days' journey from Combeia there is another mountain in which diamonds are found.

¶ We will now declare the estate and condition of the Sultan of this Combeia, who is called the Sultan Machamuth [Mahmûd Baigâra]. About forty years ago he captured this kingdom from a king of the Guzerati [Gujarâtî], which Guzerati are a certain race which eats nothing that has blood, and never kills any living thing. And these same people are neither Moors nor heathens. It is my opinion that if they were baptized, they would all be saved by virtue of their works, for they never do to others what they would not that others should do unto them. Their dress is this: some wear a shirt, and some go naked, with the exception of a piece of cloth about their middle, having nothing on their feet or on their legs. On their heads they wear a large red cloth; and they are of a tawny colour. And for this, their goodness, the aforesaid Sultan took from them their kingdom.

¶ You shall now hear the manner of living of this Sultan Machamuth. In the first place he is a Mahommedan, together with all his people. He has constantly twenty thousand horsemen. In the morning, when he rises, there come to his palace fifty elephants, on each of which a man sits astride; and the said elephants do reverence to the Sultan, and they have nothing else to do. So in like manner when he has risen from his bed. And when he eats, there are fifty or sixty kinds of instruments, namely, trumpets, drums of several sorts, and flageolets, and fifes, with many others, which for the sake of brevity I forbear mentioning. When the Sultan eats, the said elephants again do reverence to him. When the proper time shall come, I will tell you of the intelligence and understanding which these animals possess. The said Sultan has mustachios under his nose so long that he ties them over his head as a woman would tie her tresses, and he has a white beard which reaches to his girdle. Every day he eats poison. Do not, however, imagine that he fills his stomach with it; but he eats a certain quantity, so that when he wishes to destroy any great personage he makes him come before him stripped and naked, and then eats certain fruits which are called *chofole* [areca nut], which resemble a muscatel nut. He also eats certain leaves of herbs, which are like the leaves of the sour orange, called by some *tamboli* [betel leaf]; and then he eats some lime of oyster shells, together with the above mentioned things. When he has masticated them well [chewed the betel], and has his mouth full, he spurts it out upon that person whom he wishes to kill, so that in the space of half an hour he falls to the ground dead. This Sultan has also three or four thousand women, and every night that he sleeps with one she is found dead in the morning. Every time that he takes off his shirt, that shirt is never again touched by any one; and so of his other garments; and every day he chooses new garments. My companion asked how it was that this Sultan eats poison in this manner. Certain merchants, who were older than the Sultan, answered that his father had fed him upon poison from his childhood.

¶ Let us leave the Sultan, and return to our journey, that is, to the men of the said city, the greater part of whom go about in a shirt, and are very warlike and great merchants. It is impossible to describe the excellence of the country. About three hundred ships of different countries come and go here. This city, and another of which I will speak at the proper season, supply all Persia, Tartary, Turkey, Syria, Barbary, that is Africa, Arabia Felix, Ethiopia, India, and a multitude of inhabited islands, with silk and cotton stuffs. So that this Sultan lives with vast riches, and fights with a neighbouring king, who is called king of the Ioghe, distant from this city fifteen days' journey.

¶ This king of the Ioghe [Jôgî] is a man of great dignity, and has about thirty thousand people, and is a pagan, he and all his subjects; and by the pagan kings he and his people are considered to be saints, on account of their lives, which you shall hear. It is the custom of this king to go on a pilgrimage once in every three or four years, like a pilgrim, that is, at the expense of others, with three or four thousand of his people, and with his wife and children. And he takes four or five coursers, and civet-cats, apes, parrots, leopards, and falcons; and in this way he goes through the whole of India. His dress is a goat skin, that is, one before and one behind, with the hair outwards. His colour is dark tawny, for the people here begin to be more dark than white. They all wear a great quantity of jewels, and pearls, and other precious stones, in their ears, and they go dressed *all'apostolica* [*i.e.* in a loin cloth, *langôtî*], and some wear shirts. The king and some of the more noble have the face and arms and the whole body powdered over with ground sandal-wood and other most excellent scents. Some of these people adopt as an act of devotion the custom of never sitting on any high seat; others, as an act of devotion, never sit on the ground; others adopt the custom of never lying at full length on the ground; others, again, that of never speaking. These always go about with three or four companions, who wait upon them. All generally carry a little horn at their neck; and when they go into a city they all in company sound the said little horns, and this they do when they wish alms to be given to them. When the king does not go, they go at least three or four hundred at a time, and remain in a city three days, in the manner of the Singani [gipsies]. Some of them carry a stick with a ring of iron at the base. Others carry certain iron dishes which cut all round like razors, and they throw these with a sling when they wish to injure any person; and, therefore, when these people arrive at any city in India, every one tries to please them; for should they even kill the first nobleman of the land, they would not suffer any punishment because they say that they are saints. The country of these people is not very fertile; they even suffer from dearth of provisions. There are more mountains than plains. Their habitations are very poor, and they have no walled places. Many jewels come into our parts by the hands of these people, because through the liberty they enjoy, and their sanctity, they go where jewels are produced, and carry them into other countries without any expense. Thus, having a strong country, they keep the Sultan Machamuth at war.

¶ Departing from the said city of Combeia, I travelled on until I arrived at another city named Cevul [Châul], which is distant from the abovementioned city twelve days' journey, and the country between the one and the other of these cities is called Guzerati. The king of this Cevul is a pagan. The people are of a dark tawny colour. As to their dress, with the exception of some Moorish merchants, some wear a shirt, and some go naked, with a cloth round their middle, with nothing on their feet or head. The people are war-like: their arms are swords, bucklers, bows and spears made of reeds and wood, and they possess artillery. This city is extremely well walled, and is distant from the sea two miles. It possesses an extremely beautiful river, by which a very great number of foreign vessels go and return, because the country abounds in everything excepting grapes, nuts, and chestnuts. They collect here an immense quantity of grain, of barley, and of vegetables of every description; and cotton stuffs are manufactured here in great abundance. I do not describe their faith here, because their creed is the same as that of the King of Calicut, of which I will give you an account when the proper time shall come. There are in this city a very great number of Moorish merchants. The atmosphere begins here to be more warm than cold. Justice is extremely well administered here. This king has not many fighting men. The inhabitants here have horses, oxen, and cows, in great abundance.

¶ Having seen Cevul and its customs, departing thence, I went to another city, distant from it two days' journey, which is called Dabuli [Dabul,

Dâbhôl], which city is situated on the bank of a very great river. This city is surrounded by walls in our manner, and is extremely good. The country resembles that above described. There are Moorish merchants here in very great numbers. The king of this place [Dabuli] is a pagan, and possesses about thirty thousand fighting men, but according to the manner of Cevul before mentioned. This king is also a very great observer of justice. The country, the mode of living, the dress, and the customs, resemble those of the aforesaid city of Cevul.

¶ I departed from the city of Dabuli aforesaid, and went to another island, which is about a mile distant from the mainland, and is called Goga [Goa], and which pays annually to the King of Decan ten thousand golden ducats, called by them *pardai* [pagoda]. These *pardai* are smaller than the seraphim of Cairo, but thicker, and have two devils stamped upon one side of them, and certain letters on the other. In this island there is a fortress near the sea, walled round after our manner, in which there is sometimes a captain, who is called Savain [Sâvâi, Cabaim, Sabayo, *i.e.* the 'Adil-shâhî king of Bîjâpur], who has four hundred Mamelukes, he himself being also a Mameluke. When the said captain can procure any white man, he gives him very great pay, allotting him at least fifteen or twenty *pardai* per month. Before he inscribes him in the list of able men, he sends for two tunics made of leather, one for himself and the other for him who wishes to enlist; each puts on his tunic, and they fall to blows. If he finds him to be strong, he puts him in the list of able men; if not, he sets him to some other work than that of fighting. This captain, with four hundred Mamelukes, wages a great war with the King of Narsinga [Vijayanagar Empire], of whom we will speak at the proper season. I departed thence, and, travelling for seven days on the mainland, I arrived at a city which is called Decan [*i.e.* Bîjâpur].

¶ In the said city of Decan there reigns a king who is a Mahommedan. The above-mentioned captain is in his pay, together with the said Mamelukes. This city is extremely beautiful, and very fertile. The king of it, between the Mamelukes and others of his kingdom, has twenty-five thousand men horse and foot. There is a beautiful palace in this city, in which there are forty-four chambers before you arrive at that of the king. This city is walled after the manner of the Christians, and the houses are very beautiful. The king of the said city lives in great pride and pomp. A great number of his servants wear on the insteps of their shoes rubies and diamonds, and other jewels; so you may imagine how many are worn on the fingers of the hand and in the ears. There is a mountain in his kingdom where they dig out diamonds, which mountain is a league distant from the city, and is surrounded by a wall, and is kept by a great guard. This realm is most abundant in everything, like the above-mentioned cities. They are all Mahommedans. Their dress consists of robes, or very beautiful shirts of silk, and they wear on their feet shoes or boots, with breeches after the fashion of sailors. The ladies go with their faces quite covered, according to the custom of Damascus.

¶ The above-mentioned King of Decan is always at war with the King of Narsinga, and all his country is Mahommedan. The greater part of his soldiers are foreigners and white men. The natives of the kingdom are of a tawny colour. This king is extremely powerful, and very rich, and most liberal. He also possesses many naval vessels, and is a very great enemy of the Christians. Departing thence, we went to another city, called Bathacala [Sadâsivagarh].

¶ Bathacala, a very noble city of India, is distant from Decan five days' journey. The king thereof is a pagan. This city is walled, and very beautiful, and about a mile distant from the sea. The king is subject to the King of Narsinga. This city has no seaport, the only approach to it being by a small river. There are many Moorish merchants here, for it is a district of great traffic. The above-named stream passes close to the walls of the city, in which there is a great quantity of rice, and a great abundance of sugar, and especially of sugar candied, according to our manner. We begin here to find nuts and figs, after the manner of Calicut. These people are idolaters, also after the manner of Calicut, excepting the Moors, who live according to the Mahommedan religion. Neither horses, nor mules, nor asses, are customary here, but there are cows, buffaloes, sheep, oxen, and goats. In this country no grain, barley, or vegetables are produced, but other most excellent fruits, usual in India. I quitted this place, and went to another island, which is called Anzediva [Anjediva], and which is inhabited by a certain sort of people who are Moors and pagans. This island is distant from the mainland half a mile, and is about twenty miles in circumference. The air is not very good here, neither is the place very fertile. There is an excellent port between the island and the mainland, and very good water is found in the said island.

¶ Travelling for one day from the aforesaid island, I arrived at a place called Centacola, the lord of which is not very rich. A great quantity of cow beef is met with here, and much rice, and good fruits customary in India. In this city there are many Moorish merchants. The lord of it is a pagan. The people are of a tawny colour: they go naked and barefooted, and wear nothing on the head. This lord is subject to the King of Bathacala. Travelling thence for two days, we went to another place called Onor [Onore, Honâwar], the king of which is a pagan, and is subject to the King of Narsinga. This king is a good fellow, and has seven or eight ships, which are always cruising about. He is a great friend of the King of Portugal. As to his dress, he goes quite naked, with the exception of a cloth about his middle. There is a great deal of rice here, as is usual in India, and some kinds of animals are found here, viz., wild hogs, stags, wolves, lions, and a great number of birds, different from ours; there are also many peacocks and parrots there. They have beef of cows, that is, red cows, and sheep in great abundance. Roses, flowers, and fruits, are found here all through the year. The air of this place is most perfect, and the people here are longer lived than we are. Near the said district of Onor there is another place, called Mangolor [Mangalore], in which fifty or sixty ships are laden with rice. The inhabitants are pagans and Moors. Their mode of living, their customs, and their dress, are like those above described. We departed thence, and went to another city, which is called Canonor [Cannanore].

¶ Canonor is a fine and large city, in which the King of Portugal has a very strong castle. The king of this city is a great friend of the King of Portugal, although he is a pagan. This Canonor is the port at which the horses which come from Persia disembark. And you must know that every horse pays twenty-five ducats for customs duty, and then they proceed on the mainland towards Narsinga. There are many Moorish merchants in this city. No grain nor grapes grow here, nor any productions like ours, excepting cucumbers and melons. Bread is not eaten here, that is to say, by the natives of the country, but they eat rice, fish, flesh, and the nuts of the country. At the proper time we will speak of their religion and customs, for they live after the manner of those of Calicut. Here we begin to find a few spices, such as pepper, ginger, cardamums, mirabolans, and a little cassia. This place is not surrounded by a wall. The houses are very poor. Here also are found fruits different from ours, and which are also far superior to ours. I will make the comparison when the proper time comes. The country is well adapted for war, as it is full of hollow places artificially made. The king of this place has 50,000 Naeri [Nairs], that is, gentlemen who fight with swords, shields, lances and bows, and with artillery. And yet they go naked and unshod, with a cloth around them, without anything on their heads, excepting when they go to war, when they wear a turban of a red colour passed twice round the head, and they all have them tied in the same manner. They do not use here either horses, mules, camels, or asses. Elephants are sometimes used, but not for battle. At the proper time we will speak of the vigour exerted by the King of Canonor against the Portuguese. There is much traffic in this place, to which two hundred ships come every year from different countries. Having spent some days here we took our way towards the kingdom of Narsinga, and travelled on the mainland for fifteen days towards the east, and came to a city called Bisinegar.

¶ The said city of Bisinegar [Vijayanagar] belongs to the King of Narsinga [*i.e.* Narsingha, King of Vijayanagar], and is very large and strongly walled. It is situated on the side of a mountain, and is seven miles in circumference. It has a triple circle of walls. It is a place of great merchandise, is extremely fertile, and is endowed with all possible kinds of delicacies. It occupies the most beautiful site, and possesses the best air that was ever seen: with certain very beautiful places for hunting and the same for fowling, so that it appears to me to be a second paradise. The king of this city is a pagan, with all his kingdom, that is to say, idolaters. He is a very powerful king, and keeps up constantly 40,000 horsemen. And you must know that a horse is worth at least 300, 400, and 500 *pardai*, and some are purchased for 800 *pardai*, because horses are not produced there, neither are many mares found there, because those kings who hold the seaports do not allow them to be brought there.

¶ The said king also possesses 400 elephants and some dromedaries, which dromedaries run with great swiftness. It occurs to me here to touch upon a subject worthy of notice, viz., the discretion, the intelligence, and the strength of the elephant. We will first say in what manner he fights. When an elephant goes into battle he carries a saddle, in the same manner as they are borne by the mules of the kingdom of Naples, fastened underneath by two iron chains. On each side of the said saddle he carries a large and very strong wooden box, and in each box there go three men. On the neck of the elephant, between the boxes, they place a plank the size of half a span, and between the boxes and the plank a man sits astride who speaks to the elephant, for the said elephant possesses more intelligence than any other animal in the world; so that there are in all seven persons who go upon the said elephant; and they go armed with shirts of mail, and with bows and lances, swords and shields. And in like manner they arm the elephant with mail, especially the head and the trunk. They fasten to the trunk a sword two *braccia* long, as thick and as wide as the hand of a man. And in that way they fight. And he who sits upon his neck orders him: "Go forward," or "Turn back," "Strike this one," "Strike that one," "Do not strike any more," and he understands as though he were a human being. But if at any time they are put to flight it is impossible to restrain them; for this race of people are great masters of the art of making fireworks, and these animals have a great dread of fire, and through this means they sometimes take to flight. But in every way this animal is the most discreet in the world and the most powerful. I have seen three elephants bring a ship from the sea to the land, in the manner as I will tell you. When I was in Canonor, some Moorish merchants brought a ship on shore in this manner, after the custom of Christians. They beach ships the prow foremost, but here they put the side of the vessel foremost, and under the said ship they put three pieces of wood, and on the side next the sea I saw three elephants kneel down and with their heads push the ship on to dry land. Many say that the elephant has no joints, and I say that it is true that they have not the joints so high as other animals, but they have them low. I tell you, moreover, that the female elephant is stronger and more proud than the male, and some of the females are mad. The said elephants are as large as three buffaloes, and they have a skin like that of the buffalo, and eyes like those of a pig, and a trunk reaching to the ground, and with this they put their food into their mouth as also their drink; for their mouth is situated beneath their throat, and almost like a pig or a sturgeon. This trunk is hollow within, and I have many times seen them fish up a *quattrino* from the ground with it. And with this trunk I have seen them pull down a branch from a tree which twenty-four of our men could not pull to the ground with a rope, and the elephant tore it down with three pulls. The two teeth which are seen are in the upper jaw. The ears are two *palmi* every way, some more, some less. Their legs are almost as large at the lower extremity as at the upper. Their feet are round like a very large trencher for cutting meat on, and around the foot there are five nails as large as the shell of an oyster. The tail is as long as that of a buffalo, about three *palmi* long, and has a few scattered hairs. The female is smaller than the male. With respect to the height of the said elephant, I have seen a great many thirteen and fourteen *palmi* high, and I have ridden on some of that height; they say, moreover, that some are found fifteen *palmi* high. Their walk is very slow, and those who are not accustomed to it cannot ride them, because it upsets their stomach, just as it does in travelling by sea. The small elephants have a pace like that of a mule, and it is a pleasure to ride them. When the said elephants are to be ridden, the said elephant lowers one of the hind legs, and by that leg it is mounted; nevertheless, you must help yourself or be helped to mount. You must also know that the said elephants do not carry a bridle or halter, or anything bound on the head. The said elephant, when he wishes to generate, goes into a secret place, that is, into the water in certain marshes, and they unite and generate like human beings. In some countries, I have seen that the finest present which can be made to a king is the parts of an elephant, which said king eats the said parts; for in some countries an elephant is worth fifty ducats, in some other countries it is worth one thousand and two thousand ducats. So that, in conclusion, I say that I have seen some elephants which have more understanding, and more discretion and intelligence, than any kind of people I have met with.

¶ This King of Narsinga is the richest king I have ever heard spoken of. This city is situated like Milan, but not in a plain. The residence of the king is here, and his realms are placed as it might be the realm of Naples and also Venice; so that he has the sea on both sides. His Brahmins, that is, his priests, say that he possesses a revenue of 12,000 *pardai* per day. He is constantly at war with several Moorish and pagan kings. His faith is idolatrous, and they worship the devil, as do those of Calicut. When the proper time comes we will state in what manner they worship him. They live like pagans. Their dress is this: the men of condition wear a short shirt, and on their head a cloth of gold and silk in the Moorish fashion, but nothing on the feet. The common people go quite naked, with the exception of a piece of cloth about their middle. The king wears a cap of gold brocade two spans long, and when he goes to war he wears a quilted dress of cotton, and over it he puts another garment full of golden piastres, and having all around it jewels of various kinds. His horse is worth more than some of our cities, on account of the ornaments which it wears. When he rides for his pleasure he is always accompanied by three or four kings, and many other lords, and five or six thousand horse. Wherefore he may be considered to be a very powerful lord.

¶ His money consists of a *pardao*, as I have said. He also coins a silver money called *tare*, and others of gold, twenty of which go to a *pardao*, and are called *fanom*. And of these small ones of silver, there go sixteen to a *fanom*. They also have another coin called *cas*, sixteen of which go to a *tare* of silver. In this kingdom you can go everywhere in safety. But it is necessary to be on your guard against some lions which are on the road. I will not speak of their food at the present time, because I wish to describe it when we shall be in Calicut, where there are the same customs and the same manner of living. This king is a very great friend of the Christians, especially of the King of Portugal, because he does not know much of any other Christians. When the Portuguese arrive in his territories they do them great honour. When we had seen this so noble city for some days we turned towards Canonor. And when we had arrived there, at the end of three days we took our way by land and went to a city called Tormapatani.

¶ Tormapatani [Dharmapatam] is distant from Canonor twelve miles, and the lord of it is a pagan. The land is not very rich, and is one mile from the sea, and it has a river not very large. There are many vessels of Moorish merchants here. The people of this country live miserably, and the greatest riches here consist of Indian nuts, and these they eat there with a little rice. They have plenty of timber here for building ships. In this land there are about fifteen thousand Moors, and they are subject to the Sultan or pagan lord. I do not speak of their manner of living at present, because it will be described in Calicut, inasmuch as they are all of one and the same faith. The houses in this city are not too good, for a house is worth half a ducat, as I will explain to you further on. Here we remained two days, and then departed and went to a place which is called Pandarani [Pantalâyini], distant from this one day's journey, and which is subject to the King of Calicut. This place is a wretched affair, and has no port. Opposite to the said city, in the sea three leagues or thereabout, there is an uninhabited island. The manner of living of this Pandarani, and their customs, are the same as those of Calicut. This city is not level, and the land is high. We departed hence and went to another place called Capogatto [Kapata], which is also subject to the King of Calicut. This place has a very beautiful palace, built in the ancient style, and there is a small river towards the south, and it is four leagues distant from Calicut. There is nothing to be said here, because they follow the manner and style of Calicut. We departed hence and went to the very noble city of Calicut. I have not written about the manner of living, the customs and faith, the administration of justice, dress, and country of Chiavul and of Dabul, of Bathacala, nor of the King of Onor, nor of Mangalor, nor of Canonor, nor, indeed, of the King of Cucin [Cochin], nor of the King of Caicolone [Kâyankullam], nor of that of Colon [Quilon], neither have I spoken of the King of Narsinga. Now I will speak of the king here in Calicut, because he is the most important king of all those before mentioned, and is called Samory [Zamorin], which in the pagan language means "God on earth."

CHAPTER VII

CONCERNING CALICUT

HAVING nearly arrived at the head of India, that is to say, at the place in which the greatest dignity of India is centered, it has appeared to me fitting to bring the First Book to an end and commence the Second; as, moreover, I have to lay before every kind reader matters of greater importance and comfort to the intellect, and of courage, so far as our favourite labour of travelling through the world may assist us and our intelligence may serve us, submitting, however, everything to the judgment of men who may, perhaps, have visited more countries than I have.

¶ Calicut is on the mainland, the sea beats against the walls of the houses. There is no port here, but about a mile from the place towards the south there is a river, which is narrow at its embouchure and has not more than five or six spans of water. This stream flows through Calicut and has a great number of branches. This city has no wall around it, but the houses extend for about a mile, built close together, and then the wide houses, that is, the houses separate one from the other, cover a space of about six miles. The houses are very poor. The walls are about as high as a man on horseback, and the greater part are covered with leaves, and without any upper room. The reason is this, that when they dig down four or five spans, water is found, and therefore they cannot build large houses. However, the house of a merchant is worth fifteen or twenty ducats. Those of the common people are worth half a ducat each, or one or two ducats at the most.

¶ The King of Calicut is a pagan, and worships the devil in the manner you shall hear. They acknowledge that there is a God who has created the heaven and the earth and all the world; and they say that if he wished to judge you and me, a third and a fourth, he would have no pleasure in being Lord; but that he has sent this his spirit, that is the devil, into this world to do justice: and to him who does good he does good, and to him who does evil he does evil. Which devil they call Deumo [*dêvan*, godling], and God they call Tamerani [Tamburân, Lord]. And the King of Calicut keeps this Deumo in his chapel in his palace, in this wise: his chapel is two paces wide in each of the four sides, and three paces high, with a wooden door covered with devils carved in relief. In the midst of this chapel there is a devil made of metal, placed in a seat also made of metal. The said devil has a crown made like that of the papal kingdom, with three crowns; and it also has four horns and four teeth, with a very large mouth, nose, and most terrible eyes. The hands are made like those of a flesh-hook, and the feet like those of a cock; so that he is a fearful object to behold. All the pictures around the said chapel are those of devils, and on each side of it there is a Sathanas [the goddess Kâlî] seated in a seat, which seat is placed in a flame of fire, wherein are a great number of souls, of the length of half a finger and a finger of the hand. And the said [other] Sathanas [Narsingh] holds a soul in his mouth with the right hand, and with the other seizes a soul under the waist. Every morning the Brahmins, that is the priests, go to wash the said idol all over with scented water, and then they perfume it; and when it is perfumed they worship it; and some time in the course of the week they offer sacrifice to it in this manner: They have a certain small table, made and ornamented like an altar, three spans high from the ground, four spans wide, and five long; which table is extremely well adorned with roses, flowers, and other ornaments. Upon this table they have the blood of a cock and lighted coals in a vessel of silver, with many perfumes upon them. They also have a thurible, with which they scatter incense around the said altar. They have a little bell of silver which rings very frequently, and they have a silver knife with which they have killed the cock, and which they tinge with the blood, and sometimes place it upon the fire, and sometimes they take it and make motions similar to those which one makes who is about to fence; and finally, all that blood is burnt, the waxen tapers being kept lighted during the whole time. The priest who is about to perform this sacrifice puts upon his arms, hands, and feet some bracelets of silver, which make a very great noise like bells, and he wears on his neck an amulet (what it is I do not know); and when he has finished performing the sacrifice, he takes both his hands full of grain and retires from the said altar, walking backwards and always looking at the altar until he arrives at a certain tree. And when he has reached the tree, he throws the grain above his head as high as he can over the tree; he then returns and removes everything from the altar.

¶ When the King of Calicut wishes to eat he uses the following customs: you must know that four of the prinicpal Brahmins take the food which the king is to eat and carry it to the devil, and first they worship him in this manner: they raise their clasped hands over his head, and then draw their hands towards them, still clasped together, and the thumb raised upwards, and then they present to him the food which is to be given to the king, and stand in this manner as long as a person would require to eat it; and then the said Brahmins carry that food to the king. You must know that this is done only for the purpose of paying honour to that idol, in order that it may appear that the king will not eat unless the food has been first presented to Deumo. This food is in a wooden vessel, in which there is a very large leaf of a tree, and upon this leaf is placed the said food, which consists of rice and other things. The king eats on the ground without any other thing. And when he eats, the Brahmins stand around, three or four paces distant from him, with great reverence, and remain bowed down with their hands before their mouths, and their backs bent. No one is allowed to speak while the king is speaking, and they stand listening to his words with great reverence. When the king has finished his meal, the said Brahmins take that food which the king did not require and carry it into a court yard and place it on the ground. And the said Brahmins clap their hands three times, and at this clapping a very great number of black crows come to this said food and eat it. These crows are used for this purpose, and they are free and go wherever they please, and no injury is done to them.

¶ It is a proper, and at the same time a pleasant thing to know who these Brahmins are. You must know that they are the chief persons of the faith, as priests are among us. And when the king takes a wife he selects the most worthy and the most honoured of these Brahmins and makes him sleep the first night with his wife, in order that he may deflower her. Do not imagine that the Brahmin goes willingly to perform this operation. The king is even obliged to pay him four hundred or five hundred ducats. The king only and no other person in Calicut adopts this practice. We will now describe what classes [or castes] of pagans there are in Calicut.

¶ The first class of pagans in Calicut are called Brahmins. The second are Naeri [Nairs], who are the same as the gentlefolks amongst us; and these are obliged to bear sword and shield or bows or lances. When they go through the street, if they did not carry arms they would no longer be gentlemen. The third class of pagans are called Tiva [Tiyan], who are artizans. The fourth class are called Mechua [Mukkuvan], and these are fishermen. The fifth class are called Poliar [Pulayan], who collect pepper, wine, and nuts. The sixth class are called Hirava [Vettuvan], and these plant and gather in rice. These two last classes of people, that is to say, the Poliar and Hirava, may not approach either the Naeri or the Brahmins within fifty paces, unless they have been called by them, and they always go by private ways through the marshes. And when they pass through the said places, they always go crying out with a loud voice, and this they do in order that they may not meet the Naeri or the Brahmins; for should they not be crying out, and any of the Naeri should be going that way and see their fruits, or meet any of the said class, the above mentioned Naeri may kill them without incurring any punishment: and for this reason they always cry out. So now you have heard about these six classes of pagans.

¶ The dress of the king and queen, and of all the others, that is to say, of the natives of the country, is this: they go naked and with bare feet, and wear a piece of cotton or of silk around their middle, and with nothing on their heads. Some Moorish merchants, on the other hand, wear a short shirt extending to the waist; but all the pagans go without a shirt. In like manner the women go naked like the men, and wear their hair long. With respect to the food of the king and the gentlemen, they do not eat flesh without the permission of the Brahmins. But the other classes of the people eat flesh of all kinds, with the exception of cow beef. And these Hirava and Poliar eat mice and fish dried in the sun.

¶ The king being dead, and having male children, or brothers, or nephews on his brother's side, neither his sons, nor his brother, nor his nephews become king; but the heir of the king is the son of one of his sisters. And if there be no son of a said sister, the nearest [collateral] relation of the king succeeds him. And this custom prevails because the Brahmins have the virginity of the queen; and likewise when the king travels, one of these Brahmins, although he might be only twenty years of age, remains in the house with the queen, and the king would consider it to be the greatest favour that these Brahmins should be familiar with the queen, and on this account they say that it is certain that his sister and he were born of the same person, and that there is more certainty about her than of his own children, and therefore the inheritance falls to the sons of the sister. Also on the death of the king all the people of the kingdom shave their beards and their heads, with the exception of some part of the head, and also of the beard, according to the pleasure of each person. The fishermen also are not allowed to catch any fish for eight days. The same customs are observed when a near relative of the king dies. As an act of devotion, the king does not sleep with a woman or eat betel for a whole year. This betel resembles the leaves of the sour orange, and they are constantly eating it. It is the same to them that confections are to us, and they eat it more for sensuality than for any other purpose. When they eat the said leaves, they eat with them a certain fruit which is called *coffolo*, and the tree of the said *coffolo* is called *arecha*, and is formed like the stem of the date tree, and produces its fruit in the same manner. And they also eat with the said leaves a certain lime made from oyster shells, which they call *cionama* [chunam].

¶ The pagan gentlemen and merchants have this custom amongst them. There will sometimes be two merchants who will be great friends, and each will have a wife; and one merchant will say to the other in this wise: "*Langal perganal monaton ondo?*" that is, "So-and-so, have we been a long time friends?" The other will answer: "*Hognan perga manaton ondo*"; that is, "Yes, I have for a long time been your friend." The other says: "*Nipatanga ciolli?*" that is, "Do you speak the truth that you are my friend?" The other will answer, and say: "*Ho*"; that is, "Yes." Says the other one: "*Tamarani?*" that is, "By God?" The other replies: "*Tamarani!*" that is, "By God!" One says: "*In penna tonda gnan penna cortu*"; that is, "Let us exchange wives, give me your wife and I will give you mine." The other answers: "*Ni pantagocciolli?*" that is, "Do you speak from your heart?" The other says: "*Tamarani!*" that is, "Yes, by God!" His companion answers, and says: "*Biti banno*"; that is, "Come to my house." And when he has arrived at his house he calls his wife and says to her: "*Penna, ingaba idocon dopoi*"; that is, "Wife, come here, go with this man, for he is your husband." The wife answers: "*E indi?*" that is, "Wherefore? Dost thou speak the truth, by God, Tamarani?" The husband replies: "*Ho gran patangociolli*"; that is, "I speak the truth." Says the wife: "*Perga manno*"; that is, "It pleases me." "*Gnan poi*"; that is, "I go." And so she goes away with his companion to his house. The friend then tells his wife to go with the other, and in this manner they exchange their wives; but the sons of each remain with him. And amongst the other classes of pagans above-mentioned, one woman has five, six, and seven husbands, and even eight. And one sleeps with her one night, and another another night. And when the woman has children, she says it is the child of this husband or of that husband, and thus the children go according to the word of the woman.

¶ The said pagans eat on the ground in a metal basin, and for a spoon make use of the leaf of a tree, and they always eat rice and fish, and spices and fruits. The two classes of peasants eat with the hand from a pipkin; and when they take the rice from the pipkin, they hold the hand over the said pipkin and make a ball of the rice, and then put it into their mouths. With respect to the laws which are in use among these people:—If one kills another, the king causes a stake to be taken four paces long and well pointed at one end, and has two sticks fixed across the said stake two spans from the top, and then the said wood is fixed in the middle of the back of the malefactor and passes through his body, and in this way he dies. And this torture they call *uncalvet.* And if there be any one who inflicts wounds or bastinadoes, the king makes him pay money, and in this manner he is absolved. And when any one ought to receive money from another merchant, there appearing any writing of the scribes of the king, (who has at least a hundred of them,) they observe this practice:—Let us suppose the case that some one has to pay me twenty-five ducats, and the debtor promises me to pay them many times, and does not pay them; I, not being willing to wait any longer, nor to give him any indulgence, shall take a green branch in my hand, shall go softly behind the debtor, and with the said branch shall draw a circle on the ground surrounding him, and if I can enclose him in the circle, I shall say to him these words three times: "*Bramini raza pertha polle*"; that is, "I command you by the head of the Brahmins and of the king, that you do not depart hence until you have paid me and satisfied me as much as I ought to have from thee." And he will satisfy me, or truly he will die there without any other guard. And should he quit the said circle and not pay me, the king would put him to death.

¶ Early in the morning these pagans go to wash at a tank, which tank is a pond of still water. And when they are washed, they may not touch any person until they have said their prayers, and this in their house. And they say their prayers in this manner:—They lie with their body extended on the ground and very secret, and they perform certain diabolical actions [or motions] with their eyes, and with their mouths they perform certain fearful actions [or motions]; and this lasts for a quarter of an hour, and then comes the hour for eating. And they cannot eat unless the cooking is performed by the hands of a gentleman, for the ladies only cook for themselves. And this is the custom among the gentlemen. The ladies wait to wash and perfume themselves. And every time that a man wishes to associate with his wife, she washes and perfumes herself very delicately; but, under any circumstances, they always go scented and covered with jewels, that is to say, on their hands and in their ears, on their feet and on their arms.

¶ In general they practise every day with swords, shields, and lances. And when they go to war, the King of Calicut maintains constantly one hundred thousand people on foot, because they do not make use of horses, only of some elephants for the person of the king. And all the people wear a cloth bound round the head, made of silk and of a vermilion colour, and they carry swords, shields, lances, and bows. The king carries an umbrella instead of a standard, made like the stem of a boot: it is formed of the leaves of a tree, and is fixed on the end of a cane, and made to keep off the sun from the king. And when they are in battle, and one army is distant from the other two ranges of a crossbow, the king says to the Brahmins: "Go into the camp of the enemy, and tell the king to let one hundred of his Naeri come, and I will go with a hundred of mine. And thus they both go to the middle of the space, and begin to fight in this manner. Although they should fight for three days, they always give two direct blows at the head and one at the legs. And when four or six on either side are killed, the Brahmins enter into the midst of them, and make both parties return to their camp. And the said Brahmins immediately go to the armies on both sides, and say: "*Nur manezar hanno*." The king answers: "*Matile?*" that is, "Do you not wish for any more?" The Brahmin says: "No." And the adverse party does the same. And in this manner they fight, one hundred against one hundred. And this is their mode of fighting. Sometimes the king rides on an elephant, and sometimes the Naeri carry him. And when they carry him they always run. And many instruments sounding always accompany the said king. To the said Naeri he gives as pay to each four *carlini* the month, and in time of war he gives half a ducat. And they live on this pay. The before-mentioned race have black teeth, on account of the leaves which I have already told you they eat. When the Naeri die they are burnt with very great solemnity, and some preserve their ashes. But with respect to the common people, after death some bury them within the door of their house; others, again, in their garden. The money of the said city is struck here, as I have already told you in Narsinga. And inasmuch as, at the time when I was in Calicut, there were a very large number of merchants there from different countries and nations, I being desirous of knowing who these persons were, so different one from the other, asked, and was informed that there were here very many Moorish merchants, many from Mecca, a part from Banghella [Bengal], some from Ternasseri [Tenasserim], some from Pego [Pegu], very many from Ciormandel [Coromandel coast of India], in great abundance from Zailani [Ceylon], a great quantity from Sumatra, not a few from Colon and Caicolon, a very great number from Bathacala, from Dabuli, from Chievuli, from Combeia, from Guzerati [Quilon, Kâyankullam, Bhatkal, Dabul, Châul, Cambay, Gujarât], and from Ormus. There were also some there from Persia and from Arabia Felix, part from Syria, from Turkey, and some from Ethiopia and Narsinga. There were merchants from all these realms in my time. It must be known that the pagans do not navigate much, but it is the Moors who carry the merchandise; for in Calicut there are at least fifteen thousand Moors, who are for the greater part natives of the country.

¶ It appears to me very suitable and to the purpose, that I should explain to you how these people navigate along the coast of Calicut, and at what time, and how they build their vessels. First, they make their vessels, such as are open, each of three hundred or four hundred butts. And when they build the said vessels they do not put any oakum between one plank and another in any way whatever, but they join the planks so well that they keep out the water most excellently. And then they lay on pitch outside, and put in an immense quantity of iron nails. Do not imagine, however, that they have not any oakum, for it comes there in great abundance from other countries, but they are not accustomed to use it for ships. They also possess as good timber as ourselves, and in greater quantity than with us. The sails of these ships of theirs are made of cotton, and at the foot of the said sails they carry another sail, and they spread this when they are sailing in order to catch more wind; so that they carry two sails where we carry only one. They also carry anchors made of marble, that is to say, a piece of marble eight *palmi* long and two *palmi* every other way. The said marble has two large ropes attached to it; and these are their anchors. The time of their navigation is this: from Persia to the Cape of Cumerin [Comorin], which is distant from Calicut eight days' journey by sea towards the south. You can navigate through eight months in the year, that is to say, September to all April; then, from the first of May to the middle of August it is necessary to avoid this coast because the sea is very stormy and tempestuous. And you must know that during the months of May, June, July, and August, it rains constantly night and day; it does not merely rain continually, but every night and every day it rains, and but little sun is seen during this time. During the other eight months it never rains. At the end of April they depart from the coast of Calicut, and pass the Cape of Cumerin, and enter into another course of navigation, which is safe during these four months, and go for small spices. As to the names of their ships, some are called *sambuchi* [*sambûk*] and these are flat-bottomed. Some others which are made like ours, that is in the bottom, they call *capel* [*kapal*]. Some other small ships are called *parao* [*prahu*, prow], and they are boats of ten paces each, and are all of one piece, and go with oars made of cane, and the mast also is made of cane. There is another kind of small bark called *almadia* [*al-ma'adîya*, ferry-boat], which is all of one piece. There is also another kind of vessel which goes with a sail and oars. These are all made of one piece, of the length of twelve or thirteen paces each. The opening is so narrow that one man cannot sit by the side of the other, but one is obliged to go before the other. They are sharp at both ends. These ships are called *chaturi* [*shakhtûr*], and go either with a sail or oars more swiftly than any galley, *fusta* [foist], or brigantine. There are corsairs of the sea, and these *chaturi* are made at an island which is near, called Porcai [Parrakâd].

¶ The palace of the king is about a mile in circumference. The walls are low, as I have mentioned above, with very beautiful divisions of wood, with devils carved in relief. The floor of the house is all adorned with cow dung. The said house is worth two hundred ducats or thereabouts. I now saw the reason why they could not dig foundations, on account of the water, which is close to them. It would be impossible to estimate the jewels which the king wears, although in my time he was not in very good humour, in consequence of his being at war with the King of Portugal, and also because he had the French [Frangî] disease, and had it in the throat. Nevertheless, he wore so many jewels in his ears, on his hands, on his arms, on his feet, and on his legs, that it was a wonder to behold. His treasure consists of two magazines of ingots of gold, and stamped golden money, which many Brahmins said that a hundred mules could not carry. And they say, that this treasure has been left by ten or twelve previous kings, who have left it for the wants of the republic. This King of Calicut also possesses a casket three spans long and one and a half span high, filled with jewels of every description.

¶ Many pepper trees are found in the territory of Calicut: there are also some within the city, but not in large quantities. Its stem is like that of a vine, that is to say, it is planted near to some other tree, because, like the vine, it cannot stand erect. This tree grows like the ivy, which embraces and climbs as high as the wood or tree which it can grasp. The said plant throws out a great number of branches, which branches are from two to three *palmi* long. The leaves of these branches resemble those of the sour orange, but are more dry, and on the underneath part they are full of minute veins. From each of these branches there grow five, six, and eight clusters, a little longer than a man's finger, and they are like small raisins, but more regularly arranged, and are as green as unripe grapes. They gather them in this green state in the month of October and even in November, and then they lay them in the sun on certain mats, and leave them in the sun for three or four days, when they become as black as they are seen amongst us without doing anything else to them. And you must know that these people neither prune nor hoe this tree which produces the pepper.

¶ In this place ginger also grows, which is a root, and of these same roots some are found of four, eight, and twelve ounces each. When they dig it, the stem of the said root is about three or four spans long, and is formed like some reeds. And when they gather the said ginger, in that same place they take an eye of the said root, which is like an eye of the cane, and plant it in the hole whence they have dug that root, and cover it up with the same earth. At the end of a year they return to gather it, and plant it in the aforesaid manner. This root grows in red soil, and on the mountain, and in the plain, as the mirabolans grow, every kind of which is found here. Their stem is like that of a middle-sized pear tree, and they bear like the pepper tree.

¶ I found in Calicut a kind of fruit which is called *ciccara* [jack-fruit]. Its stem is like that of a large pear tree. The fruit is two or two and a half *palmi* long, and is as thick as a man's thigh. This fruit grows on the trunk of the tree, that is to say, under the boughs, and partly on the middle of the stem. The colour of the said fruit is green, and it is formed like the pine, but the work is more minute. When it begins to ripen, the skin becomes black and appears rotten. This fruit is gathered in the month of December, and when it is eaten it seems as though you were eating musk melons, and it appears to resemble a very ripe Persian quince. It appears also, as though you were eating a preparation of honey, and it also has the taste of a sweet orange. Within the said fruit there are some pellicles like the pomegranate. And within the said pellicles there is another fruit which, if placed on the embers of the fire and then eaten, you would say that they were most excellent chestnuts. So that this appears to me to be the best and the most excellent fruit I ever ate. Another fruit is also found here, which is called *amba* [*âmb*, *amba*, mango], the stem of which is called *manga* [*manga*, mango]. This tree is like a pear tree, and bears like the pear. This *amba* is made like one of our walnuts in the month of August, and has that form; and when it is ripe it is yellow and shining. This fruit has a stone within like a dry almond, and is much better than the Damascus plum. A preserve is made of this fruit, such as we make of olives, but they are much superior. Another fruit is found here resembling a melon, and it has similar divisions, and when it is cut, three or four grains, which look like grapes or sour cherries, are found inside. The tree which bears this fruit is of the height of a quince tree, and forms its leaves in the same manner. This fruit is called *corcopal* [*papau*]; it is extremely good for eating, and excellent as a medicine. I also found there another fruit, which is exactly like the medlar, but it is white, like an apple. I do not remember by what name it was called. Again, I saw another kind of fruit which resembled a pumpkin in colour, is two spans in length, and has more than three fingers of pulp, and is much better than a gourd (*zuccha*) for confections, and it is a very curious thing, and it is called *comolanga* [melon], and grows on the ground like melons. This country also produces another very singular fruit, which fruit is called *malapolanda* [plantain, banana]. The tree which bears this fruit is as high as a man or a little more, and it produces four or five leaves which are branches and leaves. Each of these covers a man against rain and sun. In the middle of this it throws out a certain branch which produces flowers in the same manner as the stalk of a bean, and afterwards it produces some fruits which are half a *palmo* and a *palmo* in length, and they are as thick as the staff of a spear. And when they wish to gather the said fruit they do not wait until it is ripe, because it ripens in the house. One branch will produce two hundred or thereabouts of these fruits, and they all touch one against the other. Of these fruits there are found three sorts. The first sort is called *cianchapalon*; these are very restorative things to eat. Their colour is somewhat yellow, and the bark is very thin. The second sort is called *cadelapalon*, and they are much superior to the others. The third sort are bitter. The two kinds above mentioned are good like our figs, but superior. The tree of this fruit produces once and then no more. The said tree always has at its stem fifty or sixty shoots (*figlioli*), and the owners remove these shoots by the hand and transplant them, and at the end of a year they produce their fruit. And if the said branches are too green when they cut them, they put a little lime upon the said fruits to make them ripen quickly. You must know that a very large quantity of such fruits is found at all times of the year, and twenty are given for a *quattrino*. In like manner, roses and most singular flowers are found here on all the days of the year.

¶ I will describe another tree to you, the best in all the world, which is called *tenga* [coconut], and is formed like the trunk of a date tree. Ten useful things are derived from this tree. The first utility is wood to burn; nuts to eat; ropes for maritime navigation; thin stuffs which, when they are dyed, appear to be made of silk; charcoal in the greatest perfection; wine; water; oil; and sugar: and with its leaves which fall, that is, when a branch falls, they cover the houses. And these ward off water for half a year. Were I to declare to you in what manner it accomplishes so many things you would not believe it, neither could you understand it. The said tree produces the above-named nuts in the same manner as the branch of a date tree; and each tree will produce from one hundred to two hundred of these nuts, the outer part of which is taken off and used as firewood. And then, next to the second bark, there is taken off a certain substance like cotton or linen flax, and this is given to workmen to beat, and from the flower, stuffs which appear like silken stuffs are made. And the coarse part they spin, and make of it small cords, and of the small they make large cords, and these they use for the sea. Of the other bark of the said nut excellent charcoal is made. After the second bark the nut is good to eat. The size of the said fruit is [at first] that of the little finger of the hand. When the said nut begins to grow, water begins to be produced within; and when the nut has arrived at perfection, it is full of water, so that there are some nuts which will contain four and five goblets of water, which water is a most excellent thing to drink, and is also like rose-water, and extremely sweet. Most excellent oil is made from the said nut, and thus you have eight utilities from it. Another branch of the said tree they do not allow to produce nuts, but they cut it in the middle and give it a certain inclination; and in the morning and evening they make an opening with a knife, and then they apply a certain fluid and that fluid draws out a certain juice. And these men set a pot underneath and collect that juice, of which one tree will produce as much as half a jug between the day and the night. This they place over the fire and boil it one, two, and three times, so that it appears like brandy, and will affect a man's head by merely smelling it, to say nothing of drinking it. This is the wine which is drunk in these countries. From another branch of the said tree they produce in a similar manner this juice, and convert it into sugar by means of fire; but it is not very good. The said tree always has fruit either green or dry, and it produces fruit in five years. These trees are found over two hundred miles of country, and all have owners. As to the goodness of this tree, when the kings are at enmity one with another, and kill each other's children, they nevertheless sometimes make peace. But if one king cut down any of these trees belonging to another king, peace will never be granted to all eternity. You must know that the said tree lives for twenty or five and twenty years, and grows in sandy places. And when these nuts are planted to produce these trees, and until they begin to germinate, or that the tree begins to grow from them, it is necessary that the men who plant them should go every evening to uncover them, in order that the cool night air may blow over them; and early in the morning they return to cover them up, in order that the sun may not find them thus uncovered. And in this manner does this tree generate and grow. In this country of Calicut, there is found a great quantity of *zerzalino* [*juljulân*], from which they make very excellent [gingelly] oil.

¶ The men of Calicut, when they wish to sow rice, observe this practice. First, they plough the land with oxen as we do, and when they sow the rice in the field they have all the instruments of the city continually sounding and making merry. They also have ten or twelve men clothed like devils, and these unite in making great rejoicing with the players on the instruments, in order that the devil may make that rice very productive.

¶ When a merchant, that is, a pagan, is sick and in great danger, the above-mentioned instruments and the aforesaid men dressed like devils go to visit the sick man; and they go at two or three o'clock in the morning; and the said men so dressed carry fire in their mouths; and in each of their hands and on their feet they wear two crutches of wood, which are one pace (*passo*) high, and in this manner they go shouting and sounding the instruments, so that truly if the person were not ill, he would fall to the ground from terror at seeing these ugly beasts. And these are the physicians who go to see and to visit the sick man. And although they should fill the stomach full up to the mouth, they pound three roots of ginger and make a cup of juice, and this they drink, and in three days they no longer have any illness, so that they live exactly like beasts.

¶ The money-changers and bankers of Calicut have some weights, that is, balances, which are so small that the box in which they stand and the weights together do not weigh half an ounce; and they are so true that they will turn by a hair of the head. And when they wish to test any piece of gold, they have carats of gold as we have; and they have the touchstone like us. And they test after our manner. When the touchstone is full of gold, they have a ball, of a certain composition which resembles wax, and with this ball, when they wish to see if the gold be good or poor, they press on the touchstone and take away some gold from the said touchstone, and then they see in the ball the goodness of the gold, and they say: "*Idu mannu, Idu aga,*" that is, "this is good, and this is poor." And when that ball is full of gold they melt it, and take out all the gold which they have tested by the touchstone. The said money-changers are extremely acute in their business. The merchants have this custom when they wish to sell or to purchase their merchandise, that is, wholesale:— They always sell by the hands of the Cortor [Portuguese, *mercador*] or of the Lella [Arabic, *dallâl*, dealer], that is, of the broker. And when the purchaser and the seller wish to make an agreement, they all stand in a circle, and the Cortor takes a cloth and holds it there openly with one hand, and with the other hand he takes the right hand of the seller, that is, the two fingers next to the thumb, and then he covers with the said cloth his hand and that of the seller, and touching each other with these two fingers, they count from one ducat up to one hundred thousand secretly, without saying "I will have so much" or "so much." But in merely touching the joints of the fingers they understand the price and say: "Yes" or "No." And the Cortor answers "No" or "Yes." And when the Cortor has understood the will of the seller, he goes to the buyer with the said cloth, and takes his hand in the manner above mentioned, and by the said touching he tells him he wants so much. The buyer takes the finger of the Cortor, and by the said touches says to him: "I will give him so much." And in this manner they fix the price. If the merchandise about which they treat be spices, they deal by the *bahar*, which *bahar* weighs three of our *cantari*. If they be stuffs, they deal by *curia* [*corja*, corge, score], and in like manner if they be jewels. By a *curia* is understood twenty; or, indeed, they deal by *farasola* [*fârsala*, *farâsala*], which *farasola* weighs about twenty-five of our *lire*.

¶ The women of these two [lowest] classes of people, that is, the Poliari and Hirava [Pulayan and Vettuvan], suckle their children for about three months, and then they feed them upon cow's milk or goat's milk. And when they have crammed them, without washing either their faces or their bodies, they throw them into the sand, in which they remain covered up from the morning until the evening, and as they are more black than any other colour, they cannot be distinguished from little buffalo[e]s or little bears; so that they appear misshapen things, and it seems as though they were fed by the devil. Their mothers give them food again in the evening. These people are the most agile leapers and runners in the world. I think I ought not to omit explaining to you the many kinds of animals and birds which are found in Calicut, and especially about the lions, wild hogs, goats, wolves, kine, buffalo[e]s, goats, and elephants (which, however, are not produced here, but come from other places), great numbers of wild peacocks, and green parrots in immense quantities; also a kind of red parrot. And there are so many of these parrots, that it is necessary to watch the rice in order that the said birds may not eat it. One of these parrots is worth four *quattrini*, and they sing extremely well. I also saw here another kind of bird, which is called *saru* [Persian, *sâr*, starling, here the talking *mainâ*]. They sing better than the parrots, but are smaller. There are many other kinds of birds here different from ours. I must inform you, that during one hour in the morning and one hour in the evening there is no pleasure in the world equal to that of listening to the song of these birds, so much so that it is like being in paradise, in consequence of there being such a multitude of trees and perpetual verdure, which arises from the circumstance that cold is unknown here, neither is there excessive heat. In this country a great number of apes are produced, one of which is worth four *casse* [*kâsu*, cash], and one *casse* is worth a *quattrino*. They do immense damage to those poor men who make wine. These apes mount on the top of those nuts and drink that same liquor, and then they overturn the vessel and throw away all the liquor they cannot drink.

¶ There is found in this Calicut a kind of serpent [crocodile] which is as large as a great pig, and which has a head much larger than that of a pig, and it has four feet, and is four *braza* long. These serpents are produced in certain marshes. The people of the country say that they have no venom, but that they are evil animals, and do injury to people by means of their teeth. Three other kinds of serpents are found here which, if they strike a person a little, that is, drawing blood, he immediately falls to the ground dead. And it has often happened here in my time that there have been many persons struck by these animals, of which animals there are three kinds. The first resemble deaf adders; the next are scorpions; the third are thrice as large as scorpions. Of these three kinds there are immense numbers. And you must know that when the King of Calicut learns where the nest of any of these brutal animals is, he has made over it a little house, on account of the water. And if any person should kill one of these animals the king would immediately put him to death. In like manner, if any one kill a cow, he would also put that person to death. They say that these serpents are spirits of God, and that if they were not his spirits, God would not have given them such a power, that biting a person a little he would immediately fall dead. And it is from this circumstance that there are such numbers of these animals who know the pagans and do not avoid them. In my time one of these serpents entered into a house during the night and bit nine persons, and in the morning they were all found dead and swollen. And when the said pagans go on a journey, if they meet any of these animals they receive it as a good augury.

¶ In the house of the King of Calicut there are many chambers, in which as soon as evening comes they have ten or twelve vases made in the form of a fountain, which are composed of cast metal, and are as high as a man. Each of these vases has three hollow places for holding oil, about two spans high from the ground. And, first, there is a vase in which is oil with cotton wicks lighted all round. And above this there is another vase more narrow, but with the same kind of lights, and on the top of the second vase there stands another yet smaller, but with oil and lights ignited. The foot of this vase is formed in a triangle, and on each of the faces of the foot there are three devils in relief, and they are very fearful to behold. These are the squires who hold the lights before the king. This king also makes use of another custom. When one of his relations dies, as soon as the year of mourning is accomplished, he sends an invitation to all the principal Brahmins who are in his own kingdom, and he also invites some from other countries. And when they are arrived, they make great feastings for three days. Their food consists of rice dressed in various ways, the flesh of wild hogs, and a great deal of venison, for they are great hunters. At the end of the three days, the said king gives to each of the principal Brahmins three, four, and five *pardai*, and then everyone returns to his house. And all the people of the kingdom of the king shave their beards for joy.

¶ Near to Calicut there is a temple [of Srîvalayanâd] in the midst of a tank, that is, in the midst of a pond of water: which temple is made in antique style with two rows of columns, like San Giovanni in Fonte at Rome. In the middle of that temple there is an altar, made of stone, where sacrifices are performed. And between each of the columns of the lower circle there stand some little ships made of stone, which are two paces long, and are full of a certain oil, which is called *enna* [oil]. Around the margin of the said tank there is an immense number of trees all of one kind, on which trees there are lights so numerous that it would be impossible to count them. And in like manner around the said temple there are oil lights in the greatest abundance. When the 25th day of the month of December arrives, all the people for fifteen days' journey around, that is to say, the Naeri and Brahmins, come to this sacrifice [the Navarâtra Festival]. And before performing the said sacrifice, they all wash in the said tank. Then the principal Brahmins of the king mount astride of the little vessels above mentioned where the oil is, and all these people come to the said Brahmins, who anoint the head of each of them with that oil, and then they perform the sacrifice on that altar before mentioned. At the end of one side of this altar there is a very large Sathanas [idol], which they all go to worship, and then each returns on his way. At this season the land is free and frank for three days, that is, they cannot exercise vengeance one against another. In truth, I never saw so many people together at one time, excepting when I was at Mecca. It appears to me that I have sufficiently explained to you the customs and manner of living, the religion and the sacrifices, of Calicut. Wherefore departing thence, I will recount to you step by step the rest of my journey, together with all the events which happened to me in the course of it.

CHAPTER VIII

CONCERNING CAPE COMORIN, THE COROMANDEL COAST OF INDIA AND CEYLON

My companion, who was called Cogiazenor [Khwâja Junair], seeing that he could not sell his merchandise because Calicut was ruined by the King of Portugal, for the merchants who used to come there were not there, neither did they come.—And the reason why they did not come was that the [King of Calicut] consented that the Moors should kill forty-eight Portuguese, whom I saw put to death. And on this account the King of Portugal is always at war, and he has killed, and every day kills, great numbers. And therefore the said city is ruined, for in every way it is at war.—And so we departed, and took our road by a river [the backwater of Calicut], which is the most beautiful I ever saw, and arrived at a city which is called Cacolon [Kâyankullam], distant from Calicut fifty leagues. The king of this city is a pagan and is not very rich. The manner of living, the dress, and the customs, are after the manner of Calicut. Many merchants arrived here, because a great deal of pepper grows in this country, and in perfection. In this city we found some [Nestorian] Christians of those of Saint Thomas, some of whom are merchants, and believe in Christ, as we do. These say that every three years a priest comes there to baptise them, and that he comes to them from Babylon. These Christians keep Lent longer than we do; but they keep Easter like ourselves, and they all observe the same solemnities that we do. But they say mass like the Greeks. The names of whom are four, that is to say, John, James, Matthew, and Thomas. The country, the air, and the situation, resemble those of Calicut. At the end of three days we departed from this place, and went to another city called Colon [Quilon], distant from that above mentioned twenty miles. The king of this city is a pagan, and extremely powerful, and he has 20,000 horsemen, and many archers, and is constantly at war with other kings. This country has a good port near to the sea-coast. No grain grows here, but fruits, as at Calicut, and pepper in great quantities. The colour of this people, their dress, manner of living, and customs, are the same as at Calicut. At that time, the king of this city was the friend of the King of Portugal, but being at war with others, it did not appear to us well to remain here. Wherefore, we took our way by sea, aforesaid, and went to a city which is called Chayl [Kâyal], belonging to the same king, opposite from Colon

[Quilon] fifty miles. We saw those pearls fished for [here] in the sea, in the same manner as I have already described to you in Ormus.

¶ We then passed further onwards, and arrived at a city which is called Cioromandel [Negapatam on the Coromandel coast], which is a marine district, and distant from Colon [Quilon] seven days' journey by sea, more or less, according to the wind. This city is very large, and is not surrounded by walls, and is subject to the King of Narsinga. The said city is situated opposite to the island of Zailon [Ceylon], when you have passed the Cape of Cumerin. In this district they gather a great quantity of rice, and it is the route to very large countries. There are many Moorish merchants here who go and come for their merchandise. No spices of any description grow here, but plenty of fruits, as at Calicut. I found some Christians in this district who told me that the body of St. Thomas [at S. Thomé] was twelve miles distant from that place, and that it was under the guard of some Christians. They also told me that Christians could not live in that country after the King of Portugal had come there, because the said king had put to death many Moors of that country, which trembled throughout from fear of the Portuguese. And, therefore, the said poor Christians cannot live here any longer, but are driven away and killed secretly, in order that it may not come to the ears of the King of Narsinga, who is a very great friend of the Christians, and especially of the Portuguese. One of these Christians also told me a very great miracle which his priest had told him, that forty-five years ago the Moors had a dispute with the Christians, and there were wounded on both sides; but one Christian, among the rest, was much wounded in the arm, and he went to the tomb of St. Thomas and touched the tomb of St. Thomas with that wounded arm, and immediately he was cured. And that from that time henceforward, the King of Narsinga has always wished well to the Christians. My companion disposed of some of his merchandise here, and inasmuch as they were at war with the King of Tarnassari [Tenasserim] we remained here only a few days, and then we took a ship with some other merchants, which ships are called *ciampane* [*sampans*], for they are flat-bottomed, and require little water and carry much goods. We passed a gulf of twelve or fifteen leagues where we had incurred great peril because there are many shoals and rocks there; however, we arrived at an island called Zailon, which is about 1000 miles in circumference, according to the report of the inhabitants thereof.

¶ In this island of Zailon there are four kings, all pagans. I do not describe to you all the things of the said island, because these kings being in fierce war with each other, we could not remain there long, neither could we see or hear the things thereof; however, having remained there some few days, we saw that which you shall hear. And first, an immense quantity of elephants which are produced there. We also saw rubies found there, at a distance of two miles from the sea shore, where there is an extremely large and very long mountain, at the foot of which the said rubies are found. And when a merchant wishes to find these jewels, he is obliged first to speak to the king and to purchase a *braza* of the said land in every direction, (which *braza* is called a *molan* [*ammonan*, 2½ acres]), and to purchase it for five ducats. And then when he digs the said land, a man always remains there on the part of the king. And if any jewel be found which exceeds ten carats, the king claims it for himself, and leaves all the rest free. There is also produced near to the said mountain, where there is a very large river, a great quantity of garnets, sapphires, jacinths, and topazes. In this island there grow the best fruits I have ever seen, and especially certain artichokes (*carzofoli*) [but probably custard apples] better than ours. Sweet oranges, (*melangoli*,) the best, I believe, in the world, and many other fruits like those of Calicut, but much superior.

¶ The tree of the *canella* is the same as the laurel, especially the leaves; and it produces some berries like the laurel, but they are smaller and more white. The said *canella*, or cinnamon, is the bark of the said tree, in this wise: Every three years they cut the branches of the said tree, and then take off the bark of them; but they do not cut the stem on any account. There are great numbers of these trees. When they collect that cinnamon it has not the excellence which it possesses a month afterwards. A Moorish merchant told me that at the top of that very large mountain [Adam's Peak] there is a cavern to which the men of that country go once in the year to pray, because, as they say, Adam was up there praying and doing penance, and that the impressions of his feet are seen to this day, and that they are about two spans long. Rice does not grow in this country, but it comes there from the main land. The kings of this island are tributaries of the King of Narsinga, on account of the rice which comes there from the main land. The air in this island is extremely good, and the people are of a dark tawny colour. And here it is neither too hot nor too cold. Their dress is *all' apostolica*; they wear certain stuffs of cotton or silk, and go bare-footed. This island is placed under the equinoctial line, and the inhabitants of it are not very warlike. Artillery is not used here; but they have some lances and swords, which lances are of cane, and with these they fight amongst each other; but they do not kill each other overmuch, because they are cowardly fellows. Here there are roses and flowers of every kind, and the people live longer than we do. Being in our ship one evening, a man came on the part of the king to my companion, and told him that he should carry to him his corals and saffron; for he had a great quantity of both. A merchant of the said island, who was a Moor, hearing these words, said to him secretly: "Do not go to the king, for he will pay you for your goods after his own fashion." And this he said out of cunning, in order that my companion might go away, because he himself had the same kind of merchandise. However, answer was given to the message of the king, that on the following day he would go to his lord. And when morning came, he took a vessel and rowed over to the mainland.

¶ We arrived in the course of three days at a place which is called Paleachet [Pulikat], which is subject to the King of Narsinga. This district is one of immense traffic in merchandise, and especially in jewels, for they come here from Zailon and from Pego [Pegu]. There are also here many great Moorish merchants of all kinds of spices. We lodged in the house of a Moorish merchant, and we told him where we came from, and that we had many corals to sell, and saffron, and much figured velvet, and many knives. The said merchant, understanding that we had this kind of merchandise, was greatly pleased. This country is most abundant in everything which is produced in India, but no grain grows there. They have rice here in great abundance. Their laws, manner of living, dress, and customs, are the same as at Calicut, and they are a warlike people, although they have no artillery. As this country was at fierce war with the King of Tarnassari, we could not remain here a very long time. But after remaining here a few days we took our route towards the city of Tarnassari, which is distant a thousand miles from here. At which city we arrived in fourteen days by sea.

CHAPTER IX

CONCERNING TENASSERIM

THE city of Tarnassari [Mergui] is situated near to the sea: it is a level place and well watered, and has a good port, that is, a river on the side towards the north. The king of the city is a pagan, and is a very powerful lord. He is constantly fighting with the King of Narsinga and the King of Banghella [Bengal]. He has a hundred armed elephants, which are larger than any I ever saw. He always maintains 100,000 men for war, part infantry and part cavalry. Their arms consist of small swords and some sort of shields, some of which are made of tortoise-shell, and some like those of Calicut; and they have a great quantity of bows, and lances of cane, and some also of wood. When they go to war they wear a dress stuffed very full of cotton. The houses of this city are well surrounded by walls. Its situation is extremely good, after the manner of Christians, and good grain and cotton also grow there. Silk is also made there in large quantities. A great deal of brazil-wood is found there, fruits in great abundance, and some which resemble our apples and pears, some oranges, lemons, and citrons, and gourds in great abundance. And here are seen very beautiful gardens, with many delicate things in them.

¶ In this country of Tarnassari there are oxen, cows, sheep, and goats in great quantities, wild hogs, stags, roebucks, wolves, cats which produce the civet, lions, peacocks in great multitudes, falcons, goss-hawks, white parrots, and also other kinds which are of seven very beautiful colours. Here there are hares and partridges, but not like ours. There is also here another kind of bird, one of prey, much larger than an eagle, of the beak of which, that is, of the upper part, they make sword-hilts, which beak is yellow and red, a thing very beautiful to behold. The colour of the said bird is black, red, and some feathers are white. There are produced here hens and cocks, the largest I ever saw, so much so that one of these hens is larger than three of ours. In this country in a few days we had great pleasure from some things which we saw, and especially that every day in the street where the Moorish merchants abide they make some cocks fight, and the owners of these cocks bet as much as a hundred ducats on the one which will fight best. And we saw two fight for five hours continuously, so that at the last both remained dead. Here also is a sort of goat, much larger than ours, and which is much more handsome, and which always has four kids at a birth. Ten and twelve large and good sheep are sold here for a ducat. And there is another kind of sheep, which has horns like a deer: these are larger than ours, and fight most terribly. There are buffalo[e]s here, much more misshapen than ours. There are also great numbers of fish like ours. I saw here, however, a bone of a fish which weighed more than ten *cantari*. With respect to the manner of living of this city, the pagans eat all kinds of flesh excepting that of oxen, and they eat on the ground, without a cloth, in some very beautiful vessels of wood. Their drink is water, sweetened where possible. They sleep high from the ground, in good beds of cotton, and covered with silk or cotton. Then, as to their dress, they go *all' apostolica*, with a quilted cloth of cotton or silk. Some merchants wear very beautiful shirts of silk or cotton: in general, they do not wear anything on their feet, excepting the Brahmins, who also wear on the head a cap of silk or camelot, which is two spans long. In the said cap they wear on the top a thing made like a hazelnut, which is worked all round in gold. They also wear two strings of silk, more than two fingers wide, which they hang round the neck. They wear their ears full of jewels and none on their fingers. The colour of the said race is semi-white, because the air here is cooler than it is in Calicut, and the seasons are the same as with us, and also the harvests.

¶ The king of the said city does not cause his wife's virginity to be taken by the Brahmins as the King of Calicut does, but he causes her to be deflowered by white men, whether Christians or Moors, provided they be not pagans. Which pagans also, before they conduct their wives to their house, find a white man, of whatever country he may be, and take him to their house for this particular purpose, to make him deflower the wife. And this happened to us when we arrived in the said city. We met by chance three or four merchants, who began to speak to my companion in this wise: "*Langalli ni pardesi,*" that is, "Friend, are you strangers?" He answered: "Yes." Said the merchants: "*Ethera nali ni banno,*" that is, "How many days have you been in this country?" We replied: "*Mun nal gnad banno,*" that is, "It is four days since we arrived." Another one of the said merchants said: "*Biti banno gnan pigamanathon ondo,*" that is, "Come to my house, for we are great friends of strangers"; and we, hearing this, went with him. When we had arrived at his house, he gave us a collation, and then he said to us: "My friends, *Patanci nale banno gnan penna periti in penna orangono panna panni cortu,*" that is, "Fifteen days hence I wish to bring home my wife, and one of you shall sleep with her the first night, and shall deflower her for me." We remained quite ashamed at hearing such a thing. Then our interpreter said: "Do not be ashamed, for this is the custom of the country." Then my companion hearing this said: "Let them not do us any other mischief, for we will satisfy you in this"; but we thought that they were mocking us. The merchant saw that we remained undecided, and said: "*O langal limaranconia ille ocha manezar irichenu,*" that is, "Do not be dispirited, for all this country follows this custom." Finding at last that such was the custom in all this country, as one who was in our company affirmed to us, and said that we need have no fear, my companion said to the merchant that he was content to go through this fatigue. The merchant then said: "I wish you to remain in my house, and that you, your companions and goods, be lodged here with me until I bring the lady home." Finally, after refusing, we were obliged to yield to his caresses, and all of us, five in number, together with all our things, were lodged in his house. Fifteen days from that time this merchant brought home his wife, and my companion slept with her the first night. She was a young girl of fifteen years, and he did for the merchant all that he had asked of him. But after the first night, it would have been at the peril of his life if he had returned again, although truly the lady would have desired that the first night had lasted a month. The merchants, having received such a service from some of us, would gladly have retained us four or five months at their own expense, for all kinds of wares cost very little money, and also because they are most liberal and very agreeable men.

¶ All the Brahmins and the king are burnt after death, and at that time a solemn sacrifice is made to the devil. And then they preserve the ashes in certain vases [Martaban jars] made of baked earth, vitrified like glass, which vases have the mouth narrow like a small *scutella* [bowl]. They then bury this vase with the ashes of the burnt body within their houses. When they make the said sacrifice, they make it under some trees, after the manner of Calicut. And for burning the dead body they light a fire of the most odoriferous things that can be found, such as aloes-wood, benzoin, sandal-wood, brazil-wood, storax and amber, incense, and some beautiful branches of coral, which things they place upon the body, and while it is burning all the instruments of the city are sounding. In like manner, fifteen or twenty men, dressed like devils, stand there and make great rejoicing. And his wife is always present, making most exceedingly great lamentations, and no other woman. And this is done at one or two o'clock of the night.

¶ In this city of Tarnassari, when fifteen days have passed after the death of the husband, the wife makes a banquet for all her relations and all those of her husband. And then they go with all the relations to the place where the husband was burnt, and at the same hour of the night. The said woman puts on all her jewels and other objects in gold, all that she possesses. And then her relations cause a hole to be made of the height of a human being, and around the hole they put four or five canes, around which they place a silken cloth, and in the said hole they make a fire of the above-mentioned things, such as were used for the husband. And then the said wife, when the feast is prepared, eats a great deal of betel, and eats so much that she loses her wits, and the instruments of the city are constantly sounding, together with the above-mentioned men clothed like devils, who carry fire in their mouths, as I have already told you in Calicut. They also offer a sacrifice to Deumo [South Indian term, *dêvan*, a godling]. And the said wife goes many times up and down that place, dancing with the other women. And she goes many times to the said men clothed like devils, to entreat and tell them to pray the Deumo that he will be pleased to accept her as his own. And there are always present here a great many women who are her relations. Do not imagine, however, that she is unwilling to do this; she even imagines that she shall be carried forthwith into heaven. And thus running violently of her own free will, she seizes the above-mentioned cloth with her hands, and throws herself into the midst of the fire. And immediately her relations and those most nearly allied to her fall upon her with sticks and with balls of pitch, and this they do only that she may die the sooner. And if the said wife were not to do this, she would be held in like estimation as a public prostitute is among us, and her relations would put her to death. When such an event takes place in this country the king is always present. However, those who undergo such a death are the most noble of the land: all, in general, do not do thus. I have seen in this city of Tarnassari another custom, somewhat less horrible than the before mentioned. There will be a young man who will speak to a lady of love, and will wish to give her to understand that he really is fond of her, and that there is nothing he would not do for her. And, discoursing with her in this wise, he will take a piece of rag well saturated with oil, and will set fire to it, and place it on his arm on the naked flesh, and whilst it is burning he will stand speaking with that lady, not caring about his arm being burnt, in order to show that he loves her, and that for her he is willing to do every great thing.

¶ He who kills another in this country is put to death, the same as in Calicut. With respect to conveying and holding, it is necessary that it should appear by writing or by witnesses. Their writing is on paper like ours, not on the leaves of a tree like that of Calicut. And then they go to a governor of the city, who administers justice for them summarily. However, when any foreign merchant dies who has no wife or children, he cannot leave his property to whomsoever he pleases, because the king wills to be his heir. (And in this country [that is, the natives, commencing from the king] after his death his son remains king.) And when any Moorish merchant dies, very great expense is incurred in odoriferous substances to preserve the body, which they put into wooden boxes and then bury it, placing the head towards the city of Mecca, which comes to be towards the north. If the deceased have children, they are his heirs.

¶ These people make use of very large ships and of various kinds, some of which are made flat bottomed, because such can enter into places where there is not much water. Another kind are made with prows before and behind, and they carry two helms and two masts, and are uncovered. There is also another kind of large ship which is called *giunchi* [junks], and each of these is of the tonnage of one thousand butts, on which they carry some little vessels to a city called Melacha [Malacca], and from thence they go with these little vessels for small spices to a place which you shall know when the proper time comes.

CHAPTER X

CONCERNING BENGAL

LET us return to my companion, for he and I had a desire to see farther on. After we had been some days in this said city, and being, indeed, tired of that same service of which you have heard above, and having sold some of our merchandise we took the route towards the city of Banghella [Satgâon in Bengal], which is distant from Tarnassari seven hundred miles, at which we arrived in eleven days by sea. This city was one of the best that I had hitherto seen, and has a very great realm. The sultan of this place is a Moor, and maintains two hundred thousand men for battle on foot and on horse; and they are all Mahommedans; and he is constantly at war with the King of Narsingha. This country abounds more in grain, flesh of every kind, in great quantity of sugar, also of ginger, and of great abundance of cotton, than any country in the world. And here there are the richest merchants I ever met with. Fifty ships are laden every year in this place with cotton and silk stuffs, which stuffs are these, that is to say, *bairam*, *namone*, *lizati*, *ciantar*, *doazar*, and *sinabaff*. These same stuffs go through all Turkey, through Syria, through Persia, through Arabia Felix, through Ethiopia, and through all India. There are also here very great merchants in jewels, which come from other countries.

¶ We also found some [Nestorian] Christian merchants here. They said that they were from a city called Sarnau [in Siam], and had brought for sale silken stuffs, and aloes-wood, and benzoin, and musk. Which Christians said that in their country there were many lords also Christians, but they are subject to the great Khan [of] Cathai [China]. As to the dress of these Christians, they were clothed in a *xebec* [jerkin] made with folds, and the sleeves were quilted with cotton. And on their heads they wore a cap a palm and a half long, made of red cloth.

These same men are as white as we are, and confess that they are Christians, and believe in the Trinity, and likewise in the Twelve Apostles, in the four Evangelists, and they also have baptism with water. But they write in the contrary way to us, that is, after the manner of Armenia. And they say that they keep the Nativity and the Passion of Christ, and observe our Lent and other vigils in the course of the year. These Christians do not wear shoes, but they wear a kind of breeches made of silk, similar to those worn by mariners, which breeches are all full of jewels, and their heads are covered with jewels. And they eat at a table after our fashion, and they eat every kind of flesh. These people also said that they knew that on the confines of the Rumi, that is, of the Grand Turk, there are very great Christian kings. After a great deal of conversation with these men, my companion at last showed them his merchandise, amongst which there were certain beautiful branches of large coral. When they had seen these branches they said to us, that if we would go to a city where they would conduct us, that they were prepared to secure for us as much as 10,000 ducats for them, or as many rubies as in Turkey would be worth 100,000. My companion replied that he was well pleased, and that they should depart immediately thence. The Christians said: "In two days' time from this a ship will sail which goes towards Pego, and we have to go with it; if you are willing to come we will go together." Hearing this we set ourselves in order, and embarked with the said Christians and with some other Persian merchants. And as we had been informed in this city that these Christians were most faithful, we formed a very great friendship with them. But before our departure from Banghella, we sold all the rest of the merchandise, with the exception of the corals, the saffron, and two pieces of rose-coloured cloth of Florence. We left this city, which I believe is the best in the world, that is, for living in. In which city the kinds of stuffs you have heard of before are not woven by women, but the men weave them. We departed thence with the said Christians, and went towards a city which is called Pego, distant from Banghella about a thousand miles. On which voyage we passed a gulf [of Martaban] towards the south, and so arrived at the city of Pego.

CHAPTER XI

CONCERNING PEGU

THE city of Pego is on the mainland, and is near to the sea. On the left hand of this, that is, towards the east, there is a very beautiful river, by which many ships go and come. The king of this city is a pagan. Their faith, customs, manner of living and dress, are after the manner of Tarnassari; but with respect to their colour, they are somewhat more white. And here, also, the air is somewhat more cold. Their seasons are like ours. This city is walled, and has good houses and palaces built of stone, with lime. The king is extremely powerful in men, both foot and horse, and has with him more than a thousand Christians of the country which has been above mentioned to you. And he gives to each, for pay, six golden *pardai* [ducats] per month and his expenses. In this country there is a great abundance of grain, of flesh of every kind, and of fruits of the same as at Calicut. These people have not many elephants, but they possess great numbers of all other animals; they also have all the kinds of birds which are found at Calicut. But there are here the most beautiful and the best parrots I had ever seen. Timber grows here in great quantities, long, and I think the thickest that can possibly be found. In like manner I do not know if there can be found in the world such thick canes as I found here, of which I saw some which were really as thick as a barrel. Civet-cats are found in this country in great numbers, three or four of which are sold for a ducat. The sole merchandise of these people is jewels, that is, rubies, which come from another city called Capellan [Ruby Mines District in Burma], which is distant from this thirty days' journey; not that I have seen it, but by what I have heard from merchants. You must know that in the said city, a large pearl and diamond are worth more here than with us, and also an emerald. When we arrived in this country, the king was fifteen days' journey distant, fighting with another who was called King of Ava [Burma]. Seeing this, we determined to go and find the king where he was, in order to give him these corals. And so we departed thence in a ship made all of one piece, and more than fifteen or sixteen paces long. The oars of this vessel were made of cane. Understand well in what manner: where the oar takes the water it was cloven, and they insert a flat piece of board fastened by cords, so that the said vessel went with more power than a brigantine. The mast of it was a cane as thick as a barrel where they put in the provisions. In three days we arrived at a village where we found certain merchants, who had not been able to enter into the said city of Ava on account of the war. Hearing this, we returned with them to Pego, and five days afterwards the king returned to the said city, who had gained a very great victory over his enemy. On the second day after the return of the king, our Christian companions took us to speak with him. ¶ Do not imagine that the King of Pego enjoys as great a reputation as the King of Calicut, although he is so humane and domestic that an infant might speak to him, and he wears more rubies on him than the value of a very large city, and he wears them on all his toes. And on his legs he wears certain great rings of gold, all full of the most beautiful rubies; also his arms and his fingers all full. His ears hang down half a palm, through the great weight of the many jewels he wears there, so that seeing the person of the king by a light at night, he shines so much that he appears to be a sun. The said Christians spoke with him, and told him of our merchandise. The king replied: "That we should return to him the day after the next, because on the next day he had to sacrifice to the devil for the victory which he had gained." When the time mentioned was past, the king, as soon as he had eaten, sent for the said Christians, and for my companion, in order that he might carry to him his merchandise. When the king saw such beautiful corals he was quite astonished and greatly pleased; for, in truth, among the other corals there were two branches, the like of which had never before entered India. This king asked what people we were. The Christians answered: "Sir, these are Persians." Said the king to the interpreter: "Ask them if they are willing to sell these things." My companions answered: "That the articles were at the service of his highness." Then the king began to say: "That he had been at war with the King of Ava for two years, and on that account he had no money; but that if we were willing to barter for so many rubies, he would amply satisfy us." We caused him to be told by these Christians that we desired nothing further from him than his friendship,—that he should take the commodities and do whatever he pleased. The Christians repeated to him what my companion had charged them to say, by telling the king that he might take the corals without money or jewels. He hearing this liberality answered: "I know that the Persians are very liberal, but I never saw one so liberal as this man"; and he swore by God and by the devil that he would see which would be the more liberal, he or a Persian. And then he desired one of his confidential servants to bring him a certain little box which was two palms in length, worked all round in gold, and was full of rubies, within and without. And when he had opened it, there were six separate divisions, all full of different rubies; and he placed it before us, telling us we should take what we wished. My companion answered: "O, sir, you show me so much kindness, that by the faith which I bear to Mahomet I make you a present of all these things. And know, sir, that I do not travel about the world to collect property, but only to see different people and different customs." The king answered: "I cannot conquer you in liberality, but take this which I give you." And so he took a good handful of rubies from each of the divisions of the said casket, and gave them to him. These rubies might be about two hundred, and in giving them he said: "Take these for the liberality you have exercised towards me." And in like manner he gave to the said Christians two rubies each, which were estimated at a thousand ducats, and those of my companions were estimated at about one hundred thousand ducats. Wherefore by this he may be considered to be the most liberal king in the world, and every year he has an income of about one million in gold. And this because in his country there is found much *lacca* [lac], a good deal of sandal-wood, very much brazil-wood, cotton and silk in great quantities, and he gives all his income to his soldiers. The people in this country are very sensual. After some days, the said Christians took leave for themselves and for us. The king ordered a room to be given to us, furnished with all that was requisite for so long as we wished to remain there; and so it was done. We remained in the said room five days. At this time there arrived news that the King of Ava was coming with a great army to make war upon him, on hearing which, this one [of Pego] went to meet him half way with a great many men, horse and foot. The next day we saw two women burnt alive voluntarily, in the manner as I have described it in Tarnassari.

CHAPTER XII

CONCERNING MALACCA AND SUMATRA

THE next day we embarked on board a ship and went to a city called Melacha [Malacca], which is situated towards the west, at which we arrived in eight days. Near to the said city we found an extremely great *fiumara* [strait], as large as any we had ever seen, which they call Gaza [Arabic *bughâz*, a strait], which is evidently more than twenty-five miles wide. And opposite to the said river there is a very large island, which is called Sumatra. The inhabitants of it say that the circumference of it is four thousand five hundred miles. I will tell you about the said island at the proper time. When we had arrived at the city of Melacha, we were immediately presented to the Sultan, who is a Moor, as is also all his kingdom. The said city is on the mainland and pays tribute to the King of Cini [Siam], who caused this place to be built about eighty years ago, because there is a good port there, which is the principal port of the main ocean. And, truly I believe, that more ships arrive here than in any other place in the world, and especially there come here all sorts of spices and an immense quantity of other merchandise. This country is not very fertile, yet there is produced here grain, a little animal food, wood, birds like those of Calicut, excepting the parrots, which are better here than in Calicut. A great quantity of sandal-wood and of tin is found here. There are also a great many elephants, horses, sheep, cows and buffalo[e]s, leopards and peacocks, in great abundance. A few fruits like those in Zeilan. It is not necessary to trade here in anything excepting in spices and silken stuffs. These people are olive-coloured, with long hair. Their dress is after the fashion of Cairo. They have the visage broad, the eye round, the nose compressed. It is not possible to go about the place here when it is dark, because people are killed like dogs, and all the merchants who arrive here go to sleep in their ships. The inhabitants of this city are of the nation of Giavai [Java]. The king keeps a governor to administer justice for foreigners, but those of the country take the law into their own hands, and they are the worst race that was ever created on earth. When the king wishes to interfere with them, they say that they will disinhabit the land, because they are men of the sea. The air here is very temperate. The Christians who were in our company gave us to understand that we ought not to remain long here because they are an evil race. Wherefore we took a junk and went towards Sumatra to a city called Pider [Pedîr], which is distant from the mainland eighty leagues, or thereabouts.

¶ They say that in this district there is the best port of the whole island, which I have already told you is in circumference 4,500 miles. In my opinion, which agrees also with what many say, I think that it is Taprobana, in which there are three crowned kings who are pagans, and their faith, their manner of living, dress, and customs, are the same as in Tarnassari, and the wives also are burnt alive. The colour of these inhabitants is almost white, and they have the face broad, and the eyes round and green. Their hair is long, the nose broad and flat, and they are of small stature. Here justice is strictly administered, as in Calicut. Their money is gold, and silver, and tin, all stamped. Their golden money has on one side a devil, on the other there is something resembling a chariot drawn by elephants: the same on the silver and tin money. Of the silver coin ten go to a ducat, and of those of tin, twenty-five. Elephants in immense quantities are produced here, which are the largest I ever saw. These people are not warlike, but attend to their merchandise, and are very great friends of foreigners.

¶ In this country of Pider [Pedîr] there grows a very great quantity of pepper, and of long pepper which is called *molaga*. This said kind of pepper is larger than that which comes here to us, and is very much whiter, and within it is hollow, and is not so biting as that of ours, and weighs very little, and is sold here in the same manner as cereals are sold with us. And you must know that in this port there are laden with it every year eighteen or twenty ships, all of which go to Cathai, because they say that the extreme cold begins there. The tree which produces this pepper produces it long, but its vine is larger, and the leaf broader and softer, than that which grows in Calicut. An immense quantity of silk is produced in this country, a great deal is also made in the forests without being cultivated by anyone. This, it is true, is not very good. A great quantity of benzoin is also produced here, which is the gum of a tree. Some say, for I have not seen it myself, that it grows at a considerable distance from the sea, on the mainland.

¶ Inasmuch as it is the variety of objects which most delights and invites man, as well to read as to understand, it has therefore appeared to me well to add that of which I have real certainty by my own experience. Wherefore you must know that neither benzoin nor aloes-wood comes much into Christian ports, and therefore you must understand that there are three sorts of aloes-wood. The first and most perfect sort is called *calampat* [*kalambak*], and which does not grow in this island, but comes from a city called Sarnau [in Siam], which (as the Christians our companions said) is near to their city, and here this first sort grows. The second sort is called *loban* [*lubân*], which comes from a river. The name of the third sort is called *bochor* [*bakh-khûr*]. The said Christians also said that the reason the said *calampat* does not come to us is this, that in Gran Cathai, and in the kingdom of Cini and Macini [Chinese Empire], and Sarnau and Giava [Java], they have a much greater abundance of gold than we have. They also say that there are much greater lords there than there are in our parts, and that they delight more than we do in those two sorts of perfumes, and that after their death a very great quantity of gold is expended in these perfumes; and for this reason these excellent sorts do not come into our parts. In Sarnau they are worth ten ducats per pound, because there is very little of them.

¶ The aforesaid Christians made us see an experiment with the two kinds of perfume. One of them had a little of both sorts. The *calampat* was about two ounces, and he made my companion hold it in his hand as long as he could say four times, "*Miserere mei, Deus,*" holding it firmly in his closed hand. Then he made him open his hand. Truly, I never smelt such an odour as that was, which exceeded all our perfumes. Then he took a piece of benzoin as large as a walnut, and he took of that (the *calampat*) which grows in Sarnau about half a pound, and had it placed in two chambers in vases with fire within. In truth I tell you, that that little produced more odour, and a greater softness and sweetness, than two pounds of any other kind would have done. It is impossible to describe the excellence of those two kinds of scents and perfumes. So that you have now heard the reason why these said things do not come to our parts. There also grows here a very great quantity of *lacca* [lac] for making red colour, and the tree of this is formed like our trees which produce walnuts.

¶ In this country I saw the most beautiful works of art I ever saw in my life, that is, some boxes worked in gold, which they gave for two ducats each, which, in truth, with us, would be valued at one hundred ducats. Again, I saw here in one street about five hundred money-changers, and these because a very great number of merchants come to this city, where they carry on a very extensive traffic. For the sleeping of these people, there are good beds of cotton, covered with silk and cotton sheets. In this island they have an extreme abundance of timber, and they make here great ships which they call *giunchi* [junks], which carry three masts, and have a prow before and behind, with two rudders before and two behind. And when they navigate through any archipelago, (for here there is a great sea like a canal), while sailing, the wind will sometimes come in their face, they immediately lower the sail, and quickly, without turning, hoist sail on the other mast, and turn back. And you must know that they are the most active men I have ever met with. They are also very great swimmers, and excellent masters of the art of making fireworks.

¶ The habitations of the said place consist of walled houses of stone, and they are not very high, and a great many of them are covered with the shells of sea turtles, because they are found here in great quantities, and in my time I saw one weighed which weighed one hundred and three pounds. I also saw two elephants' teeth which weighed three hundred and thirty-five pounds. And I saw, moreover, in this island, serpents very much larger than those of Calicut. Let us revert to our Christian companions, who were desirous of returning to their country: wherefore they asked us what was our intention, whether we wished to remain here, or to go farther on, or to return back. My companion answered them: "Since I am brought where the spices grow, I should like to see some kinds before I return back." They said to him: "No other spices grow here excepting those which you have seen." And he asked them where the nutmegs and the cloves grew. They answered: "That the nutmegs and mace grew in an island which was distant from there three hundred miles." We then asked them if we could go to that island in safety, that is, secure from robbers or corsairs. The Christians answered: "That secure from robbers we might go, but not from the chances of the sea"; and they said that we could not go to the said island with that large ship. My companion said: "What means then might there be for going to this island?" They answered: "That it was necessary to purchase a *chiampana* [*sampan*, junk]," that is, a small vessel, of which many are found there. My companion begged them to send for two, which he would buy. The Christians immediately found two, furnished with people whom they had there to manage them, with all things necessary and proper for such a voyage; and they bargained for the said vessels, men, and necessary things, for four hundred *pardai*, which were paid down by my companion, who then began to say to the Christians: "O my very dear friends, although we are not of your race, we are all sons of Adam and Eve, will you abandon me and this other my companion who is born in your faith?" "How in our faith? This companion of yours, is he not a Persian?" He replied: "He is a Persian now, because he was purchased in the city of Jerusalem." The Christians hearing Jerusalem mentioned, immediately raised their hands to heaven, and then kissed the earth three times, and asked at what time it was that I was sold in Jerusalem. We replied: "That I was about fifteen years old." Then said they: "He ought to remember his country." Said my companion: "Truly he does recollect it, for I have had no other pleasure for many months but that of hearing of the things of his country, and he has taught me (the names of) all the members of the body and the names of the things to eat." Hearing this, the Christians said: "Our wish was to return to our country, which is distant from here three thousand miles; for your sake and for that of your companion we are willing to come where you shall go; and if your companion is willing to remain with us, we will make him rich, and if he shall desire to observe the Persian law, he shall be at liberty to do so." My companion replied: "I am much pleased with your company, but it is out of order for him to remain with you, because I have given him a niece of mine to be his wife for the love which I bear him. So that, if you are willing to come in company with us, I wish that you first take this present which I give you, otherwise I should never be satisfied." The good Christians answered: "That he might do as he pleased, for they were satisfied with everything." And so he gave them half a *curia* [*corja*, score] of rubies, which were ten, of the value of five hundred *pardai*. Two days afterwards the said *chiampanė* were ready, and we put on board many articles of food, especially the best fruits I ever tasted, and thus took our way towards the island called Bandan [Banda].

CHAPTER XIII

CONCERNING THE SPICE ISLANDS

In the course of the said journey we found about twenty islands, part inhabited and part not, and in the space of fifteen days we arrived at the said island, which is very ugly and gloomy, and is about one hundred miles in circumference, and is a very low and flat country. There is no king here, nor even a governor, but there are some peasants, like beasts, without understanding. The houses of this island are of timber, very gloomy, and low. Their dress consists of a shirt; they go barefooted, with nothing on their heads; their hair long, the face broad and round, their colour is white, and they are small of stature. Their faith is pagan, but they are of that most gloomy class of Calicut called Poliar and Hirava [Pulayan and Vettuvan]; they are very weak of understanding, and in strength they have no vigour, but live like beasts. Nothing grows here but nutmegs and some fruits. The trunk of the nutmeg is formed like a peach-tree, and produces its leaves in like manner; but the branches are more close, and before the nut arrives at perfection the mace stands round it like an open rose, and when the nut is ripe the mace clasps it, and so they gather it in the month of September; for in this island the seasons go as with us, and every man gathers as much as he can, for all are common, and no labour is bestowed upon the said trees, but nature is left to do her own work. These nuts are sold by a measure, which weighs twenty-six pounds, for the price of half a *carlino*. Money circulates here as in Calicut. It is not necessary to administer justice here, for the people are so stupid, that if they wished to do evil they would not know how to accomplish it. At the end of two days my companion said to the Christians: "Where do the cloves grow?" They answered: "That they grew six days' journey hence, in an island called Monoch [the Moluccas], and that the people of that island are beastly, and more vile and worthless than those of Bandan

[Banda]." At last we determined to go to that island be the people what they might, and so we set sail, and in twelve days arrived at the said island.

¶ We disembarked in this island of Monoch, which is much smaller than Bandan; but the people are worse than those of Bandan, but live in the same manner, and are a little more white, and the air is a little more cold. Here the cloves grow, and in many other neighbouring islands, but they are small and uninhabited. The tree of the cloves is exactly like the box tree, that is, thick, and the leaf is like that of the cinnamon, but it is a little more round, and is of that colour which I have already mentioned to you in Zeilan [Ceylon], which is almost like the leaf of the laurel. When these cloves are ripe, the said men beat them down with canes, and place some mats under the said tree to catch them. The place where these trees are is like sand, that is, it is of the same colour, not that it is sand. The country is very low, and the north star is not seen from it. When we had seen this island and these people, we asked the Christians if there was anything else to see. They replied: "Let us see a little how they sell these cloves." We found that they were sold for twice as much as the nutmegs, but by measure, because these people do not understand weights.

¶ We were now desirous of changing countries, in order to learn new things in every way. Then said the Christians: "O dear companion, since God has conducted us so far in safety, if it please you, we will go to see the largest island in the world, and the most rich, and you will see a thing which you have never seen before. But we must first go to another island which is called Bornei [? Buru], where we must take a large ship, for the sea is more rough." He replied: "I am well pleased to do that which you wish." And so we took our way towards the said island, the route to which is constantly to the southward. While on our way the said Christians had no other pleasure, night and day, than that of conversing with me upon subjects relating to the Christians and about our faith. And when I told them of the Volto Santo which is in St. Peter's, and of the heads of St. Peter and St. Paul, and of many other saints, they told me secretly that if I would go with them I should be a very great lord, for having seen these things. I doubted that after they had conducted me there I should ever have been able to return to my country, and therefore I abstained from going. When we had arrived in the island of Bornei, which is distant from Monoch about two hundred miles, we found it to be somewhat larger than the above mentioned, and much lower. The people of this island are pagans, and are good people. Their colour is more white than otherwise. Their dress consists of a cotton shirt, and some go clothed in camelots. Some wear red caps. In this island justice is strictly administered, and every year a very great quantity of camphor is shipped, which they say grows there, and which is the gum of a tree. If it be so, I have not seen it, and therefore I do not affirm it. Here my companion chartered a vessel for one hundred ducats.

¶ When the chartered vessel was supplied with provisions, we took our way towards the beautiful island called Giava [Java], at which we arrived in five days, sailing towards the south. The captain of the said ship carried the compass with the magnet after our manner, and had a chart which was all marked with lines, perpendicular and across. My companion asked the Christians: "Now that we have lost the north star, how does he steer us? Is there any other north star than this by which we steer?" The Christians asked the captain of the ship this same thing, and he showed us four or five stars, among which there was one which he said was *contrario della* (opposite to) our north star, and that he sailed by the north because the magnet was adjusted and subjected to our north. He also told us that on the other side of the said island, towards the south, there are some other races, who navigate by the said four or five stars opposite to ours; and, moreover, they gave us to understand that beyond the said island the day does not last more than four hours, and that there it was colder than in any other part of the world. Hearing this we were much pleased and satisfied.

CHAPTER XIV

CONCERNING THE ISLAND OF JAVA

FOLLOWING then our route, in five days we arrived at this island of Giava, in which there are many kingdoms, the kings of which are pagans. Their faith is this: some adore idols as they do in Calicut, and there are some who worship the sun, others the moon; many worship the ox; a great many the first thing they meet in the morning; and others worship the devil in the manner I have already told you. This island produces an immense quantity of silk, part in our manner and part wild, and the best emeralds in the world are found here, and gold and copper in great quantity; very much grain, like ours, and excellent fruits like those of Calicut. Animal food of all kinds, like ours, is found in this country. I believe that these inhabitants are the most trustworthy men in the world: they are white and of about our stature, but they have the face much broader than ours, their eyes large and green, the nose much depressed, and the hair long. The birds here are in great multitudes, and all different from ours excepting the peacocks, turtle-doves, and black crows, which three kinds are like ours. The strictest justice is administered among these people, and they go clothed *all' apostolica* in stuffs of silk, camelot, and cotton, and they do not use many arms, because those only fight who go to sea. These carry bows, and the greater part darts of cane. Some also use *zara-bottane* [*sumpîtan*] (blow-pipes), with which they throw poisoned darts; and they throw them with the mouth, and, however little they draw blood, the (wounded) person dies. No artillery of any kind is used here, nor do they know at all how to make it. These people eat bread made of corn; some also eat the flesh of sheep, or of stags, or, indeed, of wild hogs, and some others eat fish and fruits.

¶ The people in this island who eat flesh, when their fathers become so old that they can no longer do any work, their children or relations set them up in the market-place for sale, and those who purchase them kill them and eat them cooked. And if any young man should be attacked by any great sickness, and that it should appear to the skilful that he might die of it, the father or the brother of the sick man kills him, and they do not wait for him to die. And when they have killed him they sell him to others to be eaten. We, being astonished at such a thing, some merchants of the country said to us: "O you poor Persians, why do you leave such charming flesh to be eaten by the worms?" My companion hearing this immediately exclaimed: "Quick, quick, let us go to our ship, for these people shall never more come near me on land."

¶ The Christians said to my companion: "O my friend, take this news to your country, and take this other also which we will show you. Look there, now that it is mid-day, turn your eyes towards where the sun sets." And raising our eyes we saw that the sun cast a shadow to the left more than a *palmo*. And by this we understood that we were far distant from our country, at which we remained exceedingly astonished. And, according to what my companion said, I think that this was the month of June; for I had lost our months, and sometimes the name of the day. You must know that there is little difference between the cold with us and here. Having seen the customs of this island, it appeared to us that there was not much reason to remain in it, because it was necessary to be all night on guard for fear some wretch should come and carry us off to eat us. Wherefore, having called the Christians, we told them that, as soon as they could, we would return to our country. Before we departed, however, my companion bought two emeralds for a thousand *pardai*, and he purchased for two hundred *pardai* two little children who had no sexual organs; for in this island there are a kind of merchants, who follow no other trade excepting that of purchasing little children, from whom they cut off in their childhood everything, and they remain like women.

CHAPTER XV

CONCERNING THE RETURN TO CALICUT

HAVING remained in this island of Giava altogether fourteen days, we determined to return back, because, partly through the fear of their cruelty in eating men, partly also through the extreme cold, we did not dare to proceed farther, and also because there was hardly any other place known to them (the Christians). Wherefore we chartered a large vessel, that is, a *giunco* [junk], and took our way outside the islands towards the east; because on this side there is no archipelago, and the navigation is more safe. We sailed for fifteen days and arrived at the city of Melacha, and here we stopped for three days, where our Christian companions remained, whose bewailings and lamentations it would be impossible shortly to describe; so that, truly, if I had not had a wife and children, I would have gone with them. And likewise they said, that if they had known how to come in safety, they would have accompanied us. And I believe also that my companion comforted them for not coming, because they would not be obliged to give an account to the Christians of so many lords who are in their country, who are also Christians and possess immense riches. So that they remained, saying that they would return to Sarnau [Siam], and we went with our ship to Cioromandel [Negapatam]. The captain of the ship said that around the island of Giava, and around the island of Sumatra, there were more than eight thousand islands. Wherefore my companion bought in Melacha five thousand *pardai* worth of small spices, and silk stuffs, and odoriferous things. We sailed for fifteen days, and arrived at the said city of Cioromandel, and here the ship chartered in Giava was unladen. We remained in this country about twenty days, and then took a ship, that is to say, a *ciampana* [a large junk], and went to Colon [Quilon], where I found twenty-two Portuguese Christians. On which account I had a very great desire to escape, but I remained, because they were few, and I was afraid of the Moors; for there were some merchants with us who knew that I had been at Mecha and to the body of Mahomet, and I was afraid that they might imagine that I should discover their hypocrisies, wherefore I abstained from running away. Twelve days afterwards we took our route towards Calicut, that is, by the river [*i.e.* the backwater], and arrived there in the space of ten days.

¶ Now it will be an easy thing for every kind reader to perceive, by the long discourse concerning various countries contained in the above written books, that my companion and myself having become wearied, partly by the different temperatures of the air as may be imagined, partly by the different customs we met with at every step as has been described, and especially by the inhuman men not unlike beasts, determined to return. I will now recount shortly, (in order that my narrative may not be wearisome,) what happened to me on our return, because it will be useful to some either in restraining their too eager appetite for seeing the inestimable greatness of the world, or, being on their road, in knowing how to regulate themselves and use their understanding in sudden emergencies. Being then arrived in Calicut on our return, as I have shortly before written, we found two Christians who were Milanese [*i.e.* Italians]. One was called Ioan-Maria, and the other Pietro Antonio, who had arrived from Portugal with the ships of the Portuguese, and had come to purchase jewels on the part of the king. And when they had arrived in Cocin [Cochin], they fled to Calicut. Truly I never had greater pleasure than in seeing these two Christians. They and I went naked after the custom of the country. I asked them if they were Christians. Ioan-Maria answered: "Yes, truly we are." And then Pietro Antonio asked me if I was a Christian. I answered: "Yes, God be praised." Then he took me by the hand, and led me into his house. And when we had arrived at the house, we began to embrace and kiss each other, and to weep. Truly, I could not speak like a Christian: it appeared as though my tongue were large and hampered, for I had been four years without speaking with Christians. The night following I remained with them; and neither of them, nor could I, either eat or sleep solely for the great joy we had. You may imagine that we could have wished that that night might have lasted for a year, that we might talk together of various things, amongst which I asked them if they were friends of the King of Calicut. They replied that they were his chief men, and that they spoke with him every day. I asked them also what was their intention. They told me that they would willingly have returned to their country, but that they did not know by what way. I answered them: "Return by the way you came." They said that that was not possible, because they had escaped from the Portuguese, and that the King of Calicut had obliged them to make a great quantity of artillery against their will, and on this account they did not wish to return by that route; and they said that they expected the fleet of the King of Portugal very soon. I answered them, that if God granted me so much grace that I might be able to escape to Cananor when the fleet had arrived, I would so act that the captain of the Christians should pardon them; and I told them that it was not possible for them to escape by any other way, because it was known through many nations that they made artillery. And many kings had wished to have them in their hands on account of their skill, and therefore it was not possible to escape in any other manner. And you must know that they had made between four and five hundred pieces of ordnance large and small, so that in short they had very great fear of the Portuguese; and in truth there was reason to be afraid, for not only did they make the artillery themselves, but they also taught the pagans to make it; and they told me, moreover, that they had taught fifteen servants of the king to fire *spingarde*. And during the time I was here, they gave to a pagan the design and form of a mortar, which weighed one hundred and five *cantara*, and was made of metal. There was also a Jew here who had built a very beautiful galley, and had made four mortars of iron. The said Jew, going to wash himself in a pond of water, was drowned. Let us return to the said Christians: God knows what I said to them, exhorting them not to commit such an act against Christians. Piero Antonio wept incessantly, and Ioan-Maria said it was the same to him whether he died in Calicut or in Rome, and that God had ordained what was to be.

¶ The next morning I returned to find my companion, who was making great lamentation, for he thought that I had been killed. I told him, in order to excuse myself, that I had been to sleep in a Moorish mosque to render thanks to God and to Mahomet for the benefit received in that we had returned in safety, and with this he was much pleased. And in order that I might be able to know what was going on in the country, I told him that I would continue to sleep in the mosque, and that I did not want any goods, but that I wished always to be poor. And wishing to escape from them, I thought that I could only deceive them by hypocrisy; for the Moors are the most stupid people in the world, so that he was satisfied. And this I did in order that I might be able to talk frequently with the Christians, because they knew everything, from day to day, from the court of the king. I began to put my hypocrisy in practice, and pretended to be a Moorish saint, and never would eat flesh excepting in the house of Ioan-Maria, where every night we ate two brace of fowls. And I would no longer associate with merchants, neither did any man ever see me smile, and all day I remained in the mosque excepting when he (my companion) sent for me to go and eat; and he scolded me because I would not eat flesh. I replied: "That too much eating leads man to many sins." And in this manner, I began to be a Moorish saint, and happy was he who could kiss my hand and some my knees.

¶ It happening that a Moorish merchant fell sick of a very great malady, and could not by any means get natural relief, he sent to my companion, who was a great friend of his, to know if he or anyone in his house could give him any remedy. He answered that I would go to visit him; and so he and I together went to the house of the sick man and questioned him about his illness. He said to us: "I feel very bad in my stomach and bowels." I asked him if he had had any cold by which this illness might have been caused? The sick man replied: "That it could not be cold, for he did not know what that was." Then my companion turned to me and asked me: "O Iunus, dost thou know any remedy for this my friend?" I replied: "That my father was a physician in my country, and that that which I knew, I knew by the practice which he had taught me." My companion said: "Well, then, let us see if by any remedy this merchant, my very dear friend, can be relieved." Then I said: "*Bizmilei erechman erathin!*" and then I took his hand, and, feeling his pulse, found that he had a great deal of fever, and I asked him if his head ached. He replied: "Yes, it aches very much." Then I asked him if his bowels were relieved. He answered: "They had not been relieved for three days." I immediately thought to myself, this man has an overloaded stomach, and to assist him he requires an injection; and saying so to my companion he replied: "Do what you like, so that he be cured." Then I made preparation for the injection in this wise: I took sugar, eggs, and salt, and for the decoction I took certain herbs, which did more harm than good: the said herbs were such as leaves of walnuts. And in this way, in the course of a day and a night, I administered five injections to him; and it did him no good on account of the herbs, which produced a contrary effect, so that I should have been glad had I not been involved in such a task. At length, seeing that he could not obtain relief on account of the wretched herbs, I took a good bunch of purslain, and made about half a jug of liquor, and put in it the same quantity of oil, and a good deal of salt and sugar, and then strained it all well. And here I committed another blunder, for I forgot to warm it, and administered it cold as it was. As soon as the injection was administered, I tied a cord to his feet, and we hoisted him up until he touched the ground with his hands and head, and we held him up thus high for the space of half a quarter of an hour. My companion said: "O Iunus, is it the custom to do thus in your country?" I replied: "Yes, when the sick man is *in extremis*." He said that that was a good reason, for in that position the mixture would penetrate better. The poor sick man cried out and said: "*Matile, Matile, gnancia tu poi, gnancia tu poi!*" that is, "No more, no more, for I am killed; I am killed!" and so we standing there to comfort him, whether it were God or nature, his bowels began to act like a fountain, and we immediately let him down; and truly he was relieved to the extent of half a vat full, and he was well pleased. On the following day he had neither fever nor pain in his head or stomach, and, after that, he was relieved several times.

¶ The next morning, he said that he felt pain in his side. I made him take cow or buffalo butter and anoint himself and bind himself up with hemp tow, and then I told him that if he wished to be cured he must eat twice a day, and before eating, I wished him to walk a mile on foot. He replied: "*O nonal irami tino biria biria gnancia tu poi,*" that is, "If you do not wish me to eat more than twice in the day, I shall be dead very soon"; for they eat eight or ten times a day. This order appeared to him very severe. However, at last he was very well cured, and this gained great credit for my hypocrisy. They said that I was the friend of God. This merchant wished to give me ten ducats, but I would not receive anything. I even gave three ducats which I had to the poor, and this I did publicly in order that they might know that I did not want any property or money. From this time forward happy was he who could take me to his house to eat, happy was he who kissed my hands and feet; and when anyone kissed my hands, I kept my ground steadily, giving him to understand that he did an act which I deserved, as being a saint. But it was my companion above all who procured me credit, because he also believed me, and said that I did not eat flesh, and that he had seen me at Mecca, and at the body of Mahomet, and that I had always travelled in his company, and that he knew my manners, and that I was truly a saint, and that, knowing me to be of a good and holy life, he had given me one of his nieces for my wife, so that, in this way every man wished me well, and every night I went secretly to talk with the Christians, who told me, on one occasion, that twelve Portuguese ships had come to Canonor. Then I said, now is the time for me to escape from the hands of dogs, and we considered together for eight days in what manner I could escape. They advised me to escape by land, but I had not the courage, through the fear that I might be killed by the Moors, I being white and they black.

¶ One day, while eating with my companion, two Persian merchants of Canonor arrived, whom he immediately called to eat with him. They answered: "We have no wish to eat and bring bad news." We asked them: "What words are these which you utter?" They said: "Twelve ships of the Portuguese have arrived, which we have seen with our eyes." My companion asked: "What people are they?" The Persians replied: "They are Christians, and are all armed in white arms, and they have commenced building a very strong castle in Canonor." My companion turned to me and asked me: "O Iunus, what people are these Portuguese?" I answered him: "Do not speak to me of such a race, for they are all thieves and corsairs of the sea, and I should like to see them all of our Mahommedan faith." Hearing this he became very malignant, and I rejoiced much in my heart.

¶ On the following day all the Moors, having heard the news, went to the mosque to say their prayers. But first some, deputed to this office, mounted the tower of their church, as is the custom amongst them three or four times a day, and, instead of bells, began with a loud voice to call the others to this same prayer, keeping one finger constantly in their ear and saying [the *azân* or call to prayer]: "*Alla u eccubar, Allà u eccubar, aialassale aialassale aialalfale aialalfale Alla u eccubar leilla illala esciadu ana Mahometh resullala*," that is, "God is great, God is great, come to the church, come to the church, come to praise God, come to praise God, God is great, God is great, God was, God will be, Mahometh the messenger of God will rise again." And they took me also with them, saying to me that they wished to pray to God for the Moors; and so they set me publicly to make the prayer, which you shall hear, which prayer is as common with them as the Pater Noster is with us, and the Ave Maria. The Moors stand all in a row; but there are many rows, and they have a priest as we have, who, after they have well washed, begins to pronounce the prayer in this manner, saying [the *fâtiha*, daily prayer]: "*Un gibilei nimi saithan e regin bizimilei erachman erachinal hamdulile ara blaharami erachman erachin malichi iaum edmi iachie nabudu hiachie nesta himi edina sarathel mostachina ledina ana antha alyhin gayril magdubin alehyhimu ualla da lim amin alla u eccubar.*" And so I pronounced the prayer [the opening verses of the Koran] in the presence of all the people, and then I returned home with my companion. On the next day I pretended to be very ill, and remained about eight days wherein I would not eat with him, but every night I went to eat with the two Christians. He (my companion) was very much surprised, and asked me why I would not eat. I replied: "That I felt very ill, and my head felt as though it were very large and full; and I said to him that it appeared to me that it proceeded from that air, that it was not good for me." He, for the singular affection which he bore me, would have done everything to please me; wherefore, hearing that the air of Calicut was injurious to me, he said to me: "Go and stay in Canonor until we return to Persia, and I will direct you to a friend of mine, who will give you all that you require." I answered him: "That I would gladly go to Canonor, but I hesitated because of those Christians." "Do not hesitate," said he, "nor have any fear of them, for you shall remain constantly in the city." Finally, having well seen all the fleet which was preparing in Calicut, and all the artillery, and the army which had been raised against the Christians, I set out on my journey to give them notice of it, and to save myself from the hands of dogs.

¶ One day, before I set out, I arranged all that I had to do with the two Christians, and then my companion placed me in the company of those two Persians who carried the news of the Portuguese, and we took a little bark. Now, you will understand in what danger I placed myself, because there were twenty-four Persian, Syrian, and Turkish merchants, all of whom knew me, and bore me great affection, and knew well what the genius of Christians was. I feared that if I took leave of them, they would think that I wanted to escape to the Portuguese. If I departed without speaking with them, and I was by chance discovered, they would have said to me: "Why did you not speak to us?" And this I balanced in my mind. However, I determined to go without speaking to any one excepting my companion. On Thursday morning, the third of September, I set out with the two Persians by sea, and when we had got about a bow-shot in the sea, four Naeri [Nairs] came to the sea-shore, who called the captain of the vessel, and we immediately returned to land. The Naeri said to the captain: "Why do you carry away this man without leave of the king?" The Persians answered: "This man is a Moorish saint, and we are going to Canonor." "We know well," said the Naeri, "that he is a Moorish saint, but he understands the language of the Portuguese, and will tell them all we are doing here, because a great fleet is being got ready"; and they ordered the captain of the ship that he should not take me away on any account, and he acted accordingly. We remained on the sea-shore, and the Naeri returned to the king's house. One of the Persians said: "Let us go to our house," that is, to Calicut. I answered: "Do not go, for you will lose these fine *sinabaph* (which were pieces of cloth we carried), because you have not paid the king's dues." The other Persians said: "O sir, what shall we do?" I replied: "Let us go along this shore until we find a *parao*," that is, a small bark; and they were pleased so to do, and we took our way for twelve miles, always by land, laden with the said goods. You may imagine how my heart felt, seeing myself in such danger. At length we found a *parao* which carried us to Canonor. We arrived at

Canonor on Saturday evening, and I immediately carried a letter which my companion had written for me to a merchant his friend; the tenor of which letter stated that he should do as much for me as for his own person until he came; and he told him about my being a saint, and of the relationship there was between him and me. The merchant, as soon as he had read the letter, laid it on his head and said, that he would answer for me with his head; and immediately had an excellent supper prepared, with many chickens and pigeons. When the two Persians saw the chickens come, they exclaimed: "Alas, what do you do?" "*Colli tinu ille*," that is, "This man does not eat flesh"; and other things came immediately. When we had finished eating, the said Persians said to me: "Let us go a little to the sea to amuse ourselves"; and so we went where the Portuguese fleet was. Imagine, O reader, the joy I felt. Going a little farther, I saw before a certain low house three empty casks, from which I imagined that the factory of the Christians was there. Then, being somewhat cheered up, I felt a desire to escape within the said gate; but I considered that, if I did so in their presence, the whole country would be in an uproar. And I, not being able to fly in safety, noted the place where the castle of the Christians was being made, and determined to wait until the following day.

CHAPTER XVI

CONCERNING THE ESCAPE TO THE PORTUGUESE

On Sunday morning I rose early, and said that I would go to amuse myself a little. My companions answered: "Go where you please"; and so I took my way according to my fancy, and went where the castle of the Christians was being built; and when I was a little distant from my companions, coming to the sea-shore I met two Portuguese Christians, and said to them: "O sirs, where is the fortress of the Portuguese?" These two Christians said: "Are you a Christian?" I answered; "Yes, sir, praised be God." And they said to me: "Where do you come from?" I answered them: "I come from Calicut." Then said the one to the other of the two companions: "Go you to the factory, and I will take this man to Don Lorenzo," that is, the son of the Viceroy. And so he conducted me to the said castle, which is distant from the beach half a mile. And when we arrived at the said castle, the Señor Don Lorenzo was at breakfast. I immediately fell on my knees at the feet of his lordship and said: "Sir, I commend myself to you to save me, for I am a Christian."

At this juncture, we heard a great uproar in the neighbourhood because I had escaped. The bombardiers were immediately summoned, who loaded all the artillery, fearing that those of the city might come to the castle to fight. Then the captain, seeing that those of the place did not do any harm, took me by the hand and conducted me into a chamber to interrogate me concerning the affairs of Calicut, and kept me three days to talk with me; and I, being desirous of the victory of the Christians, gave them all the particulars about the fleet preparing in Calicut. These conversations being concluded, he sent me with a galley to the Viceroy his father in Cuccin, of which a knight named Joan Sarrano was captain. The Viceroy was exceedingly pleased when I arrived, and showed me great distinction, because I had informed him of all that was doing in Calicut; and I also said, that if his lordship would pardon Ioan-Maria and Piero Antonio, who made artillery in Calicut, and assure me of their safety, that I would induce them to return, and that they would not do that injury to Christians which they had done, although against their will, and that they were afraid to return without a safe conduct. The Viceroy was extremely pleased and much satisfied, and gave me the safe conduct; and the captains of our ships and our vicar promised for the Viceroy; and at the end of three days he sent me back with the said galley to Canonor, and gave me a letter which he addressed to his son, that he should give me as much money as I required for payment of the spies to be sent to Calicut. When we had arrived at Canonor, I found a pagan, who gave me his wife and children as a pledge, and I sent him with my letters to Calicut, to Ioan-Maria and Pietro Antonio, by which I advised them how the Viceroy had pardoned them, and that they might come in safety. You must know that I sent the spy five times backwards and forwards, and that I always wrote to them that they should be on their guard, and should not trust their wives or their slave; for each of them had a wife, and Ioan-Maria had a son and a slave. They always wrote to me that they would come willingly. In the last letter they said to me thus: "Lodovico, we have given all our goods to this spy; come on such a night with a galley or brigantine where the fishermen are, because there is no watch in that part, and, if it please God, we will both come with all our party." You must know that I wrote to them that they should come alone, and that they should leave their wives, their son, their goods, and the slave, and that they should only bring their jewels and money. And you must know that they had a diamond which weighed thirty-two carats, which they said was worth thirty-five thousand ducats; and they had a pearl which weighed twenty-four carats; and they had two thousand rubies, which weighed a carat and a carat and a half each; and they had sixty-four rings with set jewels; and they had one thousand four hundred *pardai*; and they also wished to save seven *spingarde* and three apes, and two civet-cats, and the wheel for repairing jewels; so that their avarice caused their death. Their slave, who was of Calicut, saw that they wanted to escape, and immediately went to the king and told him everything. The king did not believe him. Nevertheless, he sent five Naeri to their house to remain in their company. The slave, seeing that the king would not put them to death, went to the Cadi of the faith of the Moors, and repeated to him those same words which he had said to the king, and, moreover, he told him that they informed the Christians of all that was done in Calicut. The Moorish Cadi held a council with all the Moorish merchants, amongst whom were collected one hundred ducats, which they carried to the King of the Gioghi, who was at that time in Calicut with three thousand Gioghi [*jôgî*, ascetics], to whom the said Moors said: "Sir, thou knowest that in other years when thou hast come here we have shown thee much kindness, and more honour than we show thee now; the reason is this: there are here two Christians who are enemies of our faith and yours, who inform the Portuguese of all that is done in this country; wherefore, we beseech thee to kill them, and to take these hundred ducats." The King of the Gioghi immediately sent two hundred men to kill the said two Christians, and when they went to their house, they began by tens to sound their horns and demand alms. And when the Christians saw so many people increasing they said: "These want something else besides alms"; and began to fight, so that these two killed six of them, and wounded more than forty. At last, these Gioghi cast at them certain pieces of iron which are made round like a wheel [quoits], and they threw them with a sling, and struck Ioan-Maria on the head and Pietro Antonio on the head, so that they fell to the ground; and then they ran upon them and cut open the veins of their throats, and with their hands they drank their blood. The wife of Ioan-Maria escaped with her son to Canonor, and I purchased the son for eight ducats of gold, and had him baptised on St. Lawrence's day, and gave him the name of Lorenzo, because I baptised him on that same day, and at the end of a year on that same day he died of the French disease. You must know that I have seen this disease three thousand miles beyond Calicut, and it is called *pua*, and they say that it is about seventeen years since it began, and it is much worse than ours.

¶ On the twelfth of March 1506, this news of the Christians being killed arrived. On this same day the immense fleet departed from Pannani [Ponânî], and from Calicut, and from Capogat [Kapata], and from

Pandarani, and from Tormapatan [Pandalâyinî and Dharmapatam]. All this fleet was two hundred and nine sail, of which eighty-four were large ships, and the remainder were rowing vessels, that is, *paraos* [*prahu*, prow]. In which fleet there was an infinite number of armed Moors; and they wore certain red garments of cloth stuffed with cotton, and they wore certain large caps stuffed, and also on the arms bracelets and gloves stuffed; and a great number of bows and lances, swords and shields, and large and small artillery after our custom. When we saw this fleet, which was on the 16th of the month above-mentioned, truly, seeing so many ships together, it appeared as though one saw a very large wood. We Christians always hoped that God would aid us to confound the pagan faith. And the most valiant knight, the captain of the fleet, son of Don Francisco dal Meda [d'Almeida], Viceroy of India, was here with eleven ships, amongst which there were two galleys and one brigantine. When he saw such a multitude of ships, he acted like a most valiant captain: he called to him all his knights and men of the said ships, and then began to exhort and beseech them that, for the love of God and of the Christian faith, they would expose themselves willingly to suffer death, saying in this wise: "O sirs, O brothers, now is the day that we must remember the Passion of Christ, and how much pain He endured to redeem us sinners. Now is that day when all our sins will be blotted out. For this I beseech you that we determine to go vigorously against these dogs; for I hope that God will give us the victory, and will not choose that His faith should fail." And then the spiritual father stood upon the ship of the said captain, with the crucifix in his hand, and delivered a beautiful discourse to all, exhorting us to do that which we were bound to do. And then he gave us absolution from punishment and sin, and said: "Now, my sons, let us all go willingly, for God will be with us." And he knew so well how to speak, that the greater part of us wept, and prayed God that He would cause us to die in that battle. In the meantime the immense fleet of the Moors came towards us to pass by. On that same day, our captain departed with two ships and went towards the Moors, and passed between two ships, which were the largest in the Moorish fleet. And when he passed between the said ships, he saluted both of them with very great discharges of artillery; and this our captain did in order to know these two ships, and how they behaved; for they carried very great ensigns, and were captains of all the fleet. Nothing more was done that day. Early on the following morning, the Moors began all to make sail and come towards the city of Canonor, and sent to our captain to say that he should let them pass and go on their voyage, for they did not wish to fight with Christians.

Our captain sent to them to say, that the Moors of Calicut would not allow Christians to return who were staying in Calicut in their faith, but killed forty-eight of them, and robbed them of three thousand ducats between goods and money. And then he said to them: "Pass, if pass you can, but first know what sort of people Christians are." Said the Moors: "Our Mahomet will defend us from you Christians"; and so began all to sail with the greatest fury, wishing to pass, and they always navigate near the land, eight or ten miles. Our captain allowed them to come until they arrived opposite the city of Canonor. Our captain did his because the King of Canonor was looking on, and to show him how great was the courage of the Christians. And when it was the time for eating, the wind began to freshen a little, and our captain said: "Now, up brothers, for now is the time; for we are all good knights"; and began to go towards these two largest ships. It would be impossible to describe to you the kinds of instruments which they sounded, according to their custom. Our captain grappled valiantly with one of the ships of the Moors, that is, the largest, and three times the Moors threw off our grappling-irons; at the fourth time we remained fast, and immediately our Christians leaped on board the said ship, in which there were six hundred Moors. Here, a most cruel battle was fought with immense effusion of blood, so that not one escaped from this ship: they were all killed. Then our captain went to find the other very large ship of the Moors, which was now grappled fast by another of our ships; and here also a cruel battle was fought, in which five hundred Moors died. When these two large ships were taken, all the rest of the fleet of the Moors fought with desperation, and divided our sixteen ships, so that there were some of our ships which had around them fifteen or twenty of those of the Moors to fight. It was a beautiful sight to see the gallant deeds of a very valiant captain, Ioan Sarano [João Serrão], who, with a galley made such a slaughter of the Moors as it is impossible to describe. And there was a time when he had around his galley fifty vessels, some with oars and some with sails, and all with artillery. And by the grace of God, neither in the galley nor in the ships was any one of the Christians killed, but many were wounded, for the fighting lasted all that day. Once our brigantine separated a little from the ships, and was immediately placed in the middle of four of the Moorish ships; and they fought her sharply, and at one time fifteen Moors were on the brigantine, so that the Christians had all withdrawn to the poop. When the valiant captain named Simon Martin saw that there were so many Moors upon the brigantine, he leaped amongst these dogs, and said: "O Jesus Christ, give us the victory! help thy faith!" and with the sword in his hand he cut off the heads of six or seven. All the other Moors threw themselves into the sea and fled, some here, some there. When the other Moors saw that this brigantine had gained the victory, four other ships went to succour their people. The captain of the brigantine, seeing the said Moors coming, immediately took a barrel which had contained powder, and then he took a piece of a sail and thrust it in the bung-hole of the said barrel, which appeared like the stone of a mortar, and he put a handful of powder over the barrel, and standing with fire in his hand, made as though he were going to fire a mortar. The Moors, seeing this, thought that the said barrel was a mortar, and immediately turned back. And the said captain withdrew where the Christians were with his brigantine, victorious. Our captain then placed himself amongst these dogs, of whom seven ships were captured, laden in part with spices and in part with other merchandise; and nine or ten were sunk by our artillery, amongst which there was one laden with elephants. When the Moors saw so many of their ships sunk, and that the two ships, the captains of the fleet and others were taken, they immediately took to flight, some one way, some another, some by land, some by sea, some in the port, some in the opposite direction. At the conclusion, our captain, seeing all our ships safe, said: "Praised be Jesus Christ, let us follow up our victory against these dogs"; and so we all together set ourselves to follow them. Truly, to any one who had seen these dogs fly, it would have appeared that they had a fleet of a hundred ships behind them. And this battle commenced with the hour for eating and lasted until the evening. And then they were pursued all night, so that all this fleet was put to flight without the death of a single Christian; and our ships which remained here followed another large ship, which was tacking out at sea. Finally our ships prevailed over theirs, which was surrounded by us, so that all the Moors cast themselves [into the sea] to swim, and we constantly followed them to the shore in the skiff, with crossbows and lances killing and wounding them. But some saved themselves by dint of swimming, and these were as many as two hundred persons, who swam more than twenty miles, sometimes under and sometimes on the water, and sometimes we thought they were dead, when they rose again to the surface a crossbow-shot distant from us. And when we came near them to kill them, thinking that they were exhausted, they dived again under the water; so that their being able to continue swimming so long appeared like a very great miracle. At last, however, the greater part were killed, and their ship sank from the blows of our artillery. On the following morning, our captain sent the galleys, the brigantine, with some other vessels, along the shore, to see what bodies they could count. They found that those who were killed on the shore and at sea, and those of the ships taken, were counted at three thousand six hundred dead bodies. You must know that many others were killed when they took to flight, who threw themselves into the sea. The King of Canonor, seeing all this battle, said: "These Christians are very brave and valiant men." And truly I have found myself in some battles in my time, but I never saw any men more brave than these Portuguese. The next day after, we returned to our Viceroy, who was at Cuccin [Cochin]. I leave you to imagine how great was the joy of the Viceroy and of the King of Cuccin, who is a true friend of the King of Portugal, on seeing us return victorious.

¶ Let us leave the fleet of the King of Calicut, which was defeated, and return to my own affairs. At the end of three months, the Viceroy gave me, of his favour, a certain office, which was that of the factorship of these parts, and I remained in this office about a year and a half. Some months afterwards, my lord the Viceroy sent me by a ship to Canonor, because many merchants of Calicut went to Canonor, and took the safe conduct from the Christians by giving them to understand that they were of Canonor, and that they wished to pass with merchandise in the ships of Canonor, and which was not true. Wherefore, the Viceroy sent me to these merchants, and to understand these frauds. It happened at this time that the King of Canonor died, and the next king that was made was a great enemy of ours; wherefore the King of Calicut made him [king] by force of money, and lent him twenty-three pieces of artillery (*bocche di fuoco*). In 1507, there commenced a very great war on the 27th of April, and it continued until the 17th of August. Now, you shall understand what the Christian faith is, and what sort of men the Portuguese are. One day, the Christians going to get water, the Moors assaulted them, through the great hatred they bore us. Our people retired into the fortress, which was now in a good state, and no harm was done on that day. Our captain, who was called Lorenzo de Britto, sent to inform the Viceroy, who was at Cuccin, of this new occurrence; and Don Lorenzo immediately came with a *caravella*, furnished with everything that was necessary, and at the expiration of four days the said Don Lorenzo returned to Cuccin, and we remained to fight with these dogs, and we were not more than two hundred men. Our food consisted solely of rice, sugar, and nuts, and we had no water to drink within the castle; but twice a week we were obliged to take water from a certain well, which was a bow-shot distant from the castle. And every time we went for water, we always were obliged to take it by force of arms; and every time we skirmished with them, the least people that came were twenty-four thousand, and sometimes there were thirty thousand, forty thousand, and fifty thousand persons, who had bows, lances, swords, and shields, with more than one hundred and forty pieces of artillery between large and small, and they wore a kind of armour, as I have explained to you in the fleet of Calicut. Their fighting was in this wise: Two or three thousand came on at a time, and bringing with them the sounds of divers instruments, and with fireworks, and they ran with such fury, that truly they would have inspired with fear ten thousand people; but the most valiant Christians went to meet them beyond the well, and they never approached the fortress within two stones'-cast. We were obliged to be on our guard, both before and behind, because sometimes there came of these Moors by sea with sixty *praos* to take us in the midst of them. Nevertheless, every day we fought we killed ten, fifteen, and twenty of them, and not more, because as soon as they saw some of their people killed they took to flight. But on one occasion, amongst others, a mortar called the Serpent, at one discharge killed eighteen of them, and they never killed one of us. They said that we kept the devil, who defended us. This war from the twenty-seventh of April never ceased until the twenty-seventh of August. Then the fleet of the Portuguese came, of which the most valiant knight Tristan da Cugna [Tristão d'Acunha or da Cunha] was captain; to which, when it arrived at Canonor, we signalled that we were at war; and the prudent captain immediately had all the boats of the fleet armed, and sent us three hundred knights all armed in white armour, so that, had it not been for our captain, as soon as they landed we would have gone to burn the whole of the city of Canonor. Think, O kind reader, what was our joy when we saw such succour; for, in truth, we were almost exhausted, and the greater part were wounded. When the Moors saw our fleet arrive, they sent an ambassador, who was named Mamal Maricar [Mâmale Mârikkâr], who was the richest man in the country, and he came to demand peace; wherefore we sent at once to the Viceroy, who was in Cuccin, to know what was to be done. The Viceroy sent to say, that we should make peace without delay, and so it was done. And this he did only that he might be able to load the ships and send them to Portugal. Four days being past, there came two merchants of Canonor, who were friends of mine before war had been made, and they spoke with me in this manner, as you shall understand. "*Fattore, on maniciar in ghene ballia nochignan candile ornal patu maniciar patance maniciar hiriva tu maniciar cia tu poi nal nur malabari nochi ornal totu ille cura po*"; that is, "O factor, show me a man who is a *brazzo* larger than any of you, who every day has killed ten, fifteen, and twenty of us, and the Naeri were sometimes four hundred and five hundred firing at him and never once could they touch him." I answered him in this manner: "*Idu manicar nicando inghene ille Cocin poi*"; that is, "This man is not here, but is gone to Cocin." Then I thought that this was other than a Christian, and I said to him: "*Giangal ingabani manaton undo.*" One of them answered: "*Undo.*" I said to him: "*Idu maniciar nicando Portogal ille.*" He replied: "*Sui e indi.*" I said: "*Tamarani Portugal idu.*" He answered: "*Tamerani ni Patanga cioli ocha malamar Patangnu idu Portogal ille Tamaran Portugal piga nammi*"; that is, I said to him: "My friend, come here, that knight whom thou hast seen is not a Portuguese, but he is the God of the Portuguese and of all the world." He replied: "By God, thou sayest the truth; for all the Naeri said that that was not a Portuguese, but that he was their God, and that the God of the Christians was better than theirs, and they did not know him, so that it appeared to all that it was a miracle of God." See what kind of people they are, who stood sometimes ten and twelve hours to see our bell ring, and looked upon it as something miraculous, and when the bell did not ring any longer, they said in this wise: "*Idu maniciar totu, idu parangnu tot ille parangnu ille Tamarani Portogal perga nan nu*"; that is, "These people touch that bell and it speaks; when they do not touch it any longer it does not speak any more; this God of Portugal is very good." And, again, some of these Moors were present at our mass, and when the body of Christ was shown, I said to them: "That is the God of Portugal, and of the pagans, and of all the world." And they replied: "You say the truth, but we do not know Him"; wherefore it may be understood that they sin without knowledge. There are, however, some of these who are great enchanters. We have seen them grasp serpents which, if they touch [bite?] any one, he immediately falls to the earth dead. Also I tell you that they are the greatest and the most expert workmen, I believe, in all the world.

¶ Now, the time approached for the return homewards, for the captain of the fleet began to load the ships to return to Portugal, and I, having been seven years from my own house, and from my love and good feeling towards my country, and also in order that I might carry to it an account of a great part of the world, was constrained to ask leave of my lord the Viceroy, which of his grace he granted to me, and said that he wished me first to go with him where you shall know. Wherefore, he and all his company put ourselves in order in white armour, so that few people remained in Cucin, and on the twenty-fourth of November of the year above mentioned we made the assault within the port of Pannani [Ponânî]. On that day we came before the city of Pannani. On the next morning, two hours before day, the Viceroy summoned all the boats of the ships with all the people of the fleet, and told them how that was the country which made war upon us more than any other country in India, and therefore he begged us all that we would go with a good will to attack that place, which truly is stronger than any other on that coast. When the Viceroy had spoken, the spiritual father made such a discourse that every one wept, and many said that for the love of God they were willing to die in that place. A little before day, we began a most deadly war against those dogs, who were eight thousand, and we were about six hundred. But it is true that the two galleys did not do much, because they could not approach so near to the land as the boats. The first knight who leapt on shore was the valiant knight, Don Lorenzo [Lourenço d'Almeida], son of the Viceroy. The second boat was that of the Viceroy, in which I was, and at the first assault a cruel battle took place, because here the river was very narrow; and on the border of the city there were a great many mortars, of which we captured more than forty pieces. Here, in this assault, there were sixty-four Moors, who had sworn that they would die in that place or be victorious, for each of them was the master of a ship. And so in the first assault they discharged many mortars at us; but God assisted us, so that none of our people were killed here, but of them there were killed about one hundred and forty, of whom the said Don Lorenzo killed six in my presence, and he received two wounds, and many others were wounded. For a short time the battle was very severe. But after our galleys got to the land, those dogs began to retire, and, as the water began to fall, we would not follow them farther. And these dogs began to increase, and therefore we set fire to their ships, of which thirteen were burnt, the greater part new and large. And then the Viceroy withdrew all his people to the headland, and here made some knights, amongst whom, out of his grace, he also made me one, and the most valiant captain Tristan da Cugna was my sponsor. Having done this, the Viceroy began to embark his people, but continued burning many houses of the said place; so that, by the grace of God, without the death of any one of us, we took our way towards Canonor, and as soon as we had arrived, our captain had the ships furnished with provisions.

CHAPTER XVII

CONCERNING THE RETURN HOME

To those who wish to make any profession of history or cosmography, by which they may contribute both to the common advantage, as already has been many times touched upon, and to the immortality of a laborious life, there is nothing more necessary than to be the tenacious possessors of their memory, in order that, if anything has been promised by them in any previous place, they may be able to perform it free from the defect of forgetfulness; so that there may be no one who may presume to reproach them wantonly with negligence or lack of memory. Wherefore I, having promised you in my proemium to display to you part of Ethiopia [east coast of Africa] on my return from so many involuntary troubles, having now on my return an opportunity of fulfilling my promise, will enter upon it with brevity, in order that you may be able to arrive quickly at the end of the work, and I to take repose in my country.

¶ On the sixth of December we took our way towards Ethiopia and passed the gulf, a course of about three thousand miles, and arrived at the island of Mozambich [Mosambique], which belongs to the King of Portugal. And before we arrived at the said island, we saw many countries which are subject to my lord the King of Portugal, in which cities the king maintains good fortresses, and especially in Melindi [Malindi], which is a realm, and Mombaza [Mombâsa], which the Viceroy put to fire and flame. In Chilva [Khilwa, Quilon] he has a fortress, and one was building in Mozambich. In Zaphala [Sofâla], also, there is a very good fortress. I do not describe to you what the valiant captain Tristan da Cugna did, who, on his coming into India, took the cities of Gogia [Angoxa] and Pati [Patê], and Brava, a very strong island, and Sacutara [Socotra], extremely good, in which the aforesaid king keeps good fortresses. I do not describe to you the war which was waged, because I was not present at it. I am also silent about many beautiful islands which we found on our route, amongst which is the island of Cumere [Comoro], with six other islands about it, where much ginger and much sugar grow, and many singular fruits, and animal food of all kinds in abundance. I likewise do not speak to you of another beautiful island called Penda [Pemba], which is friendly towards the King of Portugal, and most fertile in everything. [No order is preserved in the above place-names.]

¶ Let us return to Mozambich, whence the King of Portugal (as also in the island Zaphala [Sofâla]) derives a very great quantity of gold and of oil, which comes from the mainland. We remained in this island about fifteen days, and found it to be small: the inhabitants of it are black and poor, and have very little food here; but it comes to them from the mainland, which is not far distant. Nevertheless, there is a very good port here. Sometimes we went on the mainland to amuse ourselves and to see the country. We found some races of people quite black and quite naked, excepting that the men wore their natural parts in a bark of wood, and the women wore a leaf before and one behind. These people have their hair bristling up and short, the lips of the mouth as thick as two fingers, the face large, the teeth large and as white as snow. They are very timid, especially when they see armed men. We, seeing these beasts to be few and vile, (we were about five or six companions well armed with *spingarde*,) took a guide in the said island who conducted us through the country, and we went a good day's journey into the mainland; and on this journey we found many elephants in troops, and, on account of these elephants, he who guided us made us carry certain pieces of dry wood ignited, which we constantly made to flame up. When the elephants saw the fire they fled, excepting once, that we met three female elephants who had their young behind them, who gave chase after us as far as a mountain, and there we saved ourselves, and travelled through the said mountain at least ten miles; then we descended on the other side and found some caverns, to which the said negroes resorted, who speak in a manner which I shall have great trouble in making you understand. However, I will endeavour to explain it to you in the best way I can. For example: when the muleteers follow their mules in Sicily and wish to drive them on, with the tongue under the palate they make a certain warble and a certain noise, with which they make the mules go on. So is the manner of speaking of this people, and with signs until they are understood. Our guide asked us if we wished to purchase some cows and oxen, as he would procure them for us cheap. We answered that we had no money, thinking he might have an understanding with these beasts, and might cause us to be robbed. He said: "There is no need of money in this affair, for they have more gold and silver than you have, for it is near here that they go to find where it grows." We asked the guide: "What would they then?" He said: "They are fond of small scissors, and they like a little cloth to bind round themselves. They are also extremely fond of some little bells for their children; they also covet razors." We answered: "We will give them some of these things, if, however, they would take the cows to the mountain." The guide said: "I will see that they shall take them to the top of the mountain and no farther, for they never pass beyond. Tell me, however, what you will give them?" One of our companions, a bombardier, said: "I will give them a good razor and a small bell." And I, in order to get animal food, took off my shirt, and said that I would give them that. Then the guide, seeing what we would give, said: "Who will drive so much cattle to the sea?" We answered: "We will drive as many as they will give." And he took the things above mentioned and gave them to five or six of these men, and demanded for them thirty cows. The brutes made signs that they would give fifteen cows. We told him to take them, for they were enough, provided they did not cheat us. The negroes immediately conducted fifteen cows to the top of the mountain. But when we had gone a little way from them, those who remained in the caverns began to make a noise; and we, thinking that it might be to follow us, left the cows and all betook ourselves to our arms. The two negroes who led the cows showed us by certain of their signs that we need not be afraid. And our guide said they must be quarrelling, because each would have wanted that bell. We took the said cows again, and went to the top of the mountain, and the two negroes then returned on their way. On our descent to come to the sea-shore we passed through a grove of cubebs about five miles, and discovered part of those elephants which we had met in going, which put us into such fear that we were obliged to leave some of the cows, which fled towards the negroes, and we returned to our island. And when our fleet was furnished with all that it required, we took our way towards the Cape of Good Hope, and passed within the island of San Lorenzo, which is distant from the mainland eighty leagues; and I think that the King of Portugal will soon be lord of it, because they have already seized two places and put them to fire and flame. From what I have seen of India and Ethiopia, it appears to me that the King of Portugal, if it please God, and he is as victorious as he has been hitherto, I think that he will be the richest king in the world. And truly he deserves every good, for in India, and especially in Cucin, every fête day ten and even twelve pagans and Moors are baptised in the Christian faith, which is daily extending by means of the said king; and for this reason it may be believed that God has given him victory, and will ever prosper him in future.

¶ Let us now return to our journey. When we had passed the Cape of Good Hope, about two hundred miles distant from the cape, the wind became contrary, and this because on the left hand there is the island of San Lorenzo [Madagascar] and many other islands, amongst which there arose a very great storm of wind, which lasted for six days. However, by the grace of God we escaped any accident. When we had passed two hundred leagues we had again a very great storm for six more days, when the whole fleet was dispersed, which went some here and some there. When the storm had ceased, we went on our way, and never saw each other again until we arrived in Portugal. I went in the ship of Bartholomeo Marchioni, of Florence, dwelling in the city of Lisbon, which ship was called *Santo Vicentio*, and carried seven thousand *cantara* of spices of all sorts; and we passed near another island called Santa Helena, where we saw two fishes, each of which was as large as a large house [whales], which, every time that they are upon the water, raise a sort of visor, I think three paces (*passi*) wide, which they let down when they wish to go under water. We were so alarmed at the force of these fishes in swimming, that we fired off all the artillery. And then we found another island called Lascension [Ascension], on which we found certain birds as large as ducks, which perched upon the ship, and they were so stupid and simple that they allowed themselves to be taken by the hand, and when they were taken they appeared very sharp and fierce. And before they were taken they looked at us like something miraculous. And this arose from their never having before seen Christians; for in this island there is nothing but fishes, and water, and these birds. Having passed this island, when we had sailed for some days we began to see the north star, and yet many say that when the north star is not seen it is not possible to navigate save by the Antarctic Pole. Let me tell you that the Portuguese always sail by the north star, although some days the said star is not seen, nevertheless the magnet performs its office and is adjusted to the Arctic Pole. Some days afterwards, we arrived in a beautiful country, that is, at the islands of the Astori [Azores], which belong to the King of Portugal. And first we saw the island of Picco, that of Corvo, the island of Flores, that of San Giorgio, La Gratiosa, the island of Faial, and then we arrived at the island of Tertiera, at which we remained two days. These islands are very fruitful. We then departed thence and went towards Portugal, and in seven days arrived at the noble city of Lisbon, which is one of the noble and good cities I have seen. I leave you to imagine, O my kind reader, the pleasure and joy I felt when I had arrived on terra firma. And as the king was not in Lisbon, I immediately set out and went to find him at a city called Almada [Almeirim], which is opposite to Lisbon. When I had arrived, I went to kiss his majesty's hand, who caressed me much, and kept me some days at his court, in order to know about the things of India. After some days, I showed to his majesty the patent of knighthood, which the

Viceroy had granted me in India, praying him (if so it pleased him) that he would confirm it, and sign it with his own hand, and affix his seal to it. When he had seen the said patent, he said that it pleased him, and so he had a diploma drawn up for me on parchment, signed with his hand, with his seal, and registered; and so I took my leave of his majesty, and came to the city of Rome.

¶ Printed at Rome by Master Stephano Guillireti de Loreno, and Master Hercule de Nani, of Bologna, at the request of Master Lodovico de Henricis da Corneto, of Vicenza. In the year M.D.X. the vith day of December.

INDEX OF PERSONS, PLACES, ETC.

NOTE—*Varthema's renderings of the names are given in parentheses*

This Edition of
THE ITINERARY OF LUDOVICO DI VARTHEMA OF BOLOGNA
is the fourth publication of the Argonaut Press and is limited to
975 copies on Japon Vellum, numbered 1 to 975. The
volume has been printed by WALTER LEWIS, M.A.,
at the University Press, Cambridge, in
the year 1928. This copy is
Number ....1..................